THE ORAL HISTORY OF
Senator John W. Warner

INTERVIEWED BY
David F. Winkler

U.S. Naval Institute • Annapolis, Maryland

Copyright © 2022

Preface

One of the great pleasures associated with being the Staff Historian at the Naval Historical Foundation is the opportunity to become associated with larger-than-life personalities. Adm. James L. Holloway III was one of those personalities. John W. Warner was another.

My association with Senator Warner actually predates my time at the Naval Historical Foundation. Coming off active duty in 1991, I decided to pursue the story behind the Incidents at Sea Agreement between the United States and the Soviet Union for my master's thesis at Washington University in St. Louis. With few official records available, my work relied heavily on oral interviews with key figures involved in the 1971–1972 negotiations. Hence, I first met the senator in his office on Capitol Hill for a riveting discussion on his first trip to Moscow in April 1971, a reciprocal Soviet navy visit to the United States, and the final trip to Moscow in May 1972 to sign the accord.

With the additional acquisition of the historical paperwork with the help of Capt. Jim Bryant, who had INCSEA agreement oversight in the Pentagon, I was able to complete my doctoral dissertation on this subject at American University in 1998. Published by the Naval Institute under the title *Cold War at Sea* in 2000 and again as an expanded version in 2017 rebranded as *Incidents at Sea,* my study identifies then–Secretary of the Navy Warner as a key figure in an effort to mitigate interactions between opposing navies that could escalate into an unforeseen conflict. One of the great honors I had came in 2012 during the fortieth anniversary of the signing of the accord, when Senator Warner and I had the opportunity to address the delegations of the U.S. and Russian navies as they met at the Naval Observatory for their annual review of the behaviors of their respective navies. Not only does this accord continue to help keep the peace between Russia and the United States but it has served as a template for several other bilateral accords between other nations and agreements between the United States and China.

Eight years before that 40th anniversary INCSEA meeting, I conducted a second interview with Senator Warner on behalf of the Library of Congress Veterans History Project, this time alongside Admiral Holloway on a stage on the National Mall as part of a tribute to honor the Greatest Generation in conjunction with the opening of the National World War II Memorial.

With Warner and Holloway, who served together as SECNAV and Chief of Naval Operations, it was a mutual admiration society and the banter on their service certainly entertained the large audience of veterans and their families. In connection with that experience, last year, in collaboration with the Friends of the National World War II Memorial and the Naval Institute Press, I wrote a book about the design and building of that memorial. In researching *Tribute to a Generation*, I learned the backstory how the senator was one of those hidden hands who helped to make the memorial reality in the face of some dogged opposition. As part of a later series of interviews, I learned he had played a critical role in fundraising for the Vietnam Memorial as well as pushed other projects honoring our veterans.

A year after doing the Mall interview, the Library of Congress asked me to do an individual sit down with Senator Warner to talk about his service in World War II as an enlisted sailor in the U.S. Navy and as a Marine officer in Korea. We met in a conference room for a twenty-minute session down the hall from his office and he started to give a talk I had heard previously at banquets that minimized his time in service at the end of the war when I cut him off to ask, "Where were you on December 7?" Needless to say, that threw him off script and we got into topics such as metal scrap drives and older kids joining the service and coming home looking spiffy in their uniforms. As the interview entered its second hour his assistant kept breaking in to say, "The VCNO is still waiting in your office," to which he snapped back, "Tell him to keep waiting." After about seventy-five minutes I escorted him back to his office and he asked if there was anything he could do for his friend Admiral Holloway at the Naval Historical Foundation. With that, Senator Warner would arrange for an appropriation of $3 million to support the Cold War Gallery of the National Museum of the United States Navy.

In 2014 I had the privilege of interviewing the senator for a fourth time at the National Museum of the United States Navy in a pairing with former NHF president Vice Adm. Bob Dunn to discuss the impact of the Japanese attack on Pearl Harbor. Captured on C-SPAN, both gentlemen spoke of the impact of the war in their home cities of Washington and Chicago and their motivations to join the service. Actually, for me the highlight of the evening was driving the senator home and stopping at Balducci's in Old Town Alexandria to pick up a few grocery items and watch him work the room as if he were running again for the Senate. He called out the baker and the butcher by their first names and let everyone know he appreciated their good service. Here was a man who really liked people.

For this final series of interviews, I credit the U.S. Naval Institute for commissioning me to conduct ten interviews covering Senator Warner's life with a focus on his service in the Navy and Marine Corps, his service as Under Secretary and Secretary of the Navy, and his time on the Senate Armed Services Committee. Though the interviews are sea service oriented, Senator Warner's words painted a panorama of the political landscape in the late twentieth century from the perspective of a point man on President Nixon's failed bid for the presidency in 1960 to his own run for the Senate, an accomplishment he credits to his second wife—Elizabeth Taylor.

Over the years Senator Warner's support of maritime heritage was demonstrated by his attendance at National Maritime Historical Society Washington Awards dinners where I often found myself as his date and at receptions the Naval Historical Foundation held at the Navy Museum to welcome incoming Secretaries of the Navy. Others will eulogize Senator Warner as the type of consensus-building get-things-done politician that Washington is sorely lacking while some will note his legacy as Liz Taylor's seventh husband. I will always remember him as a patriot, a champion of the sea-services, a believer in the importance of heritage, and a friend.

With the Senator's passing, I am grateful to his long-time Executive Assistant Paulette French for conducting a review of the transcription and performing a light edit as well as his third wife Jeanne for her hospitality during my recording sessions at his Alexandria home.

The U.S. Naval Institute Oral History Program

Researchers and authors have been drawing on the Naval Institute's Oral History Program since 1969, the year it was established by Dr. John T. Mason Jr. He and his successor, author and historian Paul Stillwell, sought to capture, preserve, and disseminate a permanent record of the stories of significant figures in naval history. In recent years, the program has expanded, with increasing numbers of historians conducting more interviews.

These oral histories are carefully fact-checked and reviewed by both historians and interview subjects before being made available. The Naval Institute is known for this high level of editorial intervention and polishing. The reader is reminded, as with all oral history interviews, that this is a record of the spoken word.

The Naval Institute wishes to acknowledge the many donors who make this program possible, in particular the generous support of the Pritzker Military Foundation of Chicago and the late Jack C. Taylor of St. Louis.

Biographical Tribute by Director of Naval History Rear Admiral Samuel J. Cox, USN (Ret.), May 2021

Fellow Flag Officers,

It is with deep regret that I inform you of the passing of former Secretary of the Navy John William Warner on May 25, 2021. Secretary Warner served as Secretary of the Navy from 1972 to 1974 and then was a five-term U.S. senator from the Commonwealth of Virginia from 1979 to 2009.

Secretary Warner was born February 18, 1927 in Washington, DC. He is the grandson of John William Warner and Mary Tinsley Warner of Amherst, Virginia. His father was Dr. John W. Warner, a physician who served as an Army doctor in World War I. His mother, Martha (Budd) Warner from St. Louis, Missouri, served as a Red Cross volunteer, helping the wounded who returned from France.

As a young man, Warner was at Griffith Stadium in Washington, DC, when news began trickling in that the Japanese had attacked Pearl Harbor. In a 2005 interview with Naval Historical Foundation historian Dave Winkler, he stated that the ballgame's announcer started to pass requests for generals and admirals in attendance to call their commanding officers immediately. It wasn't until the Warner family left the stadium that they learned why they departed the ballpark.

At the age of seventeen, he asked his parents for their permission to join the Marine Corps. His father refused, stating that after serving in muddy trenches in the Army in World War I, his son would only serve in the Navy or Air Corps.

Soon enough, he enlisted in the Navy in late 1944. He boarded a train at Washington, DC, Union Station bound for Great Lakes Training Center. On VE-Day in May 1945, he was a student at electronics school. A captain asked the students to raise their hands if they didn't drink. Not wanting to admit imbibing, he raised his hand and that's when the captain shared that the war in Europe was over. The captain then assigned Warner and other nondrinkers to shore patrol in central Chicago to maintain order among the celebrating military personnel.

He left the Navy in July 1946 as a third-class electronics technician and entered Washington and Lee University in Lexington, VA, in September 1946. He majored in general engineering courses, physics, and mathematics. During his senior year, Warner joined the Marine Corps Reserves and he was commissioned as second lieutenant upon graduating from college in June 1949.

The following September he entered the University of Virginia Law School. His law training was interrupted for a second tour of active military service when he was called to active duty as a second lieutenant in October 1950. After a tour of duty in Korea serving as communications officer for Marine Attack Squadron VMA-121 and later as communications Officer for Marine Air Group 33, he was released from active duty in April 1952. He attained the rank of captain and remained in the Marine Corps Reserve until 1961.

Graduating from law school in 1953, he was appointed law clerk to the Honorable E. Barrett Prettyman, chief judge, U.S. Circuit Court of Appeals, District of Columbia Circuit. He was admitted to the Bar in April 1954 and following a brief period in private practice was appointed a special assistant to the U.S. Attorney in 1956. In 1957 he was appointed assistant U.S. attorney, Department of Justice. He served as a trial lawyer in the U.S. Attorney's Office,

Washington, DC, until April 1960, when he joined the campaign staff of then–vice president Richard M. Nixon.

In November 1960, Warner became associated with the law firm of Hogan & Hartson and in 1964 was admitted to the firm as a general partner, specializing in corporate and banking law.

He was appointed Under Secretary of the Navy by President Nixon and sworn in on February 11, 1969 by Secretary of Defense Melvin R. Laird. He subsequently was nominated by President Nixon to be the Secretary of the Navy and sworn in by Secretary of Defense Laird on May 4, 1972. He is the first under secretary and secretary to have served in the uniform of both the Navy and Marine Corps.

In addition to duties as Under Secretary of the Navy, he was given assignments representing the Department of Defense. On July 15, 1971 he was appointed director of Ocean Affairs, with the primary responsibility of representing the Department in international affairs involving law of the sea. The president designated him head of the U.S. delegation which met in Moscow in October 1971 and again in Washington, DC, in May of 1972 to discuss incidents at sea between U.S. and Soviet naval units. Secretary Warner was a member of the Presidential Party at the Moscow Summit Meeting and signed, on behalf of the United States Government, the Executive Agreement on Incidents at Sea between the United States and Soviet Union on May 25, 1972.

For his nearly four years of service as Under Secretary and then Secretary of the Navy, Mr. Warner received the Department of Defense Distinguished Public Service Medal on January 10, 1973 from the then–secretary of defense, Melvin R. Laird. A citation accompanying the Medal, signed by Secretary Laird, said in part,

John W. Warner has provided superb leadership to the Department of the Navy during a difficult period of changing priorities, missions, and resources . . . he has brought great energy, keen foresight, broad vision and expert managerial capacity to guiding the development of new naval forces and concepts . . . and to improving the management of weapons systems acquisition . . . he has ably represented the Department of Defense in international law of the sea negotiations, and the President of the United States in negotiating an Executive Agreement on Incidents at Sea between the United States and the Soviet Union.

After leaving the Navy, President Gerald Ford asked Secretary Warner to become administrator of the American Revolution Bicentennial Administration, the federal entity responsible for organizing commemorative events in fifty states and twenty-two foreign countries in 1976. Secretary Warner joined President Ford on the flight deck of the USS *Forrestal* initiating the ringing of the bicentennial bells; similar events are planned for the country's 250th birthday in 2026.

In November 1978 Secretary Warner was elected as senator from the state of Virginia. He held this seat until 2009. Shortly before he retired; his fellow senators paid tribute to his service on the Senate floor. Senator James Webb reminisced about his decades-long friendship with the Virginian. As a twenty-five-year-old Marine captain and Vietnam War veteran, Webb was assigned to the Secretary of the Navy's staff. Warner was serving as Under Secretary of the Navy at the time. He retired then-Captain Webb from the Marine Corps in front of the Secretary of the Navy's desk. Webb followed Secretary Warner's path, becoming Secretary of the Navy Webb during the Reagan administration. Senator Sheldon Whitehouse shared two sea stories in his tribute. The first referenced Secretary Warner's passion and devotion to Navy sailors. Every time he visited a ship, he insisted on talking with sailors. He wanted the ground truth. Secretary Warner was frequently observed to be closing his eyes while talking during Senate hearings. Senator Whitehouse shared that the habit wasn't one of disrespect. Rather, it was one of concentration and deliberation. Five days after he retired from the Senate in 2009, Secretary of the Navy Donald Winter named a *Virginia*-class fast attack submarine after Senator Warner—the USS *John Warner* (SSN-785). Commissioned in 2015, it was the first *Virginia*-class boat named after a person. His stature and efforts on behalf of his beloved Navy were such that the USS *John Warner* was only the thirteenth Navy ship named after a living person in the last century.

Upon his retirement from the Senate, Secretary Warner returned to Hogan Lovells in 2009 (formerly Hogan and Hartson) as a senior advisor. Senator Warner was a true American patriot who volunteered to serve in the U.S. Navy during World War II just as soon as he was old enough. He volunteered to serve as a U.S. Marine Corps officer in the Korean War, flying as a bomb damage assessment observer over enemy territory. His tenure as Secretary of the Navy during a critical period in the Cold War was marked by a seminal agreement to reduce Cold War tensions with the Soviet Union—the US/USSR Incidents at Sea (INCSEA) Agreement of 1972. He was an avid student of naval history and supporter of naval history programs. In his recent years he was a vocal leading advocate for a new national museum of the U.S. Navy. We will truly miss him, but his legacy will live on.

Rest in Peace, Secretary Warner.

Very respectfully,

Samuel J. Cox (SES)

Deed of Gift

The U.S. Naval Institute is hereby authorized to make available in any format it chooses, from bound-book hard copy to electronic/digital Internet access and as part of videorecordings, the audio recordings, transcripts, and videorecordings of the oral-history interview series conducted concerning the life and career of the Honorable John. W. Warner. Disposition, repositories, and access shall be at the discretion of the Naval Institute.

John W. Warner's legal representative, the undersigned, does hereby release and assign to the U.S. Naval Institute the rights and title to these interviews, with the exception that the undersigned and family retain the right to use the material for personal, noncommercial purposes. The copyright in the oral, transcribed, and videorecorded versions shall be held by the U.S. Naval Institute. All recordings, transcriptions, and videorecordings of the interviews shall remain the property of the U.S. Naval Institute.

Signed and sealed this 4th day of April 2022.

Signed name Jeanne Warner, Trustee

Printed name Jeanne Warner Trustee

Interview Number 1 with John W. Warner, USN (Ret.)
Date: October 13, 2017

David Winkler (DW): This is David Winkler, and here I am at Senator [John W.] Warner's office. It is October 13th, 2017. It's the Navy's 242nd birthday, which is an appropriate date to start this interview, and I want to thank you. What I want to do today is cover your early years, talk about growing up in Washington, DC, but I guess to open up, let's talk a little bit about your parents.

John Warner (JW): I think that's always important. Well, first, it's a privilege to do this. I gave a speech last night at the Metropolitan Club, it's the annual dinner we have to honor the Navy, and it's well attended by a wide range of all ranks, from several four-stars down to several humble souls like me, Petty Officer Third Class John Warner, radio technician, enlisted in Christmas week of 1944 in the wake of the Battle of the Bulge at seventeen, and reported on active duty early January or wherever it started. Actually, I had to reenlist again in January for some technical reason. But anyway, that's the beginning of my career.

As a keynote to my speech last night, I said—and I meant it from the heart—"Whatever successes I've had in life, I attribute to two strong parents," which I'll deal with shortly, "and to the training that the United States Navy gave me and thousands of other teenagers like me during the World War II period." It was absolutely a wonderful training syllabus, and it shaped us humble, irascible, undisciplined youngsters up beautifully.

Then, of course, came the end of the war very abruptly in Japan, and I was under orders with others. We were to ship out to go in for the invasion of Japan, and the order was very abrupt. It said, "All ships will turn around and come back. The war is over." So I never made it out of CONUS [Continental United States] in that conflict, but in later years, which I'll go into, I joined the Marines and I did have a tour in Korea with the 1st Marine Air Wing during that conflict. It was 19fifty to '52.

DW: Well, let's walk it back. Just talk about your father and mother specifically.

JW: So let's go back to the beginning of time. My father was a medical doctor, surgeon, later surgeon in gynecology, and he was highly respected and a very successful young doctor. He had received his training initially at Washington and Lee University, class of 1903 and I, later in 1946, followed in his footsteps at Washington and Lee. But he went from Washington and Lee to become a headmaster of a boys' school up in the northern part of Virginia on the West Virginia border, and he boarded with a doctor, and the doctor said, "John, if you drive my horse and buggy, you can have your room and board," and that was very helpful to a struggling headmaster. He was the entire faculty of the one-room schoolhouse they had. They were all boys, I think twenty of them.

So anyway, one day the doctor turned to him after several years and said, "John, you've watched me and participated with me in every medical procedure known to mankind. Why don't you go off and get a degree, make yourself legal, and you're on your way." He went to New York University Medical School, finished it with distinction. He was on the last of the horse-drawn ambulances in New York. This was about 1906 or '07, and the reason is there were so many outlying regions around the otherwise burgeoning New York City, but there were no paved roads and only a horse-drawn ambulance could get in to provide their services to bereaved people. That's just a little anecdote.

So anyway, along came World War I. He volunteered and went to France as a captain, U.S. Army Medical Corps, served in France for, I think, about fifteen months and was in three major battles. He was injured and was gassed. He went through all of it. His main job was taking care of triage and sewing up, saving as many lives as he could once they got the wounded to the field hospitals. So he was always very modest about it, but he was decorated for his valor and his service. It's interesting that today I'm working with the World War I Commission as we honor the 100th anniversary of that conflict.

My mother worked as a volunteer Red Cross worker in the hospitals, specifically on the wards of the returning veterans and caring for them. Mother and Father didn't meet until many years later, but both of them did their public service in that historic conflict. They met. My father was calling on a very wonderful family to provide medical help, and my mother was visiting at the house at the time, and she was suddenly called in to help Father administer whatever he was trying to do with the ill person. He had to make subsequent calls to the residence, and out of that brief several meetings grew a beautiful romance and eventually a marriage and eventually my birth on February 18th, 1927, in Washington, DC, at a hospital where Father was at that time Chief of Gynecology, which was a new expertise in the medical field, emerging then as a contemporaneous—not contemporaneous, but collaterally with the specific various specialties in medicine.

So Mother was very insistent that she not raise her children on the crowded streets of New York, so they both picked up and moved themselves to Washington, DC, where my father's brother was working at the Washington Cathedral as an assistant to the dean of the cathedral. He had just finished his training as an Episcopal minister and was given a small parish right there, St. Albans, on the cathedral grounds, and he remained at that parish and eventually became the head priest at the parish, and he remained there forty years.

So my life as a young boy was largely involved with that part of Washington, DC, because Father and Mother located our home just two blocks from the cathedral, and I romped and played on the grounds as that magnificent edifice was slowly being built. I remember it ever so well. So I had a wonderful life. I was in the Boy Scouts, which was a good thing. I needed discipline in those days, and they provided it. I remember very clearly where I put to use one of my first lessons in the Boy Scouts. I'll get to that momentarily.

But I grew up, and then our country was totally involved quickly and totally involved in World War II. I say "totally" because while those who fought valiantly and gave life and limb on the battlefronts, both in the European conflict and the conflict in the Pacific, well, those were the battlefields. Every bit of America was geared up to survive as a nation the forceful attacks, particularly by the Japanese, surprise attack on Pearl Harbor Day, and in Europe. My father had once commented he used to sit day after day and go over with me the newspapers and the battles raging throughout Europe, and he said, "They're fighting in the same countries that we fought in in 19seventeen, 'eighteen."

So anyway, those are chapters in history, but I lay that foundation because, again, back to the entirety of America was involved, because at home the nation had to impose rationing of food, rationing of gasoline, rationing of clothes sales. I mean, I think you got one pair of, two at the most, shoes a year. You had shoe stamps and we had food stamps and had gasoline stamps. Cars were given three gallons. I can't remember was it three gallons a week or three gallons a month, but it was very small. Now, others, like Father, being a physician who had to go out at all hours of the night, hospital calls, they had larger stipulations of the amount of fuel that they were entitled to. As a matter of fact, my recollection is it was "A" tags for the three gallons on your windshield, "B" for something else, and "C" was for people who had special needs to perform their duties and requiring extra petroleum.

I point this out because that one restriction imposed on our lives in such a way, imposed and curtailed our lives in such a way as you lived in your own segment of a city or a village, and you rarely got out of it. There was no means to transport you. We did have an active rail system, railroad system, in those days. There, of course, was bus travel, streetcar travel, but we walked to school. My schools were—well, I went to two of them, but, basically, the main school I walked to was about two and a half miles away, two to three miles. I should measure it some day.

DW: Was that Wilson High School?

JW: Yes, Woodrow Wilson High School, up in a little place called Tenleytown. But there was a streetcar that operated along the main avenue, which cut down your walking considerably, but often I walked all the way. But we accepted all those hardships because, believe me, the United States was in peril, as well as all the nations in the free world. The Axis powers in Europe, the Japanese attacks in the Pacific just laid waste to our armed forces for a while, as well as crimping the home front to where we had a very restricted amount of freedom and life to do what we wanted.

But all those things had their virtues. You learned to live in your village. Of course, we were Washington, DC, the nation's capital, but there was a Northwest section of Washington. Washington is sort of divided into four quadrants. I remember up in our section each house that had a member of the family in the armed forces proudly had a sticker. It was about 4-by-6 inches in red, white, and blue, and people proudly put it on their front doors. We have a son or a daughter wearing the uniform of the United States Navy, Army, Air Corps, Marines. And then, unfortunately, those little stickers were removed and replaced with a gold star, which indicated that loved one had given their life in the cause of freedom somewhere, mostly likely on the far-flung battlefields. So the gold star origin of mothers is pretty much in that period of time, and on our little block we had them. There was no doubt about it.

Then you had the constant flow through your community of the older boys who'd signed up, coming home on brief leave before they left to go overseas, or coming back from overseas on a brief leave, and, boy, it left an indelible impression. Here you remember this particular boy, wherever he was, on the playing fields. We used to have a baseball lot, just a sandlot. Boy, that was used around the clock because it was a wonderful ball field. It seemed like you'd be playing ball with somebody and then they'd say goodbye, "My draft number's up," or, "I'm going to enlist, and I'll see you when I see you, guys." Off they'd go and then they'd come back, proudly wearing their uniforms, and that was a tremendous incentive to all those of us coming along in age groups, recognizing that soon we would be subject to a draft unless beforehand we volunteered and enlisted.

You were able to enlist in the Armed Services at age seventeen, provided you had the written consent of your parents to do so. Well, I was in a constant argument with my parents. School seemed to me irrelevant, and the excitement that I experienced vicariously from the returning veterans, man, I wanted to wear one of those uniforms. I remember so well the Army Air Corps outfitted its troops, and you could wear it home, the lovely leather jackets, flight jackets, and, oh, it was just a moving experience to see. They were on the sandlot one day, and then the next they were coming home, and the next you heard there was just the occasional letter, and then, of course, misfortune could strike, as it did to many of our families in the neighborhood.

So we had a lot of incentive, those of us who were seventeen, to join up as quickly as we could, because you could select whether you wanted to be a sailor in the Navy or a Marine or an Army guy or Army Air Corps. The recruiters were all there in every part of the city. You had recruiting signs with an arrow pointing "Sign up here. Volunteers. Recruits needed. Volunteers needed."

So the Battle of the Bulge was an extraordinary event because it was totally unanticipated. America had, in June of 1944, June 6th, mounted a huge invasion of Europe on the beaches of Normandy, and once they were able to collect themselves, get off the beach and begin to move inland, we were rolling back quite successfully elements of the German army and had the momentum in the war, clearly, battle after battle, but it ended in a victory from our perspective.

Then all of a sudden, to the total surprise of millions and millions of people in the whole United States, the Germans, under the concealment of a period of about ten days of bad weather, when the airplanes, which were our principal means of tracking the German army units, they couldn't fly down. They couldn't fly, and therefore under the cover of Mother Nature's clouds,

Hitler amassed almost everything he had left that could move and hurled an attack against the United States and our allies with devastating speed and effectiveness, and that became known as the Battle of the Bulge. Our casualties in that battle, which lasted from, let's say, the first week somehow of December '44, up until, I think, late January, that battle was the highest total of killed and wounded we had in any one single engagement in World War II.

So I sat down with Father and Mother and I said, "Hey, you know, we've got to go." I had gone to summer school to get as much as I could finished of my high school training. And Father relented, because he understood war and he understood how proud that they would be to have a son in the military. So up on the front door of our house, 3forty9 Lowell Street, NW, Washington, two blocks from the Washington Cathedral, went the sticker. "We have a son in uniform, proudly serving in the Navy."

So that started off. I come back to the Boy Scouts. We were on a train, took three days to get on these old trains, because the rail system was so heavily taxed with military traffic. The passenger trains all had lowest priority on the use of the rails, highest priority given to troop trains, which were sailing down the rails on the East and West Coast to the ports of embarkation, loaded with soldiers, sailors, airmen, and Marines who had just finished their training and were headed to their port of embarkation, their units to be shipped out. Then you had the trains laden with military arms. I remember ever so vividly the flatcars with artillery pieces chained down to them, transporting them to the ports of embarkation to have the supplies for the troops being sent over. And the boxcars all sort of marked with everything from ammunition to canned food. I mention canned food because you lived on canned food largely out in the far-flung battlefronts of the world.

So my life was going to the ball field, walking to school. Oh, you could go to the movies. We had wonderful movies, and that was the principal way of learning and seeing pictures of the war, the old *Movietone News*. It was always a ten-minute segment in all the films. It cost, I think, ten or fifteen cents to go to the movies, and I remember I had a little allowance of twenty-five cents a week or whatever it was.

And, oh, I'd throw in this. We were all urged to do odd jobs, everybody. They said, "Put your hands to saving America." Well, oddly enough, we lived in villages and the women largely used to walk long distances to the food stores because there was no gas to drive there with any frequency, and they would be laden with heavy bags of groceries. They urged all the children to get their little wagons—and I had a wagon. I'd been a newspaper boy, so I had a beautiful wagon. You went up to the stores and properly with good discipline queued up in a line, and as the women came out, they would hire you. The fee, the first five blocks was ten cents. The next ten blocks, fifteen cents. The further away you got a little out, the paid [*sic*] scale went up. And we all went up with our wagons and loaded them up with the groceries for the wonderful care the mothers were giving their families, and they followed dutifully the wagons. We would offload them and carry the bags up to the front porch and put them down and collect our handful of pennies and nickels and dimes. But it added up at the end of the day. You might have as much as a dollar, and that was pretty big money in those days. So we were doing our war effort, and it was really an important one because to carry a heavy bag of groceries for four, five, eight, ten, blocks is not easy. So those are little remonitions [*sic*] I had. But back to enlisting in the Navy.

So the day came, I went to Union Station right here in Washington, DC, and I think my father took me down, and I got on the train. My mother was with him, and she handed me a little box and said, "Before you get to your destination, I'll ask you to open the box, not now, just as you're coming into your destination." Well, I was puzzled by it, but I abided by her wishes, and got on the train, and the train was loaded with nothing but military guys, enlistees, and people on leave, people on hospital, lot of guys with bandages on, clearly visible. They'd gotten a few days off to go home. The cost of the train trip was negligible. I mean, servicepersons could travel at a very small amount of money.

But we were under orders, first set of orders I ever had, to report to duty at Great Lakes Naval Station on a certain date, and off we went, and, boy, I'll tell you, that was an eye-opener. I lived in this rather confined lifestyle of church on Sundays, schools, family parties, and you mixed and mingled with, frankly, the families whose homes you could walk to. This was in not necessarily the wealthiest part of the city, but Cleveland Park, where I was, was considered really quite upscale and nice. So I was not attuned to what a factory worker was like or what work would be if your family worked in a steel mill. I'd had some exposure to farms. My father put me on farms to work in the summertime, and I encountered the farmhands, who were people of meager education and so forth. But it was an eye-opener that night when we arrived, three days later from departure, literally sleeping on the train as the cars were standing idly by and letting the fast trains move through.

We were taken off the train, but before we pulled into this train station at Great Lakes on the trip to Chicago, my recollection we changed trains in Chicago. That was a big rail terminal in

America, one of the three or four biggest. I dutifully got Mother's little box out and opened it up. It was one or two o'clock in the morning. I had a dimly lit car, most of the people were asleep, and read the note and said, "Dear Son, How proud Daddy and I are for your service," and everything, "but I insist that before you arrive at your duty station, you have clean underwear on." Well, I swear, I didn't know what to do. Here we're on this crowded train. There was a little pissoir, of course, in each car or every other car, or however it was, and I wasn't about to let the other guys see me changing my underwear. So I just had to make a quick executive decision. I raised the window of the railroad car and tossed it out, said a little prayer of forgiveness, and that was the last I saw of it.

So I arrived in my well-worn and well-used underwear, probably four, five days, at Great Lakes, and we were marched into a big gymnasium, and a chief petty officer got up on a big table and in a very firm voice he screamed, "Attention!" Well, Boy Scouts, I learned what that means, and I snapped to, but I noticed that very few boys were snapping to. The others hadn't the vaguest idea what "Attention!" meant. That was the level of learning in those days as it relates to military training.

So then the chief petty officer said, "All those who can't read and write, I want you to raise your hands, and I'm insistent, do not be reluctant. There are quite a few of you. We all know that statistically. Raise your hands." And quietly, a considerable number, I'd say 25 percent of these guys, raised their hands. They could not read nor write.

Then the petty officer said, "All right, I'm going to teach you your first lesson in the military, and that is you've got to always look out for your fellow soldier, sailor, and Marine. No matter who he or she or where they are, you've got to learn to live with them, work with them, and mutually help, because there could be a day that your survivability is dependent on that person who can still act when for whatever reason you can't, to protect your life." I'll never forget that. And he said, "Now, those guys who can, go and help those who can't read and write." Of course, I was proficient in reading and writing, may not have been the best student in the world, but I'd been through high school all right, most of it, that is. I never finished high school. And I helped fill out the forms. And that little lesson stayed with me to this day here, in my ninety-three-year-old life, and I often quoted it on the floor of the Senate when we were in quarrelsome moods and not reaching any results and nobody was conceding one thing or another. I told the story of interdependency of the military on fundamental rule "You've got to learn to respect and work with your fellow serviceperson."

So with that, I'm going to hold my breath for a minute. I get out of breath. But that's the entry.

DW: Did we cover why you decided on the Navy versus the Army?

JW: Well, my mother, bless her heart—I should bring a picture—always dressed me up in a sailor suit. I mean, at age five it was quite the fashionable thing to dress one or two of your children in sailor suits. I don't know why it was, but the women did it. And I never saw anybody dressed in an Army suit. [Laughs] But sailor suits were worn. And she wanted me to be in the Navy. Mother thought that that was safer, the more elegant—and it was—branch of service. I wanted to be in the Marine Corps, I had my heart set on it, and Father said, "No." He said, "I sewed up so many infantrymen in my lifetime, and so many I've had to recognize there was nothing you could do but keep him doped up till he died." Triage is the decision of who lives and who dies. It's one of the most burdensome things a doctor could perform.

So I gave up and went in the Navy, and then five years later, after I finished two years or a little less in the Navy, went on to school on the GI Bill to my father's school, Washington and Lee. In September of 1946, even though the war was over, had been over for some time, demobilization, you had sixteen million men and women all over the world in uniform, and they wanted to do it equitably, and I'm totally supportive of the challenge that America had of taking all these men and women posted all over the world and fairly letting those who'd come first go out. And then so you hung on, performed what such duties as they required, until your age group was let out.

So it wasn't then till well after the war was over, the war ended in August of 1945, and it was basically a little less than a year before my number came up, and I accepted that. We went on with our training. I remember at this time we were decommissioning a battleship. It's a long story. A few of the sailors who were on it during the war were still on it, helping us preserve it, and we got to learn a lot of sea stories and got to feel very close to the ship we were working on, storing it for whenever it might be used again.

DW: So when the war ended, you were at Great Lakes, right?

JW: No, no. I'd finished Great Lakes, finished the training cycle. I actually did a short tour at the Naval Research Laboratory for advanced training in electronics. We were beautifully trained. You've got to think that as World War II came on, we were just learning about—of course, radios had been in existence for some time, and the military, of course, was using them on ships and aircraft and the like, but they were very primitive and they were constantly refining. In World War II, they accelerated all types of technology so that the type of communication equipment we had pre–World War II didn't have any resemblance to what was being built in 1944, '45. I mean, we'd made a huge advancement. But you had to have people properly trained who understood right at the beginning with the fundamentals. I mean, what is electronics and electricity? Well, it's electrons flowing through a solid wire, and how the attenuation of their acceleration takes place every step they go along the wire, and you just kind of figure you've got to keep the pressure to push these electrons through. And then when it comes into the equipment, some of it goes into capacitors for storage, in transformers for storage. Other parts go straight into operate the speakers in the radio and the radio tubes and the antenna. And, believe me, there were a lot of people didn't have the first idea about how these radios worked, yet we had in all the military units, particularly those forward, all kinds of communication equipment. Therefore, we were put down close to the books and the training stations to learn all these things.

[telephone interruption]

JW: Let me just deal with whatever this is. And it was quite complicated. I'll finish this in a minute.

[End of October 13, 2017, recording]

Interview Number 2 with John W. Warner, USN (Ret.)
Date: November 13, 2017

David Winkler (DW): Today is November the 13th, 2017, the 75th anniversary of the Naval Battle of Guadalcanal. This is David Winkler. I'm here with former Secretary of the Navy, retired senator John Warner on our second session, and I wanted to follow up some World War II questions. You were mentioning about enlisting in the Navy?

JW: Well, by that count, you've got to remember, I'm seventeen, it's the fall of 1944. As a matter of fact, it was Christmas week. I finally convinced the family to let me go, and I went down to the old Washington Navy Yard and enlisted Christmas week, I think between Christmas and New Year's.

I had wanted to go in the Marines but my father said, "I spent fourteen months in France and never ever hardly had dry underwear, rain, rain, wet, cold, and everything." So he said, "You're not going there." And so anyway, I went in the Navy happily.

I had to reenlist again in January because they opened up a special school for training what I called "[unclear] kids." There was an exam called the Eddie test. Captain Eddie was a submariner of great renown. Unfortunately, he was in a crash, injured, burst an eardrum, so he could no longer be active in combat situations, but he devised a highly concentrated program to train young persons, enlisted, to understand how to repair every single piece of equipment in the Navy through which an electron flowed, radios, radar, fire controls, everything, and it was a nine-month intensive course of training and very selective. So you had to take the Eddie test. Well, in school I'd majored in mathematics and science and physics, flunked French and Spanish, and I boned up for this test, and I hit bingo on it, and they said, "Well, we'll change your original enlistment," which I got at Christmas '44, "and switch you over to this other program." So all took place in January, and then I soon left for boot camp at Great Lakes, and that was an experience. Did I talk about the train ride?

DW: Yes.

JW: And the little underwear my mother threw—

DW: Yes, yes.

JW: Did I talk about the first night, the guys that couldn't read and write?

DW: Yes.

JW: Okay. Did I talk about the severity of the weather when you're in formation at five thirty in the morning?

DW: No.

JW: You'd fall out on your face, it was so cold. The wind was blowing. Then we had these old mock rifles, you know, and you'd hear a crash, down would go the rifle, and then the other guy would slump. It was really cold. It was rough training.

They were bringing over raw footage from the battlefronts and playing it, because as strict as they were in the military and boot camp and things like that, seventeen-, eighteen-year-olds, they're just undisciplined. But they used to show us these films. Usually on Sunday we'd go into mandatory. We'd go in, and, boy, I'd tell you, it was right off the battlefield. It was just a voiceover describing the casualties and what happened. Then the petty officer would come out when the lights would go on and say, "Now hear this. You're next, and if you don't learn what we're trying to teach you, you see what happens. You've got to know how to take care of yourself and take care of your buddy, the man on your right or the man on your left, respectively." That was rule number one: get to know the guy on your left or your right. But the theory was wherever you were in the military, your life was sometimes dependent on the other person's ability to do the same things you could do. So, really, it was wonderful training, and then I remember—did I tell you about the shore patrol?

DW: No, you didn't, not in the last go-round.

JW: Well, the captain called us all in. We were up in the center of Chicago at a closed high school, but they had a lot of good laboratories, and that's where we had most of training with books and laboratory, equal time, and that was the lab. We built radios, we repaired old equipment, and it was a great team, great, great training course.

But he called us in, we had about 2fifty guys, and the captain locked the doors. He said, "How many of you guys don't drink a lot?" Well, no self-respecting sailor admits to anything. So he pounded away. Finally, "How many of you drink?" He had these questions, but he was trying to sort out the guys who would be responsible. So out of 2fifty, I think he took twenty five of us and made us all shore patrolmen. He said, "Tonight at seven o'clock, the president of the United States is going to go on radio and announce that Germany has surrendered, and there will be an outpouring in the Loop down in Chicago, and your job is to do what you can to maintain discipline."

Well, all the liquor had given out in the first hour and the bars couldn't get any resupply, so there wasn't any alcohol problems at all, and there really wasn't any problems. Everybody was joyous. Mainly we were all dancing and kissing girls, and everybody wanted to kiss everybody, so it was quite a night. I arrived back. I gave the first girl that kissed me an armband, the next one the whistle, the third one the billy club. I don't know what else I had to give them, and that's all. At five o'clock in the morning, I wandered back. It was a memorable night. That was the only combat I saw during World War II.

DW: But that's before the dropping of the A-bomb.

JW: Oh, no. That was May 8th.

DW: So we dropped the bomb against Japan two months later.

JW: That was the 6th of August.

DW: And do you remember where you were when that news broke out?

JW: I was out in advanced school finishing up this course. No, I wasn't. I think about this time I was reported into the Atlantic Fleet, yeah, at Bayonne, New Jersey, which was not an interesting place. The war had been over. I mean, it was over, and we were ready to go aboard ship, we had ships assigned to us and everything else, and the order came out, no more ships in the Pacific. The Atlantic had been secured. So we just spent our time bringing ships in and doing the preliminary work so that they could be self-sufficient without heavy crews, just a token crew, until the rotation they could fit them into, proceeded to transfer them into mothballing. It was a very unheroic, unromantic job. I remember our job was to analyze all the electronics on the ship and whether we should save it or junk it. We had all kinds of tests, programs, and they were liberal with liberty, got a lot of time off. So we were just really waiting out until our number came up in an orderly process. "First in, first out" was the general rule. But they pinned a little—sewed it on your uniform, a little—we called it a ruptured duck. It was something of a takeoff on the eagle. So we went home.

DW: So you were in Bayonne, New Jersey, when you found out about the A-bomb explosion.

JW: Yeah, yeah.

DW: And the reaction was?

JW: It was over. It dragged on for a while. I think a lot of the papers reported the *Missouri*. I don't know exactly what day that was. That was the formal surrender.

DW: Yes, September 2nd.

JW: September 2nd.

DW: Yes. Were you on one of the battleships that came in from the East Coast doing work?

JW: I'll tell you what. I was assigned—you've got to be assigned to a pocket battleship. There were only three of them made: *Alaska* and the *Guam.* Check out these names. It's rather interesting. I've forgotten the name of the third one.[1]

They were assigned to this naval shipyard at Bayonne, New Jersey, and they were absolutely beautiful-built boats—ships. They were finished the last year of the war. They were designed to operate with heavy armament. I think we had 14-inch guns, didn't have eighteens, and at high speeds. They called them pocket battleships, patterned after some class that Germany had. Well, here they are. I never found out the answer to this until I was Secretary of the Navy. Here are three brand new ships towed in and given priority to be decommissioned. I'm saying to myself, "Hey, all these rust buckets we got around here, certainly the Navy could use these three ships." Oh, no, the orders were immediate, pull the electronics and all other pieces of equipment that wouldn't work, being just tied up in a shipyard.

Later when I was Secretary of the Navy, I went back and researched it, and the reason that they saved these three to get rid of them is they were working out quite well in their missions, and the old Navy did not want any 12-inch battlewagons. Let me see. Did we have a ten-inch gun? We had a smaller gun. It wasn't an eighteen-inch.

DW: We had a 16- and then an 8-inch was on the cruiser, so this would have been somewhere—I think it was a 12-inch.

JW: It was a 12-inch gun. They were fearful that Congress would build more of these things when the Navy was determined, if they were going to have another round of shipbuilding post World War II, they wanted the big stuff. So you did not want these three little ships operating with the fleet in such a way that Congress would say, "Well, this ship, while it isn't equal in fire power to an old battlewagon, it's almost, and it's much cheaper and it's much faster."

So that's that chapter. Home I went. The sad part about it was I'd seen my father off and on, on leave. He was dying of cancer. I remember I arrived home. I had my little sailor suit on. You were ordered to wear your suit home with the gold badge on it for sixty or a hundred days.

---

[1] *Hawaii* was the third ship of the class of six planned battlecruisers that never was commissioned. The other three ships of the class were never laid down. *Alaska* and *Guam* saw service during the last year of the war. The ships were designed in response to the German introduction of the *Scharnhorst.*

You could wear your uniform to what you were doing, even though you started as a civilian, because a lot of people had no clothes. There were no clothes manufactured of any considerable number for the people in this country during that whole period. The war machine swung over entirely to uniforms and other things that were related to defending ourselves, like military equipment. Suit factories were slowly starting up, but then they didn't have immediately the materials, so it was a long time until we really had clothes of any quantity.

Anyway, my father was in bed, he was a terminal cancer situation, and he was a cancer doctor. He knew that time was running out, and he said he wanted me to go to his old school, Washington and Lee University, where he was an honor student, quite a wonderful student.

DW: So you went to Washington and Lee?

JW: Washington and Lee University, his school. He called up the president and got him on the phone, and I could only hear half the conversation. He hung up the phone and said, "You're in. Bring a certified check for $fifty0. That's to cover tuition until your GI Bill, then you're allowed to get a refund," or what it was, "and report on the 12th of September." So I went, and he died the first two months I was there. That's the only thing I've ever been cheated on in life, was the loss of my father when I'd reached an age where I could hold an adult conversation.

DW: So you're out there in Lexington, Virginia.

JW: It was a wonderful period in the history of America. I mean, everything was exciting. The new cars were slowly—I don't know, maybe late fall '46, the first ones came off the assembly line. My father had filed for a new car, put down a down payment, and, of course, there was no delivery. The war came on so quickly. But that auto company, even though my father was dead, took a piece of paper, one sheet, talking about this car, and they sold it to us, a Buick.

DW: So you're now at Washington and Lee, and you're there for, I guess, three years as a student? This is a cultural change for you, because you're out there in the country and you grew up in the city. So how did you handle the new environment?

JW: Well, I'll tell you what. It was hard to get into those colleges because you had an avalanche of kids, and if it hadn't been for my father, I don't know that I'd gotten in right away. So you had to be on your toes academically, and even though I joined a fraternity and did my share of hoorah-rah and beer drinking, I really buckled down. And I'd had the advantage of going through this really intense technical course. We took advanced calculus, we took advanced physics, all enlisted men going through this course, and all they were doing, cramming in our heads all advanced technology. But the college gave me credit in physics, in advanced mathematics, and I got a semester's worth of credit for that work in the Navy, and we were well trained. I mean, I went into the technical courses in my Washington and Lee University and it blew them away because of the training they'd given me in the Navy and my mental capacity to grab this stuff very quickly.

DW: Now, what was your major there?

JW: Ah, that's an interesting story. I had a terrible struggle all my life with languages. Father, who had gone to Washington and Lee, he graduated in 1903 from this little school in the valley of Virginia. It's still there. I was there to lecture last weekend. I go back once a year to lecture. My father majored in Latin and Greek in the turn of the century. That's the way you educated kids. Romance languages, classic languages, classic history, and mathematics, that was the curriculum in those days.

Anyway, I went right to the top of Washington and Lee scholastically and finished in three years, but I was beautifully trained by that school, and then came out and went to law school at the University of Virginia, and I finished my first year, and I was a law clerk here in Washington, DC to a law firm in the summer. I remember it well. I didn't have any money. Father left enough to take care of my mother. My brother and I were on our own pretty much. I only mention it because I remember this law firm was very strict, and our salaries were de minimis. Each noon every day, I had to go to court and file papers, check documents, all kinds of things, and with a wink and a nod, they would give you the expenses for taxi to go to court and back. Well, the law firm was on 15th Street. I could walk to the courthouse in fifteen minutes. You could still turn in your taxi fee, and you got lunch money, a dollar and a half, seventy-five-cent taxi fee each way, little things like that. But, god, I remember that old steam house down here called Cannon's [phonetic], and for fifty cents you could get a huge amount of roast beef sliced, shoulder roast, on a big bun. That was fifty cents. Ah, I remember those days well.

DW: So why did you want to become a lawyer?

JW: Well, it was interesting. I thought about going into advanced engineering, but I was kind of intrigued with the law. In those days in our social structure in America, there was a class of people called professionals, but it was narrowed to doctors, lawyers, and clergymen, that was it, and society looked up to them. Today we're in the mix, but in those days. I had enough GI Bill to pay for undergraduate studies and when I went back into the Korean War, I picked up another three years of eligibility, and I just decided to get the law degree. Engineering, there were plenty of engineers around, but there just weren't that many lawyers around.

DW: I think we have the reverse problem today.

JW: Yes, we have the reverse problem today. I enjoyed the academic life. I enjoyed the University of Virginia. It was a wonderful time. I lived in a boardinghouse, and I was assistant law librarian at night in the law school to supplement my GI Bill money and what little money I had. I got the job not because of any particular academic prowess, but because I was an ex-Marine back from Korea and I knew how to discipline men and had the skills of discipline, and I was pretty rough on those rowdy law students.

DW: So we got a little ahead of ourselves there. Let's talk about—because you started at the University of Virginia and then the Korean War starts.

JW: Yes. I had had a commission. I got the commission upon graduating from Washington and Lee, because the Marine Corps, if you had a two-year or thereabouts—we weren't restricted to a few months more or under, whatever—two years enlisted and you went for concentrated eight weeks of OCS at Quantico in the summer, you were given the commission the day you graduated. So I got my commission in October of 1949. I couldn't graduate in June. I was two classes short, two hours, whatever, so I had to do a summer school and then got my commission when I finished summer school. In September, I was gone.

DW: Which leads back to the question that Marine Corps officer commissioning program, you made a decision to enroll in that right when you entered Washington and Lee?

JW: No. It was a guy down in Washington and Lee that would frequently on drill weekends wear his dress blues, and he walked around. As a matter of fact, he's dead now, but I know his son. He walked around and he was a one-man recruiter. I enlisted, I enjoyed my tour, I don't regret a day of it in the Navy enlisted, but I saw the advantages of a commission and had a direct shot at the Marines. The Navy had a similar program, but I just always loved sidearms. I did a lot of hunting as a kid with rifles and shotguns, and it seems to me the Marines had a more active role. And I felt slighted throughout college because I was not a combat officer. Most of my fraternity brothers had been in combat, and they treated me all right. At least I wore the uniform, didn't try to dodge the draft or anything. So I just had a hankering that I'd like to get a commission in the reserves. Also it paid out a nice little stipend for the weekends, and I got my beer and dating money for one weekend a month.

I was down here at Anacostia. I've got a famous picture. I'm now a second lieutenant and they made me a communications officer because I'd done all the technical work in the Navy. So I'd fly along in the rear seat of the airplane. We did training weekends, and we had a marvelous gang. Nothing like the camaraderie of the aviators at a bar at night. So I did that. VMF-321 was the number of the squadron, Anacostia. We were flying all the old World War II airplanes around. God, we made endless takeoffs and landings. We melded into the pattern off of the airport down there, Washington, DC National, very easily, because we'd buck right over Maryland. I just had a good life, a lot of fun.[2]

Then I was in law school, I was going to a small infantry unit down in Charlottesville, and, bingo, the war hit, and I didn't resist at all when they sent me orders. Some guys scrambled around trying to get deferred reporting dates. I said, "Nope. Luck of the Irish. I'll come back and finish this thing."

---

[2] Naval Air Station Anacostia had been the Navy's aviation research and development center between the World Wars. That work subsequently moved to NAS Patuxent River in southern Maryland. The increase in commercial aviation traffic at Washington National (Reagan National) was such that the Navy closed Anacostia in the 1950s. Likewise the Air Force closed its airstrip at nearby Bolling Air Force Base to move its DC air operations out to Andrews AFB.

So I went on off and went to Quantico. It was an interesting experience down there, fifty young officers, all whom had gotten their lieutenants bars kind of in the last months of World War II or in the interregnum period like I had, college programs, and we were all brand new second lieutenants, some first.

The Marines had suffered a terrible blow at the Chosin Valley, and they were desperately short of young officers, so many of them had been lost in that battle, so they drove us through at full speed. Matter of fact, we were to have twenty days of retraining. They cut it to ninety and shipped us out, and I was on the way to Korea when they discovered I had the technical background. They said, "Uh-oh. No, we're going to keep you in the technical field," took me out of infantry program, put me into Radio Tech School at Quantico, and then sent me to Korea as a trained communications officer.[3]

It's an interesting experience over there. I basically didn't have the incredible hardship like the guys that had to live in foxholes, but I used to go up and visit them because I was responsible for their communication equipment, interfacing with the aviation wings, and, frankly, I wanted to go up and see how they lived anyway. They accepted me, so I lived up on the line occasionally. We had some close scrapes here and there. But I've always respected the infantry guys who had to do it seven days and nights a week. It's one thing for me to come up for a few nights and then go back. Of course, we all slept in tents; colder than hell. We had more casualties from people getting up in the middle of the night. In the days we'd have all these air raid alarms going off. We never really had any bombs dropped on us or anything. Then these guys would fall in the trenches, trying to run around and get cover. We had a lot of guys burned themselves on the tent's little stoves that we had that would radiate the only heat in the tent. They'd come in with a beer too much and fall against it and burn. So we had the usual barracks life.

Finally, the aviators, I did what they call rear-seat time as a volunteer. Those air flights used to go out, if there was a rear seat for an observer, I hopped in, because I enjoyed doing bomb damage assessment. That's when a tail plane would go in after the strike or fly with the strike going up, but the strike would take place, and as soon as the smoke and debris cleared, you

---

[3] Warner was the communications officer of Marine Air Group 33, a component of the 1st Marine Air Wing.

swooped down and took a picture, eyeballed it and photographed it and told them, "Yep, bridge still there. Missed it." Turn around, come back, hit it again.

DW: The problem with that is, is that the other side typically has got you zeroed in because they are expecting you.

JW: Yeah, there was a bit of an anti-aircraft, but it wasn't as intense as it was in Vietnam. We lost planes. We had one malfunctioning plane due to something that hit us, but we weren't concerned about it.

DW: Were you operating mostly Corsairs?

JW: Corsairs, and we had a Banshee, and we had the first jet—come on, Warner. What was the name of it?

DW: The Panther?

JW: Panther, yes. Corsairs, Panthers, and ADs we borrowed. Our squadron 121 was the first operational squadron of the new AD, which you could carry ten thousand pounds of ordnance. Big radial engine, single seat, though, so I never got a ride in one.[4]

DW: Those planes played a big role in Vietnam.

JW: It was built like a brick shithouse. I mean, that thing, they'd come back, you'd see where they'd been hit with some anti-aircraft. You got over a city target, they got different stuff to shoot up at you. Oh, yeah, they were good pilots, and we lost a few.

---

[4] Produced by Vought, the "gull winged" F4U Corsair was flown by Marine and Navy Squadrons during World War II and saw service in Korea. The straight-winged F2H Banshee entered serve in 1948 as a jet fighter and saw limited service in Korea—mostly as a reconnaissance aircraft with the Marines. In contrast the straight-winged Grumman F9F Panther saw more extensive service as a fighter-bomber in the conflict. The AD-1 Skyraider, built by Douglas, was a heavy sigle engine propeller-driven aircraft that served both in Korea and in Vietnam.

I'll never forget monitoring their flights in the radio shack that I had, and flight five divisions and three division took off, and I heard a guy on the voice box, "Hey, skipper, you're burning."

Skipper comes back, "Yeah, I got some problem. I've got to clear this village below me. I think I'll have to jump."

I listened to the whole damn thing. They said, "You're clear," and he went out over the side of his plane, but his chute streamed; it didn't pop.

So I had the coordinates, and I called the officer of the day and said, "Here's what's happened."

He said, "You got the coordinates?"

I said, "Yep."

He said, "Get some infantry guys and Jeeps and guns and go up there and find him, see if he's all right." So I remember I took it up there. I'll never forget, we were on this old beat-up road trying to get up there. There was a large crowd of people and they wouldn't get out of the way, and some woman had had an accident and was dying in the road, and they wanted to let her die before they would touch her body. It was something about their religion. I didn't understand it. In the meantime, I'm trying to go up and rescue a downed airman. So I remember we had a confrontation. I had our medic that was with us do what he could to relieve her pain, but we picked her up, moved her, and went on up there. But we lost forty minutes.

As it turned out, he'd hit the ground and was killed instantly, but I wrapped him up in his parachute and brought him back. He was such a nice man. He'd made it possible for me to be in that squadron overseas. He'd met me at the El Toro base, got to know each other, and I told him I wanted to get overseas. He said, "I'll take you. Come on."

We did everything informal in those days. We had orders and all that stuff. The Marines, "Hey, we got a job to do, let's do it with what we got. Don't worry about all the paperwork."

But I'll never forget, he gave me five days off. I had two challenges. One, I had an old beat-up 1939 Ford car, and I had a nice girlfriend, and I remember I conned my roommate into taking care of the girlfriend, and for that I sold him the car at a reduced price, because she was a nice woman, very dignified. We had a nice relationship. I was living on base, but visited her, and she ran a small shop, a small business woman. That's the way you did things in those days.

And off I went. I had five days to pack up my stuff and sign up all the papers, get the physical. Went aboard a Jeep carrier.[5] Those were carriers that were made in large numbers in World War II. They had about a third of the deckload of a big carrier, and they were quite effective ships, but they weren't that big. They had a shallow draft because they wanted to move them inland. We went through a typhoon, and that carrier went all the way over. Every Marine on that ship was so sick. My god, the sailors could deal with it, but they got us through three days. I always remember that story with all the incentives, the stories, the DEs, destroyer escorts.

DW: Yeah, they lost three of them.

JW: They rolled. I had wonderful experiences. Landed at Yokosuka, and we'd been at sea. Storm delayed us, I think about fifteen to eighteen days. Our mascot died, a dog, of seasickness, and we had to have a formal at-sea burial.

DW: Oh, my.

JW: There was a lot of friction between the sailors and the Marines, as there always is. They don't mix very well. But the ship was just out of mothball, and they didn't have time to clean it up well with Cosmoline. Every uniform, everything we had was messed up from Cosmoline. We were pissed off at the Navy for making us get all dirty and everything. So we were glad to get off, and I remember we made a beeline for BOQ to have our first drinks. Then there, these rascals conned us, said, "There isn't anything to drink in Korea. You'd better buy ahead." So we all bought bottles of liquor and threw some stuff out of our footlockers to make room. The footlockers were shipped by sea, and all the humans jumped on cargo planes, and only to get over there and find we had plenty of beer. [Laughter] They just wanted to make a buck for their BOQ bar. Oh, god. So I had a marvelous experience.

---

[5] The Navy deployed several *Commencement*–class escort carriers for the Korean War.

Then coming home, I opted to fly all the way in a four-engine plane, and it was coming back for repairs. We lost two engines on the way, and I kept looking at that ocean, "Oh, god." After going through all the stuff in Korea, and now this is the way to—but we got through. But we had to land in Guam and have an engine put back on and taken off, put on. So I had a lot of fun. I put in a lot of flying time. I had a little book in those days, used to call it something, logs all your flying time.

DW: Logbooks? Now, when you did all this time up in the air, you logged that, did that get you flight pay?

JW: No. It got me a flight jacket, though. They finally admitted me to the flight officers' bar, presented me with a fur jacket, and that jacket's now on display at Quantico, among my memorabilia in the museum down there.

DW: Excellent. All right.

JW: Oh, my. I really enjoyed all of it. It's fun to tell you about it. I just look at these kids today and think, I wonder if they're up for doing the same thing that my generation did. Everything was an adventure.

DW: Okay. Are there any other things about Korea, your time on active duty in the Marine Corps that you want to—

JW: I finished the Marine Corps. I was offered a chance to get out of the Corps when I came back. I mean, very briefly, we returned from overseas, processing unit, and the officer very nicely said, "Do you want out or do you want to stay in the reserves?"

I said, "No, I owe the Corps a lot. I'll stay." So I stayed in the reserves for, I think, ten to twelve years.

My wife, a lovely lady, filed for divorce, but anyway, she said, "It's the Marine Corps or me. You're gone away every summer. You only have two weeks' vacation, you go off on these two-week training trips."

So one time I was going down to Yemassee, South Carolina, in July to a naval justice refresher course, and the train left Union Station at nine o'clock to go down to Yemasee. When I packed my bag the night before and put it in the hall, had a guy pick me up and drive me to the train station, her bag is there. She said, "I decided I'm going with you. I made arrangements for somebody to care for the children. I want to see what this is all about."

I said, "Okay." I'm excited.

So some guys brought their wives occasionally. If you went to a big base, you could stick 'em in a BOQ. So we went down, and she was pregnant with our third child, about five or six months' pregnant, and hot as hell,100 percent humidity, 100 degrees. I was only a first lieutenant and I therefore drew the top floor on a BOQ. She had to walk up four flights, down four flights. But the first night, they gave us a parade, and she liked that. The second night, we discovered the outdoor movies, we'd go and sit, and it was very nice. I've forgotten the third night, but I remember the fifth night. I'm waking up and she's got a—women had these steel heels in those days, thin heel. She's banging the shit out of me with a shoe. She says, "It's the Marine Corps or me. I can't take it."

I said, "Okay, okay. Calm down." So I calmed her down. I said, "I can't quit. It's dereliction of duty. But I'll put you on the train and then we'll talk about it when I got home." Well, we talked about it when I got home. So I had to go out at fourteen years long, six short of the twenty to get my retirement.

DW: Now, you mentioned, did the Marines have a Judge Advocate General program?

JW: That was all Navy. No, I just took it because of the fact I liked the law. No, I never was able to get—they tattooed onto me the MOS 2fifty2 serial number,[6] but they did that training all the way through.

DW: I think that's probably a good time and place to break for today.

[End of November 13, 2017, interview]

---

[6] MOS Military Occupation Specialty Code.

Interview Number 3 with John W. Warner, USN (Ret.)
Date: November 29, 2017

David Winkler (DW): Okay. Today is November 29th [2017]. This is David Winkler with the [U.S.] Naval Institute Oral History Program, seated with Senator John Warner in his office here in Washington, DC This is the third interview. What we'd like to do today is cover the period of the 19fiftys, how he got involved in politics, involved in the [Richard M.] Nixon campaign, how his legal career developed, and also a little bit, I guess, about family life background.

So you're discharged from the Marine Corps and you go back to the University of Virginia Law School?

JW: All men, no women in UVA Law at that time, and there were only, I think, eight or nine of us who had military reserve status that got called back. All the rest of them got student deferments, so they never were involved at all in the Korean War. Maybe after they graduated from law school, depending on somebody—the war pretty well over by that time. So of that group, three or four—I know three, I think it was four—were killed, and, anyway, the few of us that went, the dean took a special interest in all of us, and I really buckled down. It was hard to make the transition from Korea and the Marines to just putting your head in books and classes, but anyway, we did it.

I had the good fortune of winning a clerkship with a federal judge, wonderful man, E. Barrett Prettyman,[7] of the Federal Circuit of Appeals for the District of Columbia, a very major part of the federal court system, and I served him as law clerk for a year, then went into the U.S. Attorney's Office, which is sort of a traditional training ground for people who wanted to be trial lawyers, and that was my ambition. Sure enough, I got plenty of training. I tried a couple hundred cases over the five years-plus I was in that office, and it was a marvelous experience.

In the context of that, the chief judge of the Federal Circuit Court of Appeals—Prettyman later became chief judge; he wasn't chief judge at this time—but they appointed senior members

---

[7] Elijah Barrett Prettyman (August 23,1819–August 4, 1971) served as a United States circuit judge of the United States Court of Appeals for the District of Columbia Circuit. Nominated by President Truman on September 12, 1945, he became an associate justice seat on the United States Court of Appeals for the District of Columbia and subsequently served as United States circuit judge of the United States Court of Appeals for the District of Columbia Circuit from June 25, 1948.

of the private Bar Association to the most egregious criminal case and hopefully to introduce the Bar Association to up the caliber of individuals who volunteered to take on pro bono cases, because that's quite a responsibility to take on the case of an individual who's been indicted for a federal crime, with all sorts of possibilities of confinement facing them, and they really needed better qualified lawyers than the run-of-the-mill that were stepping up to take on these cases.

And in that context, I met the senior partner, or one of the founding partners of Hogan & Hartson law firm, which occupied a position by virtue of size and reputation among the four or five top law firms in the nation's capital. I was deeply honored to get that appointment to the firm out of the U.S. Attorney's Office, because it came about because Hartson, Nelson T. Hartson,[8] was appointed to a criminal case, he took the case on, even though I said it's a potential death penalty. His defendant had killed two people. Anyway, he brought in a lot of seasoned trial lawyers and had himself flanked on right and left by high-powered and able men, but I had the facts, and the man was found guilty, and they entered into a plea agreement towards the end of the case.

Hartson then, after the case was over and he was free of all of his obligations under the pro bono appointment—he wanted to do it very carefully—he just approached me quite forcefully, saying he'd like to hire me to come work in his office. He'd watched me in this case and he was impressed, I guess. So anyway, I went to work for him. It was an absolutely marvelous experience. Again, the firm was the top half dozen firms in the nation's capital. All the firms of major consequence were in a little geographic area from K Street; that is, 15th and K. They later spread along K in years later, but at this time it was basically spread down 15th Street, and the major banks and law firms were all collocated in about four, five, six square blocks around the Federal Treasury Building there. So it was an exciting period in my life. I enjoyed my work with Hogan.

---

[8] Hogan & Hartson traces its origins to 1904 when Frank J. Hogan opened his law practice in Washington, DC Hogan's success attracted Nelson T. Hartson to the firm in 1925. Growth and further success led to the 1938 partnership between Hogan & Hartson. In twentyten the firm merged with the international firm of Lovells founded by John Spencer Lovell in eighteen99. Warner remains in the employ of the firm as of twenty19.

Then you asked about how I got into politics. Earlier in my life, the attorney general of the United States plucked out several assistant U.S. attorneys to take a leave of absence from the federal government, total leave, and serve as aides to Richard Nixon when he ran for his first try at the presidency in 1960, and I was picked as one of those, and I got to know him quite well, traveled extensively with him.

Then, of course, he didn't win; Jack Kennedy won that election. It's interesting, I'd gone to law school with [Robert F.] Bobby Kennedy, he was a year ahead of me in law school, knew him, and I'd later gotten to know Senator Kennedy. He was running for fresident and he won. So I left them and—I'm trying to think. Yes, I went directly from them to then Hogan & Hartson—I meant into the U.S. Attorney's Office, and then out of the U.S. Attorney's Office.

In the 1968 campaign, Nixon ran again, and this time my lovely wife at that time had three children, we had three children, and she did not look kindly on my going back on a traveling status and be gone all the time, so I was given the job of managing his office in Washington. Nixon kept his official presidential campaign office in New York at the Pierre Hotel, and had a very small group, but he knew me and he said, "I want you to go down and run this office in Washington, and don't worry, I'll send down plenty of people to work for you." And sure enough, we rented the Willard Hotel, which was at that time, for whatever reason, closed, no longer serving as a hotel. The building was empty, and we occupied it and had close to a thousand people, volunteers, largely. It was a fascinating experience.

Well, this time he won, and so he then said, "Wait a minute. I want you to go into—," what we called the transition office, which is where one president phases out a staff and the incoming president phases in their staff. It was fascinating, and I met a man named Melvin Laird, who was a congressman, and he came in rather unexpectedly, because originally Senator [Henry M.] "Scoop" Jackson[9] was to have been Richard Nixon's secretary of defense, but after being announced, I've forgotten the period, a couple of weeks, he suddenly decided he really didn't want to leave the Senate. So Mel Laird was picked, and he left the House of Representatives, where he'd been on the Defense Appropriations Committee of the House, and he was very knowledgeable about military matters. He was a distinguished sailor in World War II, a young

---

[9] Senator Jackson was a Democrat from Washington State.

officer aboard a destroyer, was wounded in the course of the battles over there and had quite a distinguished career, was a wonderful man.

He came in as secretary of defense. He picked me up out of the transition office, since I was working for him in screening people to go to work in the Department of Defense, and he and I did many an interview together. I was primarily the notetaker. But it was a fascinating experience, all the wonderful people that wanted to volunteer. He offered me the position of Under Secretary of the Navy, with the understanding that if all went well, the secretary, who was John Chafee, a distinguished member of the political structure out of the state of Rhode Island, he'd been governor of Rhode Island in younger life—I think three times he was governor; they only have a two-year term up there—so Chafee was made secretary. He'd been a young Marine on Guadalcanal as a private. He was later commissioned and he was a second lieutenant in the Battle of Okinawa, very courageous and wonderful man. Later in life, as we were reunited in the Senate, he became one of the best friends I've ever had in life. We lost him too early. I don't know; he had a very strange disease while in the Senate and died after about a year of struggling. Mighty fine man.[10]

Anyway, he and I were the team, and he did resign, as planned early on, and I succeeded him, as planned, and we had—excuse me for yawning—a very colorful ceremony at Eighth and I.[11] I was proud to be the only Secretary of the Navy in history ever to take the office of Secretary of Navy at a Marine base. The Navy viewed that with some umbrage.

So, moving right along—

DW: Let's roll back a little bit because we had a conversation one time about the actual Nixon campaign in '60, which you gave me some very good insights about how Nixon took the loss, and I think that might be worth sharing.

JW: Well, that's really interesting. Again, the advance man's job is to plan every detail of the candidate's visit to a community. Well, I'd planned many a trip with him. I was in on two debates, and that's the first time presidential candidates debated. It's fascinating. I remember

---

[10] Chafee died from congestive heart failure at the age of seventy-seven on October 2 1999.
[11] Eighth and I is the street intersection in SE Washington where the home of the commandant of the Marine Corps is located as well as the Marine Corps Barracks.

Bobby Kennedy, again a law school friend, was on the other side doing the same work as I was doing for Nixon, he did it for his brother John, and I remember Bobby and I sat down one time. We were at war, of course, as competitors, but we had a strong friendship. And [Jacqueline L.] Jackie Kennedy, the President's lovely wife, whom I'd known when we were teenagers, we sort of grew up together in the same little social group, was then pregnant. I said to Bobby, I said, "Bobby, she's under a lot of stress out here in this campaign."

"Oh, yeah, but she's up to it."

I remember one night in a debate, she wanted to attend. Of course, the vice president outranks the senator. So when we planned the debates, it was a joint planning between the two staffs, but if there was a difference of opinion, usually the vicepresident carried the day. On this one, it was a minor but interesting facet. I said to Bobby, "Look, if she suddenly goes into some sort of—." She was in the final stages of the pregnancy. I said, "We at least ought to build a little privacy into her accommodations," in the big room in which the debate took place, in one of the television stations.

He was always very grateful, and I remember we erected a special tent in there where she could be suddenly whisked away if she began to experience the first stages of delivery. My father had been an OB/GYN, and I had some very small knowledge of what went on in the lives of a doctor delivering children. Anyway, he was always very grateful for that. She was too.

I knew her quite well in later life, after she was sadly widowed. Her farm was right next to my farm in Middleburg, Virginia. We used to do a lot of horseback riding together.

So, back to now the '68 campaign. Of course, Nixon won, and I went in with Laird transition office.

DW: Back to 1960, the one story you related to me was—

JW: Oh, yes, this is the '60 campaign. I took him [Nixon] on his last visit, which was to go to California and cast his vote, and we were in Los Angeles, because I remember we went into one of the better hotels. Yes, because I remember the LA General Airport the next day. So my job was to basically just to accommodate [sic] him to the polling place, vote, and get him back to go to bed early.

Well, I remember sitting up with Bob Haldeman and John Ehrlichman and I, and there may have been one other staff or two, watching the returns, and Nixon came into the room in his pajamas around midnight, and he said, "Guys, go to bed. This election's not going to get solved tonight. It's hung up with lost votes in Texas, lost votes in Chicago. Let's get some rest, because we don't know what we're going to be faced with in the morning." Well, I don't know if we followed his advice.

But anyway, the phone rang in my office early the next morning, and Nixon said, "I want to go back to Washington and see the president. Get a plane. Let's go."

I remember it so well because I called up American Airlines, which chartered our planes many times, and they told me, "Well, because of the outcome of the election, it can't be predicted, we've had to suspend all our lines of credit to the campaigns."

I said, "Yeah, but I've got the vice president of the United States. I've got to get him back to Washington, DC"

Anyway, I finally got a major donor here in Washington, the head of Folger Nolan Investment and Securities, and he wired me $fifty,000. I got a plane. Anyway, took Nixon out, put all the staff on the plane, and put the plane at the end of the strip. We wanted to stay away from the press because the election was still wide open, no declaration by either candidate as to who was winning. So I put the staff on the plane, then came back and got him and Mrs. Nixon, and went out. As we were disembarking from the car out at this old muddy, dirty strip at the end, I remember puddles of oil all over the place. In those days, planes dumped all their fuel and oil coming in to land.

So there was a mechanic that had been sent out routinely to watch the plane take off, to make sure everything was all right. The guy was listening to a handheld radio, and as we walked by to get on the plane, Nixon paused to listen, and the radio explained how no one had made a declaration of winning because of the hangups in both Texas and Chicago. And Nixon, I remember, asked the mechanic, "Could I hold the radio to my ear? I want to hear every word," which he did. And he turned to an aide next to me, said, "Get the president on the phone and tell him I'm coming immediately back to Washington, but that I do not want to contest this election, because the continuity of succession to the president of the United States should never be in doubt for a minute, but I want to make that announcement after consultation with him, the president." So we set it all up.

But that was a very historic moment, and you gained from Nixon his understanding of the constitutional power which he was about to undertake, hopefully. So, later on of course, announcements were duly made, but he was consistent about never requiring a recount, for fear that he would put in jeopardy the continuity of succession. So that was the closeout of a very interesting chapter of my life.

DW: Now, at the same time, you were married, because we talked about your reserve duty and your bride wasn't too happy about your going away on weekends. I imagine this was another stress.

JW: Oh, yeah, big time, yeah. That finally caught up with me years afterwards. I had fourteen and a half years of active duty of three to four years and the rest reserve status, and I wanted to shoot for twenty so I could get medical, and also the satisfaction of having retirement as opposed to just release from active duty, but the Marines—I just hadn't been able to keep up with the number of days of what we call regular service on active duty, and I'd taken my two weeks heretofore as she was raising these children, to go off. Those are the days when young men, professional men, all they had was two weeks' vacation, and I used to spend it in the Marines. She got a little weary of that, understandably and rightfully. So I had to resign.

DW: Just out of curiosity, how did you meet your first wife [Catherine], Cathy Mellon?[12]

JW: Just at a dance at a hotel—at a country club. They had a dance at the Chevy Chase Country Club. We took immediate liking for each other and began to date each other. Then her father, Paul Mellon, noted philanthropist and a wonderful man, he said—and this was done almost invariably among the wealthier families in America, to some extent among others of lesser means, but you sent your daughter off to travel—I've forgotten the exact phrase of it, to go to Europe, to go to the usual watering holes as part of your final educational process. So her father announced that she was going overseas in the company of a woman who was a lifetime friend of her father and mother as her escort. So we had barely gotten under way, but a lovely relationship,

---

[12] In 1957, Warner married Catherine Conover Mellon, the daughter of banker and art collector Paul Mellon and his first wife, Mary Conover.

until her father announced that she was going to do this. So she was gone, and then when she came back, we stayed in contact, and it wasn't too long after that, we got engaged.

All right. Where are we now?

DW: So you came back after the campaign.

JW: I went back to Hogan & Hartson.

DW: Hogan & Hartson, and you're here in Washington through the 1960s. Now, when you get assigned to join the Nixon campaign, was that a preference to work for a Republican? At the time, you're still a DC native, correct?

JW: I had moved it from Virginia.

DW: Did you have a political affiliation at the time? Did you consider yourself an [Dwight D.] Eisenhower Republican or—

JW: Very much an Eisenhower Republican, yes.

DW: So that kind of leans your strong support for Nixon because Nixon, of course, was Eisenhower's vice president.

JW: Ike was a very interesting man. I don't presume to have gotten to know him very well. My first campaign with Nixon in '60, they brought me into the White House to train to be an advance man. It was a fascinating job of about three months, learning all the ropes of the press, the security. You had to work with the Secret Service on all your events carefully.

DW: Okay. So during the eight years between—you were involved in the '64 campaign for Goldwater?

JW: A little bit. Not much. Nixon ran for governor and I did a little bit in that campaign, not much. Too far away, California.

DW: Although he beat Nixon, obviously the day Kennedy was shot must have been memorable for you.

JW: Well, it was, because my wife's family were becoming good friends of the Kennedys, because the Kennedys had established their second home, as I said, there in the Middleburg area, and Mrs. Mellon and Mrs. Kennedy had become great friends because of their common love for gardening. So anyway, gardening was very important, so they were good friends.

I remember Paul Mellon, his office was one of the private homes that were owned by private citizens like him, right across from the White House on Farragut Square, and those homes were all later—each one may have been different to how it was transferred back to the federal government. My recollection is Mr. Mellon gave his to the federal—it seems to me a trust was set up that took and held the properties to establish Farragut Square. But all those buildings along Farragut Square, along the western corridor of Farragut Square, were taken into the custody either of the government or a federal entity, because years later, when I became head of the Bicentennial, I had two offices on that square for the purpose of bringing in foreign visitors and dignitaries and entertaining them on the 200th anniversary of our nation.

DW: So as far as your reaction to the loss of President Kennedy, it's—

JW: I remember my wife and I went to her father's office that day, because up on the top floor there was a very clear vision down Pennsylvania Avenue, and we had a parking space, his parking space and permit to get in. Basically, it was pretty heavily secured around the White House. We watched that parade leave the White House, and seems to me they were marching to Capitol Hill. I don't know.

DW: At the same time, you had President Johnson assumes [*sic*] the office. One of the issues that you'll engage with is we're getting more involved in Vietnam. From an outside perspective, sitting here in the law firm, did you have any observations about our involvement?

JW: Other than I had an intense interest in federal government, and this firm was beginning to emerge, as were other law firms, from the purity of the practice of law into the regulatory domain, and it was a slow evolution. And you've got to remember lawyers, when I was growing up, there were lawyers, doctors, and ministers in a category. They were known as professions. Engineers were around the edges, but they never quite got the—

DW: Gravitas?

JW: I don't know. Anyway, but we slowly began to move into it, and I did some pro bono work, I've forgotten, work on draft boards and things like that. But we didn't get fully into the real depth of that war, because it was cookin'.

DW: Okay.

JW: Well, it caused Lyndon Johnson to decline to run for president.

DW: So the work you were doing here—

JW: I took a leave of absence from the law firm to go to work in the White House. Well, I actually took the leave of absence for a year to run Nixon's campaign; that is, that portion of his campaign that was housed at the Willard Hotel. We used to call it the Campaign Annex. I mean, we had people in there, like I remember Nixon called up, "Give John Eisenhower a suite. He's important. Keep him busy. Spiro Agnew, keep him down there. I don't want him up here in New York. Give him a suite. Keep him happy."

DW: So in 1960, you were doing all the advance work, and in 1968, you were running the campaign.

JW: Managing "Lawyers for Nixon," "Undertakers for Nixon," "Doctors for Nixon," all these subgroups that wanted to be involved in the campaign.

DW: Now, that year the convention was in Miami, I recall?

JW: I wish I had [unclear]. I don't know. Seems to me—I can't pull it out of my head. Shameful I can't pull it out of my head.

DW: We know the Democratic Convention was in Chicago.

JW: That was a debacle.

DW: And by that time, the war had become very contested.

JW: Whew. Front and center.

DW: And I think when we sit down next time, that'll be topic number one.

JW: Yeah, sure.

DW: We can talk about how the Nixon administration, Melvin Laird—at the time during the campaign, when does Henry Kissinger come into play?

JW: Into my life, he came after I'd been at the Pentagon two years, because Laird decided to open secret negotiations with the Soviet Union, I mean really secret, to try and lessen the tensions of the Cold War as it related to the operations of our naval, surface, and air units on and over the high seas of the world, and it became the Incidents at Sea, of which you're an expert.

DW: And we're going to go in great detail on that. You could write a book on that subject.

JW: The best book has been written.[13]

---

[13] Warner is referring to the interviewer's PhD dissertation, which was republished by the Naval Institute Press in 2017 under the title *Incidents at Sea*.

DW: Okay. Why don't we close for today.

JW: Yeah. I'm somehow thoroughly punched out.

[End of November 29, 2017, interview]

Interview Number 4 with John W. Warner, USN (Ret.)
Date: December 18, 2017

David Winkler (DW): Today is December the 18th, 2017. This is David Winkler for the Naval Institute Oral History Program with Senator John Warner.

This is the fourth of our interviews. Today we're going to talk about the election of Richard Nixon, his appointment as under secretary, and then focus on the Vietnam War.

John Warner (JW): You asked about where I was on the election night for 1968. I had run his Washington office from the Willard Hotel and had about anywhere from 1,000 to 1,fifty0 young people, as well as Colonel Eisenhower had an office there, the vice president had his office there. It was a very fascinating experience and had a lot of bright, wonderful people working for me, all volunteers. And it's interesting today how many of them have become senior partners of law firms and diplomats. It was a class of young people of all colors, mixes, backgrounds, economics, you know. Wasn't any special sieve we sorted out to get people. They'd somehow gravitate to the challenge of working with a successful candidate, first to make the candidate's success and then join with him. It was just a marvelous experience for me.

Then I went to the transition office, where I was assigned to the desk that was sorting out all the applications for Pentagon and the Department of State. Then we really had to sever the two, because there were some conflicts in there, and we stuck with the Pentagon. Then eventually I was fortunate enough to get the under secretary slot, which led to then my becoming secretary.

But I wanted to inject in here just a bit of a tutorial on America's system of forming the cabinet and subcabinet. The subcabinet is the general category of all those who are not cabinet but are working as under secretaries and/or assistant secretaries and are in the uppermost structure of the cabinet offices. And that's the way we work. When there's a rollover, we try to have a seamless transfer as possible, and, generally speaking, it's done in a friendly, bipartisan way when the parties are different, as it was in this case, because Lyndon Johnson was faced with the reality that he could not win again because of a lot of incidents connected with the war. So he was stepping down, and there was some bitterness in there.

I remember when I was asked to go over and get the keys for the offices for the transition, the guy that was in the White House in charge of allocating the offices to the new transition team—and, incidentally, that's written into law that a certain number of offices in the EOB, that's Executive Office Building—that was before we had the new EOB. This is just when the old one was there. Fascinating building. At one time, the Army was in there, the Navy, State, all of them. The president's office is right next door, and all the door knobs have these classic, beautiful doorknobs with the seal of the secretary of state, secretary of the army, treasury, all that. Maybe the Treasury was separate.[14]

Anyway, the way we do it, new president comes in, he picks X, Y, and Z to be cabinet officers. Z, Y, and Z picks, as a rule, in consultation, as we used to say, with the White House, his principal subordinates, under secretary and assistants. Then you get on down into what we call the super grades, the Civil Service and so forth.

But the thing that's astonishing, here we are, it's January of 1969, Nixon took the oath of office, became president, and the war in Vietnam was at a very high pitch, and the outlook was not clear at all. We had not reached that measure of success that was anticipated. Matter of fact, you see, we had an interim secretary of defense in Clark Clifford. McNamara had resigned, not under protest, just felt his time was up, and the president turned to Clark Clifford. Clark Clifford was a very interesting man. In later life, I got to know him quite well. He was a very eminent investment banker type around Washington, New York. He was absolutely in the upper tier of successful men in the United States, and he had a very, very good grip and understanding on American politics. So, to some extent, he was quite capable to go in there. I don't recall what his military background was, but he struggled with that department, I think about eighteen months.[15]

And then there was a turnover. "Scoop" Jackson was to have been the secretary of defense until someone told him, "Scoop, if this thing doesn't work out with Nixon, you might be able to run for President someday." He was a Democrat. To Nixon's credit, he was picking a Democrat. He wanted upfront to show bipartisanship in the area of national security and defense. Anyway, Jackson was talked out of coming over.

---

[14] Warner is referring to the Old Executive Office Building (EOB), now renamed the Eisenhower Executive Office Building, a National Historic Landmark built between eighteen71 and eighteen88. The building first hosted the Departments of State, War, and Navy.
[15] Clifford, based on his legal experience, entered the Navy with an advance pay grade serving from 1944 to 1946. Reaching the rank of captain, he served as assistant naval aide and then naval aide to President Truman.

And he quickly and fortunately found Melvin Laird, a strong Republican from Wisconsin, albeit—I tease him a little bit—he did have a flavor. He had a liberal streak in him that was a little bit to the left of Nixon's basic charter, but, nevertheless, a very able man. He had been in the House I think a dozen years. He was on the Appropriations Committee and, I think, had a high position on the Subcommittee on Defense. So anyway, he gave up his seat in the House and came over, and I had the privilege of working with him in the same-sized room that you and I are sitting in, we had a room that big over in the old EOB to do the work of transition.

But the thing that was so remarkable is that within weeks, we had picked and Mel Laird had carefully picked only about half Republicans to go in, and he persuaded half the Democrats in offices in the Pentagon to stay on for a while. He did sort of evaluate the different ones, but he got a splendid group of very able men who had presidential appointments. I remember one was the secretary of the army, and I think another was the comptroller. They were in key top positions, because Laird, having been on the defense committee, he understood quite well the challenge of coming in to do that job.

And mind you, defense is isolated over here in the sense that I'd say a very high percentage of people working in defense—well, first you have the career staff of the Army, Navy, Air Force, who all aspire to be generals and admirals, but, nevertheless, spend anywhere from eight to ten or twelve years, and those men and what few women there were at that time were thoroughly capable of giving up their term as captain of a ship, reporting to Washington and taking up a desk in the Pentagon, because they were doing one portion of their work at sea operating a ship, but the ship was responding to orders from the Pentagon, so it wasn't like they were moving in a new world, and they had a lot of contacts in the Pentagon, so they assimilated into their positions very easily, the senior military, as they rotate in and out of top positions in the Pentagon, not necessarily presidential positions. As a matter of fact, very few of them get presidential positions, but they did do the chief of staff to the Army, Navy, and all the way down.

Civilians are totally different. They're brought in, and to some extent you draw on your military experience, and I had modest military experience, having served in World War II in the Navy for just about two years or less, a few months less, and then another two years in the Marine Corps, and in the Marine Corps Reserve. So I had a good understanding of defense and defense issues in the eyes of, let's say, a captain in the Marines, definitely, top rank. But all of a sudden, you are offered the job to become under secretary. You go through a careful screening process. Heavily weighted are your experiences in uniform. Don't have to have lot of medals, but at least you were there and you understand the mentality, rigidity, and challenge of being in uniform, and that applies whether you stay there a couple of years or thirty years.

But suddenly you're given an *enormous* amount of responsibility, not the least of which is the life and limb of an individual or groups of individuals, namely, those military in uniform, in the case of the Navy Department, most Marines and sailors. I mean, they were laying their lives on the line, the Marines deep in the jungles of Vietnam, and Navy aboard ships and aircraft. So it's a heavy burden. Suddenly you realize it.

I remember the first day in office, I was handed a daily casualty report, and the casualty report, all deaths recorded in the last twenty-four hours, and you suddenly look at it, and in my instance, eight or ten Marines on it, two Navy pilots lost, shot down by anti-aircraft fire. The fellows on the ships had a fairly secure life. The aviators were dealing with a lot of what we call ground-to-air weaponry, and we were losing lots of them. Marines, we were just losing them like the Army was losing theirs. So it was a wake-up call.

When you take this job, you screen for qualifications, you go up to Capitol Hill. Congress then has a hearing. You've got to testify, and you've got a good bit of homework to convince Congress, and Congress realizes you're a new boy on the block, but, "Have you studied this? Have you studied that?"

"Yes, yes." So you kind of go to school.

But then comes the day that you arrive at the Pentagon, and the Pentagon was built originally to be a hospital for the wounded they anticipated we were going to experience if this war went on, and that was its original use. Well, they shifted gears somehow and it developed into a huge office complex. But I walked into my office, as did other presidential appointees, and there on your desk is a six-inch stack of papers, and you're assigned military aides. They carefully don't chuck all the ones that are in there out. They keep them, and you learn to like them, and then in time, they go back to active-duty assignments. You pick some new guys and you have a voice in it. The system very well schools young men and women.

Very few women then, very, very few, but there were a couple of fine women. You could just only count them on one hand in the Pentagon and maybe secretariat. I made the decision that we should have a woman as admiral. That didn't sit well with the admirals. But the secretary writes what they call a prescription for the flag board, which is all uniform, no civilians. They screen their own fellow sailors, Marines, pick the ones that should be promoted, present the secretary with a list of names carefully. The names match each of the vacant slots, and that's it. You can overrule them and say, "I'm not taking that person," but that was rare, but you had that authority, and to that extent, you had some infusion of judgment.

But they were all in uniform and they knew what they were doing. You're a civilian coming in. That stack of papers, I didn't have the foggiest idea. I could read the casualty report and understood that, but all the decisions that I had to make or begin to make were there for the day, and these were big decisions, many of them on procurement and weapons systems and so forth. Now, some of the men had come out of the aerospace section and they had some familiarity. I'd been a trial lawyer in this law firm that I'm now in, and I never saw a defense contract, and suddenly on my desk were a stack of them to approve. You've got to have instantaneous learning, and you rely very heavily on the infrastructure that you inherit, consisting of uniformed officers. You had some enlisted working for you, but I mean in the decision making, uniformed officers, Navy and Marine Corps. That's the beauty as the Secretary of the Navy: you've got two services. And then you had a marvelous career staff of civilians, people who had elected to devote their lives to a specialty, and year after year in the Pentagon, then they moved up the pay scale, then became Senior [Executive] Service. Sometimes it had a category for the top one. And they knew their business. So they were there to help you.

But then when it came time to affix a signature, it was yours, and you were committing your department to the expenditure of huge sums of money. Multiple millions of dollars in each of those departments were allocated in every year's budget. Decisions on buy or not buy this ship, buy or not buy that airplane or submarine, and there you are. You've got no running time to really sit back and sort of watch the wheels grind and slowly move yourself into the decision. It's yours.

So you soon began to repose, quite understandably, a lot of confidence in the ability of the professional civilian corps that you inherit and the professional uniformed people you had. But the system seems to work. It's a marvelous system established by the founding fathers. The president is the commander in chief [Warner eating; cannot understand what he's saying], and therefore that title, that responsibility gives that executive branch member of the President the authority to pick all those he desires to have to do the various levels of responsibility under him, and that's how the system works. Amazing. In England, it works similarly, but they rely much more heavily on what they call the permanent civilian in the positions that they have. The European countries have a similar system, but, again, the bureaucracy [Warner eating; cannot understand what he's saying] longer than we have here.

So that was it. Now we're there. What's your next question?

DW: Okay. So you're under secretary, then, of course, there's Secretary Chafee. So could you, I guess, discuss how that relationship is built, the division of power, authority?

JW: There's nothing in statute law other than the secretary shall be in charge of the department. He or she, in the case of the incoming president putting in a whole new team, very often the secretary has little or nothing to say about who the president picks for these various jobs, but you suddenly meet each other, you recognize the enormity of your challenge, not only complexity of the world of contracts and military politics is there, believe me, mister.

DW: Mm-hmm.

JW: I'm familiar with both military system of politics, you know, ring clickers, the Annapolis guys, always felt they had the edge, you know, because they're up over the regular and all that sort of stuff. But you had to be a fast learner, but you did manage. The system works. The system worked.

The secretary is omnipotent. Now, since I left, I think some of that omnipotence has been sort of changed in various ways. I know the Pentagon, early on, when the new Defense Department was established, in the old days, there was a Secretary of the Army and a Secretary of the Navy. The Air Force was always a part of the Army, the Air Corps. But that secretary ran everything.

DW: Right.

JW: In later years, they established the Joint Chiefs, and then slowly that Joint Chiefs began to report to the president, and there was only a lateral line. You kept the Secretary of the Navy informed, but the decision ran from the Joint Chiefs straight to the president, and that's when the secretaries began to have a diminished stature and authority. But I do want to make that point.

Now, what's next? You want to know about the war itself?

DW: Well, yeah, the war, but I guess just a little bit of clarification of what was the expectation from Secretary of the Navy Chafee as far as saying, "Okay, Warner, this is what you're gonna do. This is what I want to focus you on"?

JW: Okay. There's an enormous amount of public exposure that the Navy Department has to have. The secretary does that fairly exclusively. The uniformed guys really don't like press conferences. They like to run things by the book, experience. But the secretary has to interface with the public. They have a bad loss in the battlefield, a particular military operation just didn't work out, you had heavy casualties, the secretary of defense is the first one up on the line, then the Secretary of the Navy speaking on behalf of the Marines is the next one up. If you have a problem with a ship, I mean secretary called up there and you're thrown out in that press conference. You've got to defend your service and tell them how it is. So under secretaries don't get into that unless they're going to have to fill the gap. Occasionally when they go on trips, they interface with the press. But if there's a big accident, big battle loss, ship sunk, that service secretary is out there on the line. Takes a lot of time, a tough job.

John Chafee had been governor three terms, of Rhode Island. Albeit a small state, governors have a lot of problems and the governor is responsible for that state and answerable. So he was thoroughly trained and he was excellent with the press, so that took a big piece of my life and put it to the side. He also is the one that most effectively, simply because of his title, his rank, interfaces with other nations at their top level. You go to a conference in Europe, a NATO conference, you want the secretary there, not the under secretary. So he's got to spend a lot of time on that airplane and he's got to carve out a pretty healthy bit of his time to be with his operational forces, be in Vietnam, down in the mud the best you can for safety purposes. You don't want to take any foolish exposures, but you can get right into the fighting and you can hear the guns and you can see it all. So he's got to interface with the press, he's got to interface with the services, with the world, and even beyond that, he's got to be in on a lot of the work the secretary of state is doing, if he needs consultation from the secretary of defense, so that goes under it.

So, really, the under secretary is left to do his own, and he wants the care and attention of families. I'm the one that met POW wives. I was the one that looked after their pay benefits. I was the one who made sure they were fed and clothed. I was the guy that did the daily "Let's keep everybody going." And when the time came—for instance, I remember we were losing young men in the submarine force because as we injected nuclear submarines into the fleet, it was contemporaneous with America shifting part of its power needs to nuclear power.

We were rapidly expanding nuclear power, and to train an individual in the complexity of nuclear science, power, safety, that's a lot of hard work to do it. The military sent their officers to school for two years. Well, a year, and then they had the on-hands experience of driving the submarines and nuclear-powered ships, and they were absolutely in high demand by the civilian industry. They were worth five times what a graduate of, say, MIT, albeit he'd studied nuclear power. There's a guy, his hands were dirty, having worked with it. He understood safety, understands accidents. So these young officers were finishing honorably their tour of duty, usually four to six years. That's a contract you make periodically with the Navy or Army, whatever it is. And then you're free to go out if you want to go. An Annapolis graduate graduates after four years at Annapolis, he's got a five-year commitment to stay in uniform. He can't leave. And as a result, he learns a lot.

Or she. I'm going to use "he" and mean "she." So that's key to it. So then the secretary has got the contracts, major responsibility in the procurement area, so it's personnel, pay and benefits, it's procurement, it's base structure, base maintenance, all that is under the secretary. Then you've got the assistants, got the assistant secretary, different jobs, and you've really got a lot of help there.

And the under secretary pretty well runs the assistants.

DW: Okay. I guess while we're on the subject of the assistants, some of the people come to mind that were good assistants?

JW: Excellent, yeah. Really had top-notch people.

DW: Any examples off the top of your head?

JW: Mm-hmm. A guy named Charles Bowsher.[16]

DW: Oh, yeah.

JW: [Robert] McNamara had hired him out of a big accounting firm, and he served under McNamara, then served under that interim eighteen-month person they had.

DW: Clark.

JW: And then Mel Laird had the wisdom to invite him to stay on and he worked with me for years, became a very close personal friend, as he is today, but he finally got lured out and he became [sic] top civilian jobs in the county in budgeting. And certainly the engineers that do the research and development, assistant secretary for R&D, boy, that individual's worth his weight in gold because he's so [unclear] adversity and complexity of technology. Because you take a submarine, you've got electronics, you've got structural members [unclear], you've got nuclear power. Boy, those guys really have a lot of training. Secretary of personnel management, usually, pretty much, it's parallel to civilian. The rest of them are all unique.

DW: Okay.

JW: And industry is always looking to hiring [sic] those people. And industry wants to hire them for two reasons. One, they've got a lot of experience, but equally important is, two, they know the people left back in the building and they know who's in charge and who's got the answer to this, rather than somebody fumbling around trying to find out what it is.

---

[16] Charles Arthur Bowsher served as the 5th Assistant Secretary of the Navy (Financial Management and Comptroller) from 1967 to 1971 in both the Johnson and Nixon administrations.

DW: So that leads us to the big topic at the time. I visited you a session or two ago and you related a story about how Melvin Laird sent you and John Chafee to one of these war protests to get an assessment. Was that early in your tenure?

JW: I'd like to say it was within the first eighteen months.

DW: Okay.

JW: Because Laird saw in Chafee and, to a lesser extent, me, but, nevertheless, I had good credentials, he needed to know what the hell was going on out there, and he didn't want it filtered through four levels of memo writers, so he told us Monday, take off our Brooks Brothers suits, find an old car, don't have a driver. Secretary had a Cadillac. Under secretaries had a step down from a Cadillac but above a Ford with a rumble seat. And get an old beat-up car and drive down to the Mall, and there was a million-person march, peace march.

And that was a trip I'll never forget. It started the wheels running in Laird's mind that the war, as we were prosecuting it—to fight a successful war of long duration, you've got to have the home front with you, and the home front was eroding very rapidly. And sadly, the home front took their wrath out not on the Secretary of the Navy, although I was pelted with eggs many a time, but took it out on the uniformed people.

Just unexplainable to me how a guy coming back from Vietnam, having gone through that tortuous experience, only to get home and everybody, "Ah, I don't want that uniform." They told them when they got discharged, take the uniform off, buy some cheap blue jeans. It was a sad period of our life.

And he recognized, Mel Laird, that we had to phase this thing out, and what we did was to begin to train the Vietnamese, South Vietnamese, to learn to operate our equipment, maintain the equipment, and then "Here's the key. Goodbye. We're gone."

But it didn't work very well. A lot of political dissension, the country divided. Just did not work well, and a lot of blood and grief over it. Too bad. You know, if you're going into war, you'd better decide to go in with the—let me have that cookie—go in with the intention to win it and do whatever you had to do to win it, and we were up against an impossible crumbling political structure in South Vietnam, full of intrigue, full of graft, and there was just no political tenacity, because for a century they'd basically been ruled by very strong, ruthless rulers, you know, and this idea of their having democracy and all that stuff.

DW: You also had the French. It was a French colony for about a—

JW: Oh, yeah. And the French found it totally unimaginable, totally, quit, marched off, and they said to themselves as we went in, "C'est la guerre, old boy. You'll soon understand why we packed up and went home."

DW: True. Although the North Vietnamese certainly gave them a push to force the issue.

JW: We had just the finest people, as the community does today. I guess you think of your own generation being the best. Most of the senior officers, if not all, were World War II veterans.

And they'd been young officers, had to make the difficult decision, do we make a career out of a military or go out and jump into the sea of prosperity, as America was developing, and the wives were tugging at your coattails. But we support you. Really fine, fine people who decided to make a career out of it.

DW: So as under secretary, how much did Vietnam affect your portion of the weekly planning for example? Because, you know, one of your jobs is to provide the forces the training, as you mentioned, retention, acquisition of weapons, but then you mentioned, of course, you dealt with wives of the POWs. But as far as prosecuting the war and the strategy, that wasn't on your plate?

JW: No. Now, secretary of defense had a weekly meeting Monday morning, and the under secretaries were invited to sit in the back row. Now, it wasn't like the old rule that in a British household children would be seen but not heard, but it was a vestige of that. You were there to become totally familiar with what the [unclear] from the top to the secretary, what they had to do, because when the secretary took a trip, he was on the end of a long airplane flight somewhere, and you had to make decisions that were parallel to those that he made with regularity.

DW: So, at the time, the Chief of Naval Operations was Admiral Moorer?

JW: Admiral Moorer. He was a wonderful man, very much the old barrel-chested—there was a phrase called "the old barrel-chested" battleship sailors. And he fit that role, but he was a battle-tested aviator. Now, he flew the multi-engine planes, very little single-engine, and, of course, that is a pecking order of its own. It's not written down anywhere, but the single-engine fighter pilot is the ultimate. The single-engine torpedo bomber, dive bomber, fighter, they were the crème de la crème. The Navy had a number of multi-engine planes and they did some bombing missions, but that was left to the Army Air Corps in those days which became the Air Force.

DW: I recall he was a PBY pilot at the Battle of Midway.

JW: Yeah, that's right. He was PBY, Battle of Midway, and he was very courageous. I think he had several—I remember his highest award was Silver Star, which is quite a recognition.

Your Navy Crosses went to the submariners. You've got to understand there were a great percentage of them. I mean, you take that boat out, you just suddenly sever all communications with the real world except listening. You're on the receiving end, very little on the transmitting end. And you've got *huge* distances to transit and have to come up at night, and your survivability is dependent on recharging your batteries, and you hope there's not a full moon. Then you fire your torpedoes, and a high percentage of them malfunctioned. Still when I was there, they were malfunctioning.

I'll never forget one guy came back one time. Now, Vietnam didn't really have any torpedo exploits, but in World War II, this old guy told the story he couldn't explain to his squadron commander why he had so few hits that were effective. He said, so one day he spotted a small uninhabited island, and he put some of his crew and camera crew in a little dingy that you blew up with air, told them to go in, get on the beach and get in a safe place, because he was going to fire two torpedoes just at the rocks. Can't miss rocks. And sure enough, those two poor torpedoes boomed in and hit the rocks and they were still there. He took them back and showed him to his boss. "This is what I'm dealing with."

They got Navy Crosses, a good many of them, because the vice chief under Moorer had two Navy Crosses.

DW: The chief—

JW: "Chick" Clarey.[17]

DW: That's right.

JW: Wonderful man. He was my nomination to succeed Moorer, but the Secretary of Navy, in consultation with the secretary of defense, has the authority. I remember sitting in the room and I argued. I said, "Look, Chafee's going to leave in six months. It basically is my call."

Laird said, "No, you're not secretary yet, not until Congress confirms you." And he let Chafee pick a liberal, and that guy, he personally piled up on the rocks. He never amounted to anything.

DW: Well, speaking of Admiral Zumwalt[18] going back to Vietnam, because that was his—I guess he must have impressed Secretary Laird when he went over there.

JW: To his credit, he ran the riverine forces, because there was no real textbook explanation of what the riverine was to do, and his forces were operating at great personal risk, because you take those river deltas down there and estuaries from the sea and the rivers that emptied into the sea, and you take a small naval boat, which they had, and you're trying to resupply a regiment that got cut off from its supplies up the river, you try and get up that river with all the canopy and cover on both sides, these guys, the bad boys that hang out in those bushes blow right the side of your vessel with fifty-yards range. Couldn't miss. And there were a high number of casualties.

DW: So did you go over to Vietnam yourself as under secretary?

JW: Oh, yeah, about three or four times.

---

[17] Bernard Ambrose "Chick" Clarey, a graduate of the USNA class of 1934, served in submarines in World War II and as Vice Chief of Naval Operations in the late 1960s. At the time he was serving as Commander in Chief U.S. Pacific Fleet.

[18] President Nixon nominated Admiral Elmo Zumwalt to be the CNO in April 1970.

DW: Can you talk a little bit about those visits?

JW: Well, in the first place, I don't know of another word, but it's enormously exciting, and in the case of myself and being rambunctious, an ex-Marine, I wanted to push it to the edge. I'll never forget one time I was up on a fire base and it was active incoming and outgoing to operate this base, because it was also a protected side to the base from enemy fire. One side of the base was clearly exposed to enemy fire and receiving enemy fire, but the other, we were able to get helicopters in, take the wounded out.

I went up to see this base operate. It was brilliant, the way these men did it at high risk, and I remember going along a row of stretchers and these guys, I mean, the blood was clearly showing through the bandages. They were in bad shape. A whirlybird was to come in and pick them up and take them out, and I watched that operation. Those whirlybirds come in, they strap them on the side of the Hueys, and as they went, I got the feeling of what can you do. The guy's sitting there, he's stuffed full of morphine, and the clock's ticking on his life. So I went up, and they used to toe tag. They had toe tags, how much morphine he'd gotten, where the injuries were. I mean, a trained doctor could pick up a toe tag and pretty well get a good grasp of what the problem is as they were unfolding him, sending him into the operating room.

Incidentally, that operating room was a job my father had in World War I. That was the triage center. We didn't try and do triage out in the field. We tried to send them all back, which is a wise thing to do, because corpsmen are wonderful, beautifully trained individuals, hugely brave, but they are not doctors. And really you need a physician to make the decision, "Let's try and save this life. There's nothing we can do. Keep him full of morphine, make him as comfortable as you can till he dies."

But where was I? Oh, on the fire base.

So the whole line of stretchers there. So I would take the toe tag and wiggle it, and if there was any consciousness to the guy, I'd just say, "Looks like you're going to be all right." I was shooting from the hip.

Now fast-forward, I'm in the Senate, chairman of the Armed Services Committee, and you have to really meet personally all four-stars, candidates to be four-stars.

DW: Right.

JW: And particularly [the] candidate to be CNO. Well, this guy was going to be picked to be candidate for Commandant Marine Corps, so he was in there. A whole lot of financial stuff you've got to go through, a general orientation, looks like that. And got up to leave, and this man turned to me, the nominee to be the next commandant, and everything had gone beautifully well. He said, "Mr. Chairman, this is not the first time we've met."

"Huh?"

Said, "No, I remember. I'm on the fire base and I'm getting ready to be shipped out, and you came over and grabbed my toe tag. You said, 'You're going to be all right.'" He says, "Here I am. You were right." That was Krulak.[19]

DW: Okay.

JW: You have personal stories like that. That's the joy and the benefit of doing these jobs. You just remember.

DW: Now, this is obviously up in I Corps, northern area of the country, because that's where the Marines were assigned during the Vietnam War, up towards the DMZ and along the Cambodian border, very hilly, rugged countryside.

JW: The Marines were given some pretty tough terrain. There's always a push-pull between the Army and the Marine Corps that'll never change. You go back to World War I. Pershing, frankly, didn't want any Marines in the AEF, but Secretary of the Navy made the decision "They're coming."

I'll tell you another little story, kind of interesting. Pershing fought it, but finally Secretary of the Navy went to Wilson. Wilson said, "You're secretary. You tell Pershing what to do."

---

[19] Charles Chandler Krulak served as the 31st commandant of the Marine Corps from July 1, 1995, to June 30, 1999.

He took them, and at first they wanted to make them in charge of the hospitals and the food and resupplying the frontline Army units. Pershing finally relented. They fought the famous Battle of Belleau Wood, where the Marines were under terrific odds, heavy casualties, made their future Corps secure forever.

Anyway, go on. What else?

DW: So, continuing. As under secretary, you got to Vietnam, and probably besides going into in-country to visit with Marines, well, you probably met with the coastal forces and any—

JW: I spread myself around, but I remember one mission. I wish I could remember the name of the battle. The peace talks were under way, and they were on again, off again. I got to know Kissinger fairly well during that period, because he's the one that selected me to go to Russia—

DW: Okay.

JW:—to do incidents at sea. Anyway, Kissinger persuaded Mel Laird. He really wanted to grind it in, so we started flying around the clock, and took all our ships and had ship-to-shore surface bombardment all the way up the coast. Linebacker.

DW: That's it.

JW: Operation Linebacker. And it was done at Christmastime, so I said to my staff, "I think it's important that I go." And Admiral Clarey, who was CinCPac, knew of my interest. He said, "I will go with you." So the two of us, for four or five days, were visiting ships. Every ship that a helicopter could lower you on we visited. We visited twenty-two ships in seventy-two hours. That's a lot going down the rope and back up the rope. We had some close calls because the water was rough that time of year.

DW: I think the impetus for that was the sailors had been over there and the morale was a little—

JW: Very, very bad. And there were certain parts of the aircraft carrier where officers couldn't go in. There's not been much written about that.

It was not a pretty story. As a matter of fact, I kind of accidentally found out about it. No dispatches on it. So I looked into it when I was over there, when I was on the very carriers. They said, "We got a war fighting, we're doing around-the-clock flying. We just have to deal with it someday, but right now we have to, as the Brits say, pull our forelock and agree with the facts what they are."

DW: This is the sixties and seventies. You had the drug culture, and I think that was a problem.

JW: It was coming on. It wasn't that bad. Our worst problem was the home front turned against the uniform.

DW: Now, during your time, during this period, you had the North Vietnamese Easter Offensive in 1972. You're transitioning from an under secretary to secretary, and, of course, you're involved in the Incidents at Sea talks with the Russians, so you're talking about the decision to go hard against the North Vietnamese with Linebacker, and eventually we do negotiate a peace treaty in Paris, and that ends the war in January of 1973. Then we have the release of the prisoners.

JW: Was it January of '73?

DW: That's correct.

JW: What did we do, put out a ceasefire, didn't we? The end of the fighting.

DW: That's correct. Everybody stays in place, which I think the South Vietnamese government wasn't happy about.

JW: No, no, they weren't, yet they were not competent enough to take over the whole thing. Boy, the chapters after that were sad. I was there through, I think, June, April or June of '74, though.

So I must have seen a lot of it, but I was gone to the next job, which was the Bicentennial. Nixon wanted me to do that.

I remember seeing the television, in total disbelief of those helicopters taking off and the civilians hanging on the wheels and everything else, dropping, falling as they left the embassy. Not a pretty sight.

DW: Well, the happier news was when we had our POWs come back. Did you have an opportunity to meet with them and their wives?

JW: Oh, yes. Frequently I made a thing—Sybil Stockdale was the one that endeared herself to her fellow colleagues, widows. She would be the spokesman for the group, and she was the right person at the right time, wonderful. She always kept her head high.

But the most difficult job, I had none more difficult than this one. When the POWs came home, we knew, because we had very good intel out of the prison camps, that several of them had literally become turncoats and were squealing facts that were used against some of those being brutally treated in the prisons, attempted escapes or they won't sign this, a number of things that took place. And those guys had literally sold out, so there wasn't any question about getting rid of them, but should we court-martial them. And I'll tell you an interesting fact. I don't know if it's ever been written up, but it's truthful. I decided in most instances not to do the court-martial because had they been convicted, and as far as I knew, the facts were absolutely there to convict, there weren't that many. I think you could count them on certainly your ten fingers. You had, on the other end, you had a very faithful wife and children, often. And you court-martial them and strip them of their retirement or their salary, the whole thing, that wife gets punished. She never lost confidence. She fought her way. Boy, I was really criticized for that, but I felt we could not turn our backs on those widows. I think later on, people forgave me in many respects, after they looked at the severity of it. What the hell. I mean, he's finished. He's drummed out.

DW: Right.

JW: He's worthless in the job market, he's worthless, but that woman who steadfastly got up every morning and dressed those kids and got them out to school, helped them with their homework, you couldn't indirectly punish her.

DW: Okay. At that time, well, John McCain was one of those prisoners, and, of course, his father had been with the Seventh Fleet, so did you have opportunity to meet him for the first time?

JW: That is correct. When he came back—I've been trying to put it together, but I think I was with his father when his father first met him, but I can't reconstruct it well enough, because I went down to Annapolis the other day and I fussed over that. Just one of those things. I couldn't pull it out. Because it's clear that he came back, and I don't remember whether it was his squadron or what it was, was in Florida, but he wanted to go back to report to the then–commanding officer of the squadron that he was once in technically,

But what I do remember is I asked him if I could help him. He said, "Give me a day or two to sort out things." Then he contacted me, and we plotted out a good format for his reentering uniform and responsibilities. It was clear to me—and he felt pretty much the same way—he said, "I've really got to read four years of back newspapers. I don't know what's happened." So we sent him into the War College. He thrived in that, always with a sense of humility.

DW: Any other prisoners of war that—I know I've met "Eve" [Everett] Alvaraz [Jr.] and some of the other Navy veterans who—a fellow by the name of Ken Coskey hired me to work as a historian, and he was a prisoner of war. So most of these individuals went on to do good things.

JW: Yeah, they did. I remember the one that came to the Senate, though. He was in a wheelchair. Wow. It was very hard for him. Then I think he committed suicide. Come on. Help me out. You'll have to pull aside some POW—

DW: Yeah.

JW: —who studied the history. I can see him wheeling around the Senate chamber. I always befriended him. He knew exactly who I was and what I'd done. [unclear]. He was very gracious towards me. Some southern state.

DW: Was he Navy?

JW: Navy.

DW: Okay.

JW: He was an admiral, I think, got promoted to admiral when he got back.

DW: Ooh. Okay.

JW: Wasn't Jim Stockdale.

DW: No, no. He went out to the War College.

JW: I met one of them down at McCain's last appearance at the Academy. He introduced himself, came up. Very nondescript, lovely person, said, "I was in the camp with John."

DW: I've had correspondence with, like, Bob Shoemaker, who retired as an admiral. He was like, I think, the second-longest POW, and he's the one who's kind of credited with inventing that tap code. So I saw him about two years ago.

So, as far as personalities while you were over there, some of the naval commanders you may have run into? Did you run into Zumwalt while you were over there?

JW: We never crossed paths. Oh, I think we went to some funerals together. It wasn't that I was—I tried my best and he tried his best, but we both were just different philosophical—anyway, my last appointment was the new chief, you know, the admiral, the history guy.

DW: Holloway?

JW: Holloway. I appointed him CNO to succeed Zumwalt. Zumwalt was embittered, and at that point we severed all relationships, because he wanted one of the Bagley boys,[20] but secretary of defense at that time, Schlesinger was the secretary. He turned out to be a very highly respected CNO.

DW: One of the things that Vietnam did for the Navy was that it really stressed us as far as ship replacements, parts, cost. We were fighting basically with World War II naval infrastructure, and I think one of your concerns as under secretary must have been building programs to replace some of these ships.

JW: Oh, yeah, we went through several classes of cruisers. The submarines, we established the *Virginia* class. I remember making that decision, which was just an attack boat. [He meant *Los Angeles* class—*Virginia* is a new cruiser in the 1970s]

That was such a well- and orderly-run branch of the service, I'd be less than kind if I didn't say that they really knew what they were doing. Rickover[21] was very active. I was quite close to him as a personal friend. He didn't like Moorer, because Moorer was not happy with all the things that he was able to get out of Congress, and he overruled Moorer before Congress more than one time. So, boy, if you overrule CNO! That's not a happy event.

DW: Okay.

JW: And then he didn't like Chafee very much because Chafee was liberal, and he couldn't tolerate that. And he had his own fiefdom and was working and working well, and he just at first tolerated me and then we became friends, and we were friends right up through that crisis. I was part of the architecture that established, with Ronald Reagan—I was in the Senate—the positions and funding it, because he had a separate little entity, a fiefdom all of his own. He helped advise us on civilian nuclear power, and it seemed to me the ideal thing, but, boy, it blew up in our face.

---

[20] Worth H. Bagley and David H. Bagley both achieved the rank of admiral.
[21] The director of Naval Reactors, Admiral Hyman G. Rickover.

Well, listen, let's look forward to another one. I like to do this.

DW: Okay. That's cool.

[End of December eighteen, 2017, interview]

Interview Number 5 with John W. Warner, USN (Ret.)
Date: February 23, 2018

David Winkler (DW): Today is Friday, February 23rd [2018]. This is David Winkler for the [U.S.] Naval Institute, with Senator John Warner, and today we'd like to talk about the Russians. It just so happens I was contacted by Russian television yesterday, and they wanted me to talk about the *Yorktown-Caron* incidents in the Black Sea back in 1988. We had the collision between the Russians.

It might be worth noting—we're going to talk about the Incidents at Sea Agreement, but while that's topical, it's the twentieth anniversary of that incident, you were in the Senate at the time. We had these two Russian ships. We were doing innocent passage, I recall, in the Black Sea, and these guys came out and rammed us. Do you have any recollections?

John Warner (JW): You know, I don't have a recollection of it, Dave, so I'm fearful of trying to tread on areas that I can't recall. The Incidents at Sea Agreement was in effect.

But I've been up through that Black Sea passage.[22] I'll never forget proceeding up towards Russia, the Turks had put huge—I mean six-foot—mines in embankment, and they had a trap door. If you pulled the trap door, the thing rolled down the side of the hill and splashed right into this narrow passageway. So one guy could run along and pull those ropes, and within ten minutes, he would have closed the passageway, which is quite narrow there, a mile or so, pretty well close that passageway up. The Chief of Naval Operations of Turkey—I was on official visit—took me there to show me, with great pride, and he explained that they went all the way back prior to World War I.

DW: That's right. They had the Gallipoli, and I think the British and the French tried to run the straits, and didn't work out too well for the British and the French. They lost several ships. Was this back when you were Secretary of the Navy?

JW: Yes.

---

[22] The Bosporus Strait.

DW: So that was kind of an interesting trip. What were some of the other interesting visits you made? I know you spent a lot of time out in Southeast Asia with the Seventh Fleet. You probably traveled to, like, Japan and Formosa and some places like that.

JW: I went to all those areas, yeah, because, you see, I was Navy Under Secretary and Secretary five and a half years, and that was quite a long tenure. As such, I went to all the areas where we had U.S. naval facilities. It was a marvelous chapter in my life. I learned a lot and discharged my duty with reasonably good grades.

DW: Okay. Well, let's see about—and just going by region, you mentioned you had a very interesting visit with Turkey. I guess the British—you probably had a very good relation with the Royal Navy?

JW: Had quite a nice relationship. I went up to Holy Loch, where we had our submarine base. I visited almost all the British facilities, not that many. Then, of course, you see, CinCUSNavEur was located in London at that time, four-star position, and they occupied the same quarters that Eisenhower was billeted in during his tenure there in World War II, preparing for the invasion. Very historic. It was right there on the square with our embassy, which now has been rebuilt—

DW: I guess that was Grosvenor Square?

JW: I'll never forget one time, I just remember this so well, there were four four-star admirals, U.S. admirals, however, the occasion was in London, and I had two British four-star admirals, and I rent—not rented—the famous hotel there, it's a small one but well-known, called the Cunard International Hotel,[23] and actually I'd spent my honeymoon there at that time, probably ten years before that day. And I remember we had had dinner. We had a big round table put up in the restaurant for us. They were all in full uniform, and the people were coming in, any excuse to come in and dine and look at this collection of old sea dogs. It was rather interesting. That was

---

[23] Today it's a Novotel (London West).

just an aside. Cunard was just a block or two from the embassy and the quarters for CinCUSNavEur.

DW: During this time with the British, I guess we were sharing our knowledge as far as nuclear propulsion and ballistic missiles, because—

JW: Well, there is a side chapter to that, with which I had some involvement. We had probably the best sharing relationship with Great Britain. I least I know of none better. Yes, good, bad, or indifferent, I mean in terms—"better" perhaps is not the correct word. More comprehensive, covered a lot of systems, air, sea and undersea.

Great Britain at that time were contemplating the construction of their first nuclear submarines, and I had some involvement in the negotiations, and Rickover, of course, was very active in the negotiations. Rickover and I had a difference of opinion. Let's put it politely that way. It was pretty strong, the difference, but over a week's time of debating it, he finally came around largely to my point of view. But I felt that Great Britain, with the initial design phases of their submarine, we should go ahead and share with our strong ally the propulsion plant in large measure that we had in our then-current missile boats. It was for the purpose of trying to save them some money. Why should they go off and spend the extraordinary sums of money required to do all of the research and testing of a new concept that they would have had to develop, when we could, I think, quite safely—and it did turn out to become quite a safe exchange—share with them the propulsion designs that we were then using for our reactor installation and save them billions of dollars? And they were everlastingly grateful to me for that. And it made good sense.

DW: Because, in effect, the British ballistic submarines were kind of a force multiplier deterrent.

JW: Absolutely. I argued that very point that you make, because the more of our close allies that are working in tandem with me on the specific missions that subsurface weapons systems have, the better off we are.

DW: Now, the French, on the other hand, I think they developed totally different systems?

JW: I cannot recall the specificity of what they did. Surprisingly, we had very little to do with the French navy during my period in the Pentagon. I mean, what we did was courteous. We had the availability of their bases and so forth. But for submarines, we had Rota, Spain, which was a very major installation, and for that part of the globe down there, we had our facilities in Italy. We probably had some limited facilities down in the lower part of France, yes.

DW: Well, the French, if I recall, de Gaulle was now in power, and he kind of pulled France out of NATO, so they were—

JW: Kind of? He *did*.

DW: Yeah.

JW: And they pulled him out of Paris, you know. NATO was in Paris.

DW: That's right. You had to go to Brussels.

JW: Yeah, built a whole new set of headquarters. All of our officers had to find new quarters. I mean, the whole thing was typical de Gaulle, and, really, I think the French look back on it as a terrible era.

DW: Now, in Spain you mentioned, I guess Franco was in charge, so we had to deal with him.

JW: I personally do not recall meeting him.

DW: Okay.

JW: And our Rota installations were largely put in before I started in the Navy Secretary, so all that was in place, and it ran like clockwork and very successfully. Spain was a good host country.

DW: Well, same in Italy. We had a place in Naples. I don't know if—I think Sixth Fleet operated a cruiser out of Gaeta.

JW: Yes. But NATO South was in Naples.

DW: Yes. I've traveled there from time—well, when I was active in the fleet. So on the other side of the world, I think the strongest maritime ally—well, two of them, I would think, was Australia and Japan, and I expect that you probably had visits to Yokosuka and—

JW: Oh, yes. Considerable. But we had a limited exchange program of weaponry with Japan. With Australia, we had quite a strong exchange program of information and so forth. Australia has been involved in every war of the United States, on our side, fighting to support us, since the Revolutionary War. Of course, the Revolutionary War was against Great Britain. Understandably, they didn't get involved. But thereafter, they were absolutely in every engagement, they fought alongside of it, and that's true right through to today.

DW: Very much so. I think at the time, we were selling them *Adams*-class destroyers. I don't know if that had happened during your watch. They purchased a couple of destroyers from us, and later they would buy the FFG-7 frigates for their navy.

And, of course, the Japanese were strong allies, as far as a bulwark against the Soviet Union, which is, you know, the gist of the conversation I'd like to talk about today is the growth of the Soviet Navy and what were your concerns about that. When you came in as Under Secretary of the Navy, what were you seeing as far as trends of the Soviet navy forces?

JW: Well, in numbers, they had grown considerably. In technology, they had a progression of improvements in their weaponry and so forth, but they were still far from being a first-class navy.

DW: Okay. So the Soviets were still far from being a first-class navy.

JW: Yeah, but they had numbers of ships.

DW: During 1970, they did a big global exercise called Okean-70.

JW: Oh, yes, I remember that.

DW: How were you tracking that?

JW: Nothing unusual, but we were watching it, and other allies were sharing information with us.

DW: Okay. Did that give you an impression that they were making some progress?

JW: Oh, yes, very definitely.

DW: Okay.

JW: And they were making some significant progress in their submarines. And then, as you know, in connection with doing the agreement, I met a lot of the Soviet navy, endless number of banquets and visitations. By the way, I'll tell you one of the most classic recollections I have is their counterpart to Annapolis, which is—

DW: St. Petersburg.

JW: St. Petersburg. And there they have the old construction bays that the czar built to have his wooden ships made there, and they're as pristine today as the day that he left them. They really have taken good care of their navy.

I had one of the more amusing incidents up there. The Chief of Naval Operations of the Soviet navy was my chief counterpart in negotiations. The vice chief was next to him, and he's the one who came to Washington. But there was a third guy. It was sort of a triumvirate, because these three young naval officers during the early part of World War II were all ship commanders, and [chuckles] the only ships they had were bringing in supplies up the rivers to the, for instance, Stalingrad. That was totally supplied by a riverine force that they had. But anyway, they were roommates. They'd grown up all through the navy. It was similar linkups with men in our navy. But the superintendent of their Naval Academy was very close friends to the CNO and the Vice. They were all contemporaries.

And they decided, when I went up to Leningrad to visit the navy installations, they'd have a banquet for me, and the banquet started at three o'clock in the afternoon. I had with me, I think, the full delegation of officers traveling, because they wanted to have the benefit of that historic part of the Soviet Union, such a beautiful city, and the naval base and so forth. So you picture this banquet hall, about the size of this room, and there were some fifteen or twenty of us were in it, and the old Chief was so proud to have me there and so forth. They started the vodka and the meal at three o'clock.

DW: Oh, my.

JW: And by four o'clock, there were some people around the table who weren't sure where they were. But I had carefully laid down what I call the drinking watch and the nondrinking watch. The nondrinking watch couldn't drop a touch of alcohol and could never take their eyes off me, for fear they'd snatch me and haul me off in a corner somewhere and box me around to get some information.

Well, as guest of honor, I had limited participation, and what I did—and somebody taught me this—they serve a lot of brown bread and caviar. Of course, caviar is delicious and the brown bread is good too. And you stuff yourself as full as you can of that, and that absorbs an awful lot of alcohol and takes it through the system, but a part of it, if you're careful, you can take your napkin and pretend as if you're wiping your face, kind of lean forward and spit down on the floor through the napkin and get rid of it, a lot of it. So I was successfully doing that maneuver. And the old guy, the host, was getting drunker and drunker, and he noticed that some of them weren't drinking, and finally he said, "It's an insult to me and the Soviet navy and everything else that you're not drinking our toast." Our men were stoic; they didn't say a thing. I would say about a third of our guys were on the nondrinking, and those that were allowed to drink were very careful to never finish a glass or anything. Of course, they just constantly poured it as you went around.

So, finally, he stood up and he said, "I'm going to propose a toast now that no self-respecting man at this table can refuse to participate in."

Silence. And we're looking at each other. And he said, "Fill 'em up." So they filled up the glasses. "Stand!" Everybody stands. "We hereby toast our mothers!"

DW: "Mothers."

JW: Oh, I've told you this story.

DW: I saw it coming.

JW: And some of our guys just didn't drink it. He got so damn mad, he took his glass, threw it across the whole length of the table and smashed up on the wall behind me. They were furious about that drinking thing.

DW: That sounds like Baikov,[24] who was the Russian host.

JW: Yes, that was his name, Baikov.

DW: That was well done. So let's get back to what led us to this, because this was in April of—I'm trying to think. Actually, October of '71, where you went to Moscow, and they would come back to the United States in May of '72. Then you would go back to Moscow, May of '72.

JW: Went back with Nixon this time.

DW: This goes all the way back to Nixon. So how did you get involved in this? You were under secretary at the time.

---

[24] Admiral Ivan Ivanovich Baikov had served in the Soviet submarine force.

JW: That's correct. I'll give you the background. Because like all young men that we were in those days in the Pentagon, we were quite competitive, and I was, of course, in the Department of Navy. There was another very fine man—I'll think of his name in a minute. I'm just tired. I can't remember his name, but we'll probably get it when I give you the facts. He was assistant secretary of defense for sort of foreign affairs. I've forgotten what the other half of the title was.[25] [It was G. Warren Nutter.]

And Laird studied him—and he was a very able man—studied him carefully and studied me, and I was chosen because, (a), it was a naval agreement, and although he was a very competent man, it would be viewed by the Soviets as just, you know, another bureaucrat in the stack, because whether they had one post in their country similar to this is hard to remember. The other thing is we had an ironclad rule in INCSEA talks that all discussions stopped at water's edge, nothing subsurface.

And the submariners were *so* tough about this, because they were making some good progress in their submarine force, and they did not want any slightest chance that they picked up anything or in the understandable curtailment of operational situations that INCSEA puts on surface vessels, they didn't want any limitations on submarines operating in the proximity of the adversary ship. "Forget it. We'll do what we think's best."

So, that connection, and Rickover was very much involved in this, in the sense that he was fearful that INCSEA would leak out some of the material. But he and I had formed by that time a very close personal and friendly professional working relationship. He didn't get along with the admiralty, as you know.

DW: Admiral Zumwalt?

JW: Zumwalt wasn't yet CNO. Certainly when I first arrived, Moorer, and Moorer was chairman, too, you see. So Moorer wasn't very far away. And Moorer's deputy, Clarey, was a wonderful four-star submarine admiral, two-time Navy Cross winner in World War II, marvelous man. He was my choice for admiral over Zumwalt. Should've been.

---

[25] G. Warren Nutter was assistant secretary for defense for international security affairs from 1969–73. He was a professor of economics at the University of Virginia.

Back again, so it came down to a call, and Laird felt he wanted to stay Navy and have someone that Rickover looked upon with some respect. Now, what dealings this other fellow had with "Rick" at that time, I'm unfamiliar, but I had a very close relationship and that was known throughout the building.

I remember he had a rule, he would only see me after eight o'clock at night, and all the rest of the people had left the office, because he loved to storm and rant, and he knew his voice carried, so he just—you know. But he came in one night, ranging and raving, and I said, "Okay, exactly what is your problem?"

And he said, "I want to get married."

I said, "Well, what the hell have I got to do with that?"

He said, "A lot."

And I'm saying to myself, "Where are we going with this conversation?"

He had survived a very serious illness months before this meeting, and he was at Bethesda Naval Hospital, and a very fine nurse was assigned to him. I think there were more than one, but this one. And they fell in love. He'd lost his wife. She'd died some years prior. So they decided to get married.

So he came to see me. This was just at the time when our Navy was shifting from the old naval courts and boards to the Uniform Code of Military Justice, and there was some reach-back, you know, anywhere the subject wasn't covered in the uniform courts, they got some precedent for how it may have been covered in courts and boards. And he brought a copy of the book in with him, he slammed it on the desk, and he went through, bookmarker, and opened it up, said, "There it is." And he was at a paragraph in there, something went along this line. Uniformed officers of the Royal Navy—not uniformed. Commissioned. I mean—they had some word. Officers of the Royal Navy, but there was another modifier in there. "Are absolutely—." Let me get this straight now. Well, it was some mix-up of words that went along this line. "Uniformed officers of the Royal Navy are absolutely forbidden to engage in any activity that resembles cohabitation unless they have a dispensation from the First Sea Lord." So they were going to be legitimately married, but it was some oblique reference to homosexuality, that you will not engage in that in the Royal Navy. He said, "I've got to have your damn permission."

DW: Okay.

JW: So I gave him permission.

DW: Are you still in Main Navy or the Pentagon?

JW: No, we were all in the Pentagon at this time.

DW: Okay, okay, because Main Navy is still—

JW: On Constitution Avenue.

DW: Right.

JW: No, Nixon called me one day from his helicopter. No, he'd landed. Said, "I just landed on routine mission, came in and we did our typical letdown on Constitution Avenue," according to the windage in those days. "And I saw an old friend of mine."

I'm saying, "Oh, really?"

Said, "Yes, a four-legged rat on the roof of the Main Navy. That's the same bugger that was there when I was a lieutenant jaygee in the early part of World War II, working at Main Navy. I want to get rid of those old damn buildings, get 'em the hell out of there, and you got six months to get it done." "Bang!" went the damn phone.

So we quickly rented all kinds of spaces over in Crystal City, put Main Navy in that area, and tore it down.

DW: Okay.

JW: Yeah, he was funny. But I think one of the more interesting Rickover stories, tough ones that I had, the Navy at Annapolis built a beautiful engineering building, and I can't remember the guy who was commandant of midshipmen. Not commandant, but superintendent of the Academy. But he did not like Rickover at all. Out of courtesy, I called him up and told him I was going to name that building the Hyman G. Rickover. And he was a tough old sea dog and a hangover from World War II. Not a hangover, but a holdover. Good, fine officer, I mean old Navy, rigid and tough. And he just let me have it, but I went right ahead with it.[26]

But I got a hold of the chief engineer of construction and said, "Look, I want you to take the main bearing column in the lobby as you go in the building, I want you to strip off all that fireproofing, have the steel girders bare, and reinforce them and double up the amount of steel you got on them and everything."

He's looking at me, "What am I supposed to do that for?"

I said, "I'm going to hang something on it." I had this big plaque made, had it welded to the main bearing column right in the hallway. You've seen it, haven't you?

DW: Yes.

JW: And had Rickover come down, told him to appear on the day I was dedicating the building. "I don't want to go down."

I said, "This is an order. Go down. I want you in full uniform."

"What the hell's going on?"

"You'll find out when you get there. I'm ordering you. And bring your wife."

"What's this all about?"

So I went down and had the welders bring over a complete welding suit, put him in that welding suit out of his four-star uniform and had him weld his initials in that plate, the Hyman G. Rickover Building, and his initials. He did that weld, and welded it to the—he enjoyed every minute of it.

DW: His experience at the Naval Academy wasn't the best, I think, if I recall.

JW: Well, I'm trying to think. On my watch, I don't think he was stationed there.

DW: No. No, but I'm talking about back in the 19twentys.

---

[26] Vice Admiral William P. Mack served as the superintendent from 1972–75.

JW: Oh, yeah. Well, I've read through it. But he did reasonably well.

DW: Yeah, he did well.

JW: Mind you, he was diminutive in stature. I mean, you wonder how in the world they let him in to begin. He was Jewish, which was definitely in those days, regrettably, subject to an awful lot of disrespectful things, but he weathered them. And his first job was on a riverboat in the Yangtze River. Matter of fact, he said that's the only real sea duty he ever had.[27]

DW: Yeah, gunboat. I think he may have had command of something. But from the 19fortys on, he was an engineering duty officer. I think he rewired one of the battleships that went down at Pearl Harbor.[28]

JW: Did he?

DW: Yeah, the electric plant had to be restrung. And then, of course, he got into nuclear propulsion after the war, and the rest is history. Did it trouble you that he kind of wore two hats? Because he was over on the Navy side and also he was over on the Atomic Energy Commission.

JW: That's all right. His talents were so badly needed by the United States, the more he was able to share them and broaden the scope of his activities, the better. We never laid a finger on him. He did what he wanted when he wanted to do it.

DW: But that did cause resentment from some—

JW: Well, he got enemies wherever he went. But he made a lot of good friends. Boy, governors, helping them get grants. Oh, he knew how to play the political circuit, senators and everything. He was truly untouchable.

---

[27] Rickover did have duty on the *Nevada* and two submarines but the only ship he would command was the minesweeper *Finch* stationed at Tsingtao, where he reported as the commanding officer in July 1937.
[28] The *California*.

DW: And let's take that—well, while we're on Rickover, let's just take that up beyond his time when you were Secretary of the Navy to when you're in the Senate now. How did that relationship continue when you were in elected office?

JW: We still maintained a friendship. The mutual respect we had with one another was there. I was not directly involved. John Lehman was Secretary [of the Navy]. I was not involved in his day-by-day activities. He would come over and see me and talk from time to time, particularly when he was having a stressful period with Lehman, but, no, he was very independent, very independent.

DW: Of course, you know, Lehman eventually retired him.

JW: Well, let me step back and expand on that, and I'll give you a very objective analysis. Navy was somewhat suffering with him still in those high posts, because age had begun to take its toll, as it does to any of us. Here I am talking to you at age ninety-one. You know that occasionally I drop off to sleep, as you know. Anyway, he was very effective, still doing a lot of good work, but we were on the brink of a tremendous expansion of our own domestic use of nuclear power, primarily, of course, for heating and cooling and so forth. And I felt that to the extent he could get out and show that same leadership with the civilian community as they built their power plants, and to give them assurances to the safety of them, because he had a beautiful talk about that, all the better.

So we talked to President Reagan. I knew Reagan very well. He was very open-minded about Rickover, but he felt that the time had come. He understood that. So we devised a concept where he would become an advisor to the President on matters of domestic use of reactors, primarily for the use of generating power, heat and light all over America.

So we thought we'd give him all the trimmings of a Navy billet, but it would be a civilian billet, not the Department of Defense. Funds for payment would not come out of DOD budgets; it would come out of other budgets.

But he just did not like the idea of being pulled out of the bosom of Mother Navy. The submarine force was highly respected, you know. This country is still harboring a lot of fear about nuclear power, and he could have, I think, dispelled a lot of that fear.

So we tried to give him this job, gave him all kinds of lovely office space, office help, staffed him up beautifully, far more than anybody you could possibly think of. But he walked in that room when Reagan was going to tell him what he was going to do, retire him on the spot from the Navy, but let him continue to enjoy some assets of military life, boy, he wasn't for it, take on this other job. It just went downhill, far down.

DW: No, as somebody who was in Pennsylvania when the Three Mile Island incident occurred, there was a lack of confidence in the civilian power, so he could have done much to reinstill confidence. So, my recollection is that he then retired and was offered an office at the Navy Yard and I was told that he had two portraits in the office. One was of Benedict Arnold and the other was of John Lehman.

JW: No kidding. I didn't know that. That's a little bit of coloration.

But Lehman, I worked with Lehman on devising this thing, and others of good faith and friendship with Rickover. You remember there were some wonderful officers around. Jim Calvertwas close,[29] and then this other wonderful old four-star, he was Chief of Naval Operations, Jim—

DW: Watkins.[30]

JW: Watkins. All those guys worshipped "Rick." They hated and worshipped him, and they wanted to do everything they could. They came out and tried to counsel with him and calm him down, but he was, I think, becoming slightly mentally off the range.

---

[29] Vice Admiral James Calvert served in nuclear submarines and finished his career as the superintendent of the Naval Academy in 1972.
[30] Admiral James D. Watkins, another nuclear submariner, served as CNO from 1982–86.

DW: Okay, yeah. I did an oral history with Kin McKee.[31]

JW: Kin, knew him well.

DW: And he's the one who had to go in and do the turnover, and he discussed that. As I said, Rickover was definitely hurt by the whole process, but he was getting on in age.

JW: I mean, John Lehman is not to be blamed. He really conscientiously tried to carry out the president of the United States' wishes. It was a presidential decision. Has an oral history ever been done of Lehman?

DW: I believe—well, he's written a couple of books.

JW: Yeah. And another one's about to roll out.[32]

DW: That's right. I gave him some steers on people to talk to on that.

JW: I happen to be a friend of Lehman's, so feel comfortable.

DW: No, I don't think—unless the Naval Institute's doing one currently, nobody's done an oral history with him.

JW: Does the Naval Institute, independent of your organization, do them?

DW: Well, the Naval Historical Foundation, where I work for my day job part-time, does oral histories on a catch-can basis, but the Naval Institute really has invested some resources to do some long-term, quality, multisession, deep-type oral histories with some of the senior Navy leaders of the past two decades. So I applaud the Naval Institute for taking the initiative to do

---

[31] Admiral McKee would succeed Rickover. See: http://www.navyhistory.org/oral-history-admiral-kinnaird-mckee-usn/.
[32] In 2018, Lehman published *Oceans Ventured*, a highly acclaimed reflection on the importance of naval exercises as a component of the 1980s Maritime Strategy against the Soviet Union.

that. Like right now, for example, they're interviewing Admiral James G. Stavridis[33] and a lot of the senior officers.

JW: Stavridis is a good man.

DW: Yeah. I watched his career go up when he was a one-star, two-star. You could see he was going places.

JW: Yeah. I don't know that he had CNO managerial skills, and I don't know whether he was ever a contender for it or not.

DW: He definitely was very good at international affairs.

JW: Analytical and international.

DW: So he always got those overseas jobs.

JW: And he liked them.

DW: Yeah.

JW: My recollection, he had NATO South, didn't he?

DW: I believe so.[34]

JW: And I know he's up at some college, university.

DW: I think he's at Tufts, The Fletcher School.

---

[33] Admiral Stavridis became the first naval officer to serve as Supreme Allied Commander in Europe in 2009, retiring from that post in twenty13. Among his post–military career duties is the chair of the board for the U.S. Naval Institute.
[34] Actually we were thinking U.S. Southern Command, a billet he had from 2006 to 2009.

JW: President or—

DW: Dean.[35] He's chairman of the board of the Naval Institute, whereas Admiral Fallon is the chairman of Naval Historical Foundation.

JW: Do they get along?

DW: I believe so, believe so.
 Okay. Getting back to the Incidents at Sea Agreement. So we were talking about you're assigned to head up this delegation. The Russians had approached us about doing the Safety at Sea talks, and you have to hook up with somebody at State Department.

JW: A fellow named Herbert Okun.

DW: Yeah. Talk a little bit about how that—

JW: Well, the State felt that they had as much of a deal. And Bill Rogers was secretary of state, and I was privileged to be a friend of his. He said, "You know, you're doing something normally the State Department does, but we can understand. The military aspects of it, they should have a military personage in it."
 But I said, "Well, just appoint me. Appoint a deputy."
 It's kind of like the title of the Secretary of the Navy is equivalent to the four-star but above, whatever "above" means. So I was the chairman, but above the deputy, who was from the State Department, Herb Okun. Did you ever interview him?

DW: Yes.

JW: He's still alive somewhere.

---

[35] Stavridis stepped down as dean of the Fletcher School of Law and Diplomacy at Tufts University in August 2018.

DW: Could be.[36]

JW: So it worked out. Bill Rogers couldn't have been better.

There's another chapter of this that I'd like to tell you. As we ground on, it was over a period of two years, with visitations from their delegation here, visitation of the U.S. delegation there, and so forth. We basically devised the four corners of the instrument, but they weren't ready to have it stamped "done." They began to drag their feet in all kinds of different directions. I think, bottom line, the Navy really didn't want the damn thing.

They wanted it for one reason, and that is to show the world that we have reached that point where we're sitting across the table from the United States of America and the biggest navy in the world. They wanted to have that status. But the rest of it was a lot of bullshit. "If we want to harass your damn ships, we want to do it. We want to surveil them and scrape the paint of them doing it, so what?" Anyway, we—

DW: Just to clarify whose side is pushing back on this—

JW: The Soviet side.

DW: The Soviet side. Okay.

JW: Yeah, because I think down deep, they realized that, "My god, this is going to be a nuisance."

DW: Yeah. Because I know you mentioned that the submarine folks on our side were kind of leery about this.

JW: Well, they were always leery, but they got their zone totally sealed off, and I don't know of any slip-up that we made.

---

[36] Herb Okun would also serve as the chief negotiator for the SALT Treaty and go on to be the U.S. ambassador to East Germany and the UN. He passed away in twenty11.

DW: And I think our intel folks were kind of worried about this because we wanted the ability to maneuver closely to—

JW: Oh, sure. They wanted every bit of collection. But the point I wish to make, we were just, as we say in the Navy, in irons. And I'll tell you a story on "in irons" when I finish this important part. But all of a sudden, out of the blue came the announcement that Nixon was going to Russia, and it was almost as if the pope blessed this agreement. They came back to the table. "We'll do this, maybe move the comma here," but nothing was touched with that agreement, and from that point on, it was greased in. Then, of course, they did that beautiful ceremony.

DW: Right.

JW: And Henry Kissinger was off going to the head and missed it. He, to this day, "[demonstrates in heavy accent]. Could've waited a minute while I [demonstrates]." Anyway, good ol' Henry. He's funny.

But, boy, it zipped through. Then they took pride in it. They waved the flag. I think it served a purpose.

DW: Oh, it certainly has. Now, what was the "iron" story?

JW: John Chafee and I went up somewhere on the Charles River to a shipyard which had refinished the USS *Constitution*, still ship number one in our Navy. We were invited aboard to take it on its maiden voyage—I think it had been in the yard at least a year, probably more—and up the Charles with the prevailing wind so that we had a wind. There must have been several thousand small boat crafts that turned out to line the Hudson and to salute the ship as she, under full sail, was going up the river. Well, it was fascinating. Chafee and I were down on the quarterdeck and watched the sailors in bare feet go up the riggings, rigged all the sails, got the whole thing going. She didn't move. There wasn't even a cough of air.

And we sat there hour after hour, and you've got all these people picnicking and partying on their boats as far as the eye could see up the river. Finally, Chafee, he talked with me, "What the hell do you think we do?"

I said, "We've got to tow this thing up the river." And we got a tow and pulled her up the river. We were in irons.

DW: So, okay. Getting back to the Incidents at Sea Agreement. So you went to Russia for the first time, and this is where the delegation—

JW: I'd been to Russia before. I belonged to a very interesting organization in Washington. Only males, I remember that. We were international lawyers back before all these firms had all these branch offices and everything. At one time our organization did a trip to Russia, and the chief justice, we took him along. I was bag carrier, I mean literally two feet behind the big boys, but I carried the chief's bags, and that was my first trip to Russia. He was fascinated with it. Earl Warren.

DW: Okay. So how long did you stay in Russia for that trip?

JW: We probably were there four or five days. We met with all their judicial types, and chief justice of the United States was the big figure.

DW: Okay. So this was, I imagine, what, in the early sixties?

JW: I'm at Hogan & Hartson, so it was early sixties.

DW: Okay.

JW: I'm trying to think. A fellow named Charlie Rein [phonetic]—I'll go get his book somewhere—he wrote a book before he died about the trip. I can't remember what they called the organization. It was four or five consecutive summers, take two weeks and visit a part of the world. We went over and saw Tito. I mean, we got to anybody that they had to pull the big guys on it.

DW: Okay. So you got to see Tito and you got to Russia. Any other memorable—

JW: No, I can't think of any right now.

DW: So I think as a part of your delegation, did you have Tom Hayward with you?

JW: Yes, he's in the picture. He's in the official portrait.

DW: And I think Ron Kurth[37] was a member of your delegation.

JW: He was one.

DW: So that was the thing that impressed me, is that you had these naval officers that could talk the same language and talk with other delegation heads. They say, "We were more comfortable talking to these Russian naval officers than we are our own Army and Air Force." Because there's a common bond with people who are at sea.
    So I think you probably saw a little of that. You got to take that trip—I think you did some activities in Moscow. You stayed at Rossiya Hotel.

JW: Yes. I remember the toilet fell apart.

DW: Oh, really?

JW: Oh, yeah. Another interesting thing, the CNO [Admiral of the Fleet Sergei Gorshkov] wanted to properly show his respect to me and through me to the whole delegation, and he told me he wanted to take me on a trip the day after it was signed, and only I would go with him. This

---

[37] Hayward would serve as CNO from 1978 to 1982. Ronald Kurth would go on to serve as naval then defense attaché to Moscow and president of the Naval War College.

troubled the other guys a little bit. I didn't want to be so exclusive, but he is CNO, and his private plane would only seat so many. I may have taken one other person with me. I'm sure I did. I never traveled alone. Maybe it was Tom Hayward. But he wouldn't tell me where he was going to take me.

So the plane took off, and sure enough, the steward came up with a glass of vodka, so we started drinking.[38] And he said, "I want to show you a city that exemplifies the strength of Mother Russia." And we went to Stalingrad. And there he related how he was on the patrol boats that brought up the food and kept them alive as best they could and took the wounded back to someplace. He talked about the frightful cold and terrible condition everybody was in. And there in the yard is a figure of a twice-life-size woman, and she's got a big sword in her hand, and her sword is pointed. I didn't have any particular orientation whether it was east, north. He said, "That sword is pointed due west, because we don't trust you now and we'll never trust you." I mean, here we are, just signed this agreement.[39]

DW: And here we are in 2018 and it doesn't seem to be much better.

JW: Yeah.

DW: Unfortunately. Okay. So a couple of other aspects of, I guess, the Incidents at Sea and your visit. This trip, of course, to Stalingrad or I guess it was with Fleet Admiral Gorshkov, I assume? Sergei Gorshkov was the head of their Navy?

JW: No, Gorshkov didn't go with us.

DW: Right, if I recall from my book it was Kasatonov.
Okay. So during your time in Moscow, did you get to go to the Bolshoi?

JW: Oh, yeah. That was so funny. No, it was the *Swan Lake*. I got a seat right behind [Soviet Premier Leonid] Brezhnev and Nixon, you know, two rows up or something, and Brezhnev had

---

[38] Admiral Gorshkov sent regrets and sent Admiral Kasatonov in his place.
[39] The statue, "The Motherland Calls" was dedicated in 1967.

been obviously drinking over the dinner. He fell asleep and his head actually rested on Nixon's shoulder through much of the show. Funny as hell. Those guys I just don't understand.

JW: I do remember we accessed ourselves—the word is "nomenklatura." That's the upper class, where you just drive into a main boulevard, go to the center of the road and go as fast as you want, right down the main road, blowing a horn. Didn't have to have government markings or anything. They knew if you had one of the big cars, you were an official. And, man, it scared the pants off me. But these drivers knew how to handle it, and the public just got out of the way.

DW: I guess we have the Easy Pass now in this country.

JW: The other thing I remember, I'll never forget, there was a very attractive woman that was assigned to us as a guide. What's that spy organization?

DW: The KGB?

JW: KGB. She was an agent. We all knew it. Anyway, she got very friendly. She would never drink, she would never do anything, but the last night they were there, I got her a sip of wine and talked to her a little bit, and I told her, "You know, we're leaving the next day." I said, "I'll carry back with me the vivid memories of so many people on the streets carrying on as best they can, with a leg or an arm missing." The war must have been terrible. And she didn't say much for a while.

We talked a little bit more, and I came back to it. She said, "I want you to know that maybe some of them as a result of the war. Most of them are victims of alcoholism, where they drink so much, fall down, go to sleep, and that limb freezes." On the ground or wherever it is. And there's no trying to save it. I always remember that. Wow.

DW: That was an aha moment.

JW: Yeah.

DW: The Hotel Rossiya itself, you said the toilet broke. Anything else memorable?

JW: No, but you felt that you were in a place that saw a lot of history.

DW: Standing on Red Square must be a—

JW: The whole thing is a very moving experience. Remember we were early, early on in terms of Americans going behind the Iron Curtain, very early on. Matter of fact, I occupied the honor of being the highest-ranking American associated with the military ever to go behind the Iron Curtain, some phrase to that effect.

I remember going up to the embassy. They had an old tough colonel, Army colonel, he later became four-stars, awful nice guy. He's from Virginia, southwest Virginia. He took a liking to me, and I billeted with him. He actually insisted that I take his room because it was a quieter room, and we were working so hard around the clock, working on the instrument. But then the party and the receptions, you had to go to them, just constantly. So I was having trouble getting enough sleep, so he gave me his room.

Lo and behold, I went to sleep one afternoon, and he was scheduled to come back and get me up because I had to go to a reception. His door got jammed and it took hours before the carpenters could get up this massive, huge door and somehow take it apart to get it out and let me out of the room. Just the little things.

I had wonderful eggs, interesting corn beef. I liked the goulash. Rice was good, potatoes were plentiful, butter was good, ice cream was good. We never wanted for, I think, a pretty good meal. We all had a lot of caviar, which I think is good for you. I don't know.

DW: Protein.

JW: I suppose it is.

DW: The embassy, we eventually replaced that, and that became quite the fiasco—I guess you're in the Senate now and you're probably looking into that.

JW: I went over there with Sam Nunn, and then I went on another trip with Strom Thurmond. We were the first CODEL ever to go to Russia after World War II. Old Strom led the CODEL. Or did Byrd lead the CODEL? Byrd led the CODEL. I remember he and Strom divided up an hour to address Gorbachev, and each member on the delegation according to the number of years you had lined up, and I was at the end. I got two minutes of questioning, one question.

DW: That was actually, I guess, '85 we had the 40th anniversary of the end of World War II. I guess we can pick that up in our next sit-down—

JW: Sure.

[End of February 23, 2018, interview]

Interview Number 6 with John W. Warner, USN (Ret.)
Date: March 19, 2018

David Winkler (DW): Today is March 19 [2018], and we're here for a fireside chat with Senator [John] Warner. On behalf of the [U.S.] Naval Institute, this is Dave Winkler.

I think what we'd like to do today is cover the period following your tour as Secretary of the Navy. A couple of months ago, we were driving home and you told me about a phone call you got from President Nixon, was it, about this Bicentennial Commission?

John Warner (JW): I'll give you the routine. I was Secretary of the Navy, had been in the Navy secretariat under SecNav five and a half years, and Nixon was beginning to come to the reality about the consequences of Watergate, and he was very worried that it would tarnish, if not damage, the 200th anniversary celebration called the Bicentennial that America was undertaking. Congress had set up a small organization and it had been sort of stumbling along. Nixon was deeply concerned, so he had Congress rewrite the bill to create a more formidable organization, and quietly let the incumbent CEO, a nice fellow out of the New York area, who had limited experience in trying to put on events—but anyway, I'm not here to criticize him.

But anyway, he knew me very well since I had worked for him beginning in 1960 as an aide intermittently in his campaign in '60 for the presidency, and then '68 for the presidency I worked for him again. So we had been longtime associates. He wanted to make sure that the Bicentennial was given the proper support by the Congress, by the executive branch, and that it be detached and operated totally successfully apart from the rigors that he was facing with Watergate.

I'd been in the under secretary/secretary position five years, four months, and three days, and I was enjoying every moment of it, when I got a summons to come down to meet with Richard Nixon, and in the room was Al Haig. He was down taking a break in Florida, and I flew down to see him, and Haig was there in the room. He was one of his principal aides at that time. Haig was dressed in his fatigues; Nixon, open collar, very relaxed. He said, "John, I wanted to see you because I've got a problem, and I think you're the man that I know and trust most to help me dig out of this problem." He said, "The United States is preparing to celebrate its 200th anniversary of creation, and I want to be remembered as the president who gave full support to

America and urged it to, in every way, celebrate and also record in history the importance of this day and our constitutional form of government."

And I said, "Well, that's quite interesting, Mr. President. How do I fit?"

He said, "Well, about six months ago, I set up a small commission, sole purpose to help the states prepare and to coordinate the federal departments and agencies and the White House itself in how they should recognize and participate and contribute to this Bicentennial. The current person that I chose, it's not working out to his satisfaction or mine, and so a quiet turnover's going to take place, and I need you, with your energy and your background, to take over and make this thing a success."

I said, "Well, Mr. President, that's very flattering. I don't even know how to spell the word."

And he laughs and says, "I expected that. Al here has prepared a book for you." The book was five inches thick. He said, "Take it home and come back and see me in a week."

So I went home, and my wife and three little children, I hadn't seen much of them in the course of that period of time during the war in Vietnam. There were heavy pressures to travel extensively into the Pacific region and to Vietnam, and equally heavy pressures to travel into the Atlantic theater of operation, Mediterranean, because of the Cold War aspects with the then Soviet Union.

So I had long been away from home for a long time, and my wife and children were very anxious for me to do this, so I took it. I took it, and I never regretted it. Matter of fact, learned more interesting things than I ever did in my lifetime, because it took me to all fifty states and twelve different nations that participated.

It was time me to step out of the Navy job and take on the chairmanship. And, frankly, it had been a challenge for five and a half years with all the traveling, and my traveling now would be basically limited to the United States and several countries like Great Britain and France and others that were very active in our revolutionary period, in terms of supporting us. So I took it on. It was a change. I remember Nixon, when I finally agreed to do it and went to see him, he was very pleased. I was walking out of the Oval Office, and he turned on his heels and he said, "You know something, John? You've always expressed an interest in being in the U.S. Senate. Believe me, if you don't screw this up, you might get there." And the rest is history.

It was a marvelous eye-opener. Just think, unlimited support financially from the Congress, studying American history, and volunteer organizations all over America. All fifty states were involved, and several foreign countries gave magnificent gifts to America. Notably—I'll comment on it at the end of this comment—notably was Great Britain. As I'll finish up, the queen very respectfully accepted our invitation to visit the country but said she thought she'd best do it after the celebration of July 4th, 1976. "You chaps have at it. You won. Have your party, and then I'll come over to say hi." It was a wonderful experience for me, just absolutely one of a kind. Nobody will ever have a job exactly like that.

DW: But your reaction—because being Secretary of the Navy is a pretty good job.

JW: Oh, it's good. I had it five and a half years. That's a long time.

DW: What were some of the challenges that you kind of faced, as far as staffing, putting together organizations?

JW: It came together. Congress gave us literally all the money needed. I went up there annually and testified. It was a presidential commission, and I had to be confirmed by the Senate, so it was a presidential appointment. So it had adequate funding, but there was an enormous enthusiasm across the country, and we were very helpful because we not only doled out money to each of the fifty states, but we had experts in tourism and construction and events, and we really had a staff of about 375 or something, and that was just the Washington office. We had branch offices, which we collocated with the states' headquarters and had people out there working across the country. They were primarily involved in evaluating the grant process to the states, because we carefully surveyed the grants and made sure that they had a potential for contributing to the seriousness and historical perspective.

And also we—I think rather cleverly, if I may say so—devised a trademark to preserve us under the Trademark Acts, and so therefore anybody who made an artifact or wrote a book, they had to get permission to use the official Bicentennial logo, which is a very simple—you see that plate over there up in that chamber?

DW: Right.

JW: That's an interesting plate. France made that plate and, I think, two hundred plates altogether like it, and the French president Giscard d'Estaing at the time came over to the United States and personally held a cocktail party dinner, as elegant as I've ever seen on in my life, in the embassy here in Washington. The president and everybody was there, beautifully done, because of the significance of France to our efforts to seek freedom from Great Britain. And, oh, my, what an evening that was. And they only made two hundred of those plates. Each guest was told, "You can take your plate with you," so they took them all, and there were a few others, but I got that one and I cherish it.

DW: It looks like it's about a nine-inch plate with that Bicentennial logo, that star with the red, white, and blue striping.

JW: Five-point star. It was carefully designed, and that was our trademark. Because people had been abusing—they had been making Bicentennial bathtubs, you know, everything, Bicentennial bedsheets, a lot of things that didn't enhance in any way the seriousness of the event.

Oh, I had a grand time. I'll never forget Nixon. He was enormously interested in it. And then history records that we had barely gotten underway with the new commission—and I was chairman—when he faced impeachment and resigned. In the interim, I was sworn into this job on the steps of the U.S. Capitol by the vice president of the United States, Gerald Ford. Got a wonderful picture of that somewhere. Gosh, the whole Congress, I'm circled by members of the House and the Senate. I mean, it's a heady experience for a young man who was thinking then of aspiring to get to Congress.

But Ford was just so enthusiastic about everything, and he never lost the beat, once Nixon stepped out, when it came to the Bicentennial. And I'll never forget—oh, I'm repeating myself with the phrase, but it's worthy—on July 4th, 1976, he very graciously invited me to join him on his private helicopter to visit the United States on that historic day as much as we could cover. And I remember I joined him for a church service at Christ Church in Farragut Square, called the President's Chapel, I think, at around six-thirty, seven in the morning. You know, those days, he had plenty of security, but nothing overwhelming, and I remember we walked to and from the White House as the sun was coming up and got on his helicopter and took off for Valley Forge. That was our first stop.

When we got up there, we obviously noticed that the helicopter was circling and circling, couldn't see the ground for the fog cover, and the pilot came back and said, "Mr. President, this looks like a very iffy situation."

And Ford, mind you, was a naval officer during World War II. He was not an aviator, but he was on carriers as an intelligence officer, and he was not one to do things lightly. He was a real gung-ho naval man. Ford said, "Well, my ground people have wired us that there are five thousand people down there at Valley Forge waiting to see us. Captain," so-and-so, the pilot, "get this machine down there." He said, "The first little squeak you get peek of the ground, just turn off the engine and drop through that hole."

Sure enough, suddenly we dropped through that hole. Nothing perilous in safety. But there was this panorama of Valley Forge and people as far as you could see, and that was his first speech. That got in stride.

Then we went to Philadelphia, then to the famous place, Declaration of Independence.

DW: Independence Hall.

JW: And he gave another speech. Then I had organized a Tall Ships regatta. I say "I." As chairman, I worked with the local communities and everything, New York. I don't mean to possess this thing. It was strictly volunteer, millions of volunteers all across the country. And to have the Tall Ships, then we brought an aircraft carrier and parked it at the foot of the Statue of Liberty, berthed it right up against the statue. The statue is not more than fifty yards from the waterfront. On the deck of the ship, we had all the luminaries and people from far over. We had rigged up an electronic system where when Ford hit the ship's bell after his speech, he made a speech, then hit the ship's bell, when that bell rang, he pulled it, the bell rang and it triggered church bells in every city, town, and village in America. They all rang their bells from coast to coast, two-thirty, three, something like that in the afternoon. It sent chills up everybody's back.

I'll never forget there was an old master chief petty officer who was assigned to the rostrum and escort for the president, in his old sailor suit, you know, and I was a former

Secretary of the Navy, he knew who I was. And I told Ford his introductory remarks had to be four minutes, and I looked at my watch and I said, "Okay, now." And he started talking.

The chief edged over next to me and he pulled my sleeve. He said, "Your watch is off by two and a half minutes if you want to ring the bells precisely at 3:00."

So I whispered to the president, "Drag it out," which he dragged out his story for another two and a half minutes. He said, "You know, it gives me a moment to reflect on perhaps one of the most important two days of my life when I nearly lost my life during the World War II when I was a deck officer aboard a small carrier. We were in the famous fleet shift under Halsey's orders to go through a typhoon and join other elements. That typhoon was one of the worst ever experienced by the U.S. Navy." As a matter of fact, two small destroyer escorts rolled over and went down with all hands aboard. I think there were few, if any, survivors.[40]

DW: Right.

JW: You may know that answer. And he was the deck officer. The ship had been engaged in kamikaze attacks in the earlier part of the day and had experienced fire aboard it, and now things were exacerbated because so much destruction was being done by this raging storm, and Ford, as one of the deck officers, was out there fighting fires, and he, fortunately, held tight to his hose when his ship pitched, and sailors, unfortunately, working with him got washed overboard, never to be seen again. And only because he had a grip on that hose was his life spared.[41]

And he reminisced, as you can see in this picture, to me about that in those five minutes. He said, "I really should at this point in my life thank God again for saving my life, and because of it, I'm here today." And then he launched into his speech on the Bicentennial. It's a famous picture.

We chatted about this ever after. Then all the bells rang across America.

Then we got back on his helicopter and took the helicopter up the East River and down the full length of Madison Avenue. The people were all out on the streets, and he lowered that

---

[40] Three destroyers were lost, *Hull*, *Spence*, and *Monaghan*. Some survivors were recovered.
[41] The light carrier *Monterey* did not experience a kamikaze attack that day December 18, 1944, but Typhoon Cobra caused aircraft on the hangar deck to collide, resulting in a fire at 0911 (December 18) and lost steerageway a few minutes later. The fire was brought under control at 0945 Captain Stuart H. Ingersoll wisely decided to let his ship lie dead in the water until temporary repairs could be effected. Ingersoll had sent his officer-of-the-deck Ford down below to report on the fire.

helicopter to scrape the tops of the skyscrapers so that the people could do it, and it was a *beautiful* scene, nothing but massing of cheering people waving their hands. He liked it so much, turned the helicopter back around and brought it down this time along Fifth Avenue, and then off we went. We landed at the White House right there on the lawn, and he got out and he kind of almost gave me a hug, he was so happy. He said, "This is a day we'll never forget." And he went into the White House.

I had to scramble into one of his limos and go straight up to the Washington Monument, where I met Nelson Rockefeller, the vice president of the United States, and he was going to give the final address to the nation, because the president had given the three p.m. address. I got up there a little ahead of time to check out the rostrum and make everything set to greet Rockefeller. Well, in the course of doing that, we couldn't get the damn microphone working. So then [demonstrates], the sirens and motorcycles come up, and the vice president gets out of the car. A *million* people were in that ground, megaphones as far as you could see, and a beautiful sunset setting in, and it was all timed. I said, "Mr. vice president, we've got a problem."

"What is that problem?"

I said, "Somewhere in the circuitry, there's a dead something, and we've got to find it."

He said, "You don't mean it."

And he and I and electricians got down on our hands and knees [chuckles], trying to find where the problem was. I'd actually been an electronic technician's mate in the Navy and knew a little bit in those days. Well, sir, we finally found it, and he was overjoyed.

Now, the next problem with Rockefeller was containing his enthusiasm. He was a man bigger than life and *loved* life. I said, "The schedule is that you will——." I've forgotten. We had the Mormon Tabernacle Choir, *the* choir. We had musical bands of all the military. I mean, we had a show going on that you wouldn't believe. And I said, "I've got to keep this thing in the time."

"Oh, all right, John. We'll do that." But, boy, I had to almost tackle him and get him to stay on schedule and let the Mormons have their piece and the military have their piece.

I would say we got underway about ten o'clock. It was a two-hour show. And at the stroke of midnight, some fanfare and it was over, or fanfare prior to it, so the bells rang or something. It was all over, and he said to me—he was very cordial—he said, "Can I give you a ride somewhere?"

And I told him, "Mr. Vice President, I thank you. I just want to stay here. It's all over for me. I'm finished now. We've done the Bicentennial of the United States, and this marks the termination of what the commission was set up to do."

He says, "Okay." He was a great backslapper, banged me on the back.

I then melded into the crowd—nobody knew who the hell I was—and walked all the way home and watched the people dancing in the streets, celebrating. Walked all the way down Constitution Avenue, up Wisconsin Avenue, up through Georgetown to my home, which was on the corner of R Street and Wisconsin Avenue. I'll never forget it.

DW: So to pull all this off, there's a lot of brainstorming, so how was that all engineered? Who were the ideas people that pulled off, for example, the Tall Ships? I remember they had a steam train that went around the country.

JW: Oh, yeah. I remember that very well.

DW: They also had some enormous fireworks, of course. So how do you—did you have some very creative people working with you?

JW: I had wonderful people, volunteers all of them. I'd taken some of my senior staff from the Pentagon, Navy Secretary's office. Two of them resigned from the Navy Department and went on my payroll. The chief captain in the Navy who was my PAO that came with me—he's dead now—wonderful guy.

DW: Was that—

JW: Herb Hetu. Very, very intelligent man. He was a total success. My secretary, who was a very strong, vigorous woman, came, and she was a good executive in the office. And I had a staff here in Washington, somewhere around four hundred, had them all divided up, but our working modus operandi was to encourage the people in the states to conceive their own programs, and if we thought they were within the definable boundaries of American history and made a contribution, they got a grant from us. Well, we had to turn down some stuff, just too tawdry and didn't work, but by and large, the creation of it was by the people. Each state had its own Bicentennial Committee, and you would not *believe* the ferocity within these states of the people who wanted to be on that Bicentennial Committee, because it was a one-time event in the history of the country.

DW: True.

JW: And so really able people went on their boards, and then they enlisted the thinking from the universities and the schools.

I'll tell you one amusing aspect. Nixon—I hadn't been in the job more than a couple of weeks or something—called me over to the White House. He said, "You're getting along great. I'm getting some good reports from people."

I said, "I think we're making progress, Mr. President."

He says, "One thing you've got to watch out."

"Yes, sir. What's that?"

"Intellectuals. Be careful. My advice to you is to devise a series of very esoteric programs, give 'em a little funding, assign 'em to a program and to write a piece, and just slowly feed 'em. And you know something? They'll never get it done. They'll argue themselves into the moonlight of every night, and you never have to worry about their work product." He was right.

DW: Okay.

JW: We had the intellectual society, all kinds of stuff.

DW: The concern with the intellectuals is that they would get too nitty-gritty in the details and the history?

JW: Oh, yeah. I'm again in another history program for the World War I Memorial. I'm just an adjunct volunteer, but I'm heavily involved with them, and there's people in there that constantly demand—and justifiably, to a degree—to tell the other side of the story. "What *if* we hadn't gotten into that war? What *if* Germany finally realized they couldn't win the war and forged some sort of détente with France and England? What *if* you wouldn't have had the decimation of Germany? They could have sort of written their own terms of surrender and you wouldn't have had the extensive redrawing of boundaries and all the other things that happened after World War II." The guys have got a point, but they drift off into "what if" until you're just wondering when is this conversation going to end. Then they're talking about "What if Woodrow Wilson hadn't gotten sick and had a heart attack?" What if? You've got to make your forays into "what if" short.

DW: Right.

JW: I learned that trade.

DW: Right. So besides bringing some Navy staff with you, with that Tall Ships, wasn't there international naval review?

JW: Oh, yeah, there was all sorts of wonderful people. My job with the Tall Ships was to do some modest funding and turn it over to them.

DW: Okay. But the Navy kind of ran that, the international review portion? Because you did have the aircraft carrier.

JW: Yeah. I think we had some other—I don't think we got a battleship out, though. See, all those things were in mothballs.

DW: That's right. I think you had some ships from other countries.

JW: We did. I think we had a bit of a naval regatta.

DW: Yeah. Okay. The one I always remember, of course, is the Freedom Train, I guess it was.

JW: That guy's name was Ross something, R-o-s-s.[42] He put much of his own money in it, and he was an absolute—he was a very good man. He made a strong contribution. But we used to joke, he's the biggest railroad nut in the United States. I mean, his most exciting time of day is driving his own engine. He had his own engine. And he kept hitting on this Freedom Train, which was a good idea, because if you look at the history of America, it was the railroad system and their ability to link the two coasts and to bring us together as fifty states, each one with their own system. That's one of the powerful stories of this country. We take all these trains for granted now, and they, of course, have a much lesser role, given aviation and highway construction.

But remember Eisenhower, it was in the Depression era, 1935 or something, as a young major was detailed by the president to map the interstate road system of the United States. Few people realize that. And the road between here and San Francisco, some of it was a dirt road, so America had to do a lot of expansion.[43]

As I look back on it, the Navy job was the best job I ever had, but this would be the second best. I had so much fun, and Nixon was right, I got elected to the Senate.

DW: We'll talk about that, because that's an interesting story.

JW: Well, it has its twists and turns, yeah. I mentioned that we invited—we had, I think—don't hold me to the number, but about fifteen heads of state came over, and Ford gave each one of them a dinner.

And then the Queen, very thoughtfully, said, "I will come over after the July 4th"—she came on July 7th—"and let you chaps have at it. We had a lovely dinner at the White House one night, and then the next night, the queen invited the president to the Queen's House, of which the embassy is known. We went up there, and I had been called by the ambassador, because I'd worked with the ambassador on bringing over a copy of the Magna Carta, a loan for one year to the United States, and I got it done and we put it in the Capitol Building under twenty-four-hour

---

[42] The idea for the American Freedom Train is credited to successful broker Ross Rowland Jr. who first thought of the idea in 1969 and eventually landed PepsiCo as a sponsor. When President Nixon authorized national artifacts to be carried by the train, additional funding came in.
[43] Eisenhower traveled with an Army convoy on the Lincoln Highway in 1919 and was not impressed. In contrast, he appreciated the German Autobahn system when Americans invaded Germany in 1945.

military surveillance, because there's only, I think, four original 1215s. The original one, there's a sequence of three of them there. I'm getting rusty in my history.[44] This was the queen's copy, and so that's one of the reasons I was knighted by the queen. Jeanne, my wife, reminded me it was nine years ago yesterday I was knighted, went to Buckingham Palace.

DW: Wow!

JW: Knighted. I'm getting astray now. But what was I on?

DW: You were talking about all these dignitaries and heads of state coming over.

JW: Oh, yeah, and I was asked to escort Elizabeth Taylor, and that was the beginning of a rather interesting romance that came together pretty quickly, and we were married in December. Dinner was in July. We were married in December.

DW: So I guess we need to back up a little bit, because you're a single guy now, and I guess with all the travel when you were Secretary of the Navy put stresses on your previous marriage?

JW: Yeah, that was tough. Also my wife and I, I still see her regularly. Well, not regularly, but, you know, a couple times a year, and we talk because we've still got these children and we proudly shared all responsibilities raising them. The toughest part was that she really was opposed to the Vietnam War. She's ten or twelve years younger than I am, and her age group, you know, rebelled in the streets, and she got very much involved in that movement, and that sort of pulled the marriage apart, sadly.

DW: Okay, okay. And here you are, of course, the Secretary of the Navy.

JW: That was not an easy thing to be divorced as Secretary of the Navy.

---

[44] There were Charters in 1216, 1217, 1225, and 1297.

DW: Okay, okay.

JW: Because a naval wife, be it [the] secretary's wife, the CNO's wife, we worked a lot with families, and you've got to remember the POW families numbered in the hundreds of our POWs, and I made a special point of meeting with POW wives whenever they asked for an audience. I remember the organization was largely run by a woman named Sybil Stockdale, Admiral Stockdale's wife. Admiral Stockdale was given the Medal of Honor.

DW: He was the senior POW.

JW: Yeah.

DW: And so that was an organization—well, also, I guess, Ross Perot was very much involved in that.

JW: Yeah, Ross was quite anxious to be involved in it. Yes, he did.

DW: And then you mentioned earlier today the fact that it was kind of sensitive because we had John McCain.

JW: Yeah. That was during my period as Secretary of the Navy. Had no relationship to the Bicentennial.

DW: Right.

JW: But McCain, when I came there in '69, he was in the camp then. He'd been captured. His father, nicknamed "Jumpin' Jack" because he was a man of *incredible* energy, he was commander-in-chief, four-star admiral, of all military forces in the Pacific, and his son is in the lockup. And on my trips, which were regular trips out to Vietnam, I'd land, spend the night with Admiral and Mrs. McCain, and we'd go over the situation. I'd go in country, and when I came out, I spent a night and said, "This is what I think." There was a wide diversity of thinking about what was going on, right and wrong.

It's interesting, a lot of that is being revisited now. For some reason, which I think is a good reason, the Tet Offensive, which was a very distressing part of military history, is being reexamined by a lot of groups in symposiums and seminars—

DW: You had three daughters?

JW: Two daughters and one son.

DW: So they're growing up. I guess they're relatively young kids at this time.

JW: Oh, yes, very much so.

DW: Okay. So anyway, so this stresses your marriage. I know you were still together in '72 because you had this dinner where you had Kasatonov over to the house.

JW: Yeah. Oh, yeah.

DW: For the Incidents at Sea Agreement.

JW: Kasatonov being the head of the Soviet Union delegation to the Incidents at Sea, yeah.

DW: And you watched the Nixon speech announcing that he—

JW: With Kasatonov in the room.

DW: Yes, that he was going to mine the harbors.

JW: That's right. Haiphong.

DW: Yes. I think we covered that.

JW: And old Kasatonov, through the interpreter, listened very carefully, and when he finished his speech, I turned to him and I said, "Well, I wanted to share that with you."

    He said, "I'd like to have another drink."

DW: Yes.

JW: And he never mentioned it afterwards.

DW: Right. So, basically, I guess you parted amicably, I guess you would say, in the '73, '74 time frame?

JW: Sadly.

DW: Sadly.

JW: But friendly.

DW: Okay. So you're escorting Elizabeth Taylor to a reception?

JW: I'd never really met her. And we had a grand time, and I took her back to the hotel. She and I had a sip of something together, and she said, "Well, I'm going to stay a few days. You tell me you have a farm?"

    "Yeah."

    "I'd like to come down, drive out, and see your countryside."

    "Okay. Here's my number. Call me up."

    Two days later, she called me up, came down.

DW: I guess you had horses, right?

JW: Yeah. It's in a place called Middleburg [Virginia], and it's a series of two counties, Fauquier County and Blue Ridge County and the northern part of it. I'll think of it in a minute. They're famous for their stone walls. That part of the country had sort of a soft limestone, and when the settlers came out and worked their fields, they would disgorge these stones about the size, generally, of two and a half bricks or two bricks, and they'd stack them up in rows and made fences out of them. Shortly, they realized it was a very successful fence, and if built properly, you didn't have to come back; it stayed. Some of those fences built in the 1600s, seventeen00s, eighteen00s are still there, and my farm was filled with them. There are places in England called the Cotswolds—

DW: That's right.

JW: —where much the same construction with stone fences. So Elizabeth had already read about the Cotswolds. She'd visited them. My goodness, she went all over England. She said, "It's really like the Cotswolds?"
"Yeah."
So she came down to see the stone fences, and I guess around the fifth time she came down, she never left.

DW: Her background, of course, she was a movie star, Richard Burton, *Cleopatra*.

JW: Oh, yeah. I mean, she was titanic in her following.

DW: Right, right. And you wound up with her.

JW: I'm a country boy.

DW: Yeah. So for some reason, that had an appeal.

JW: That had an appeal. That and the horses. She often said, "I married you for the farm. I won't take it, but anyway, I liked it." She loved it.

DW: Okay.

JW: And she was a very good horsewoman herself. The first year or two of the marriage, we rode a lot together and fox hunted together. Then she took a terrible fall and injured her back, and she never got on another horse the rest of her life.

DW: Okay. Although she grew up in England, you never heard her really with a British accent.

JW: She could put it on. She could flick it like a switch.

DW: Okay, okay. So, no, I'd be like—you probably were pinching yourself, saying, "I'm here with Elizabeth Taylor." So you got married after the Bicentennial was over.

JW: That's correct.

DW: Okay. Now, after the Bicentennial is over, now you're unemployed.

JW: That's correct.

DW: Did you come back to the law firm?

JW: No. I had made the decision—Bicentennial was over, and, boy, that seventh day of July for me, it took four months, five months to dismantle the agency, and we gave back to the federal government all our unexpended funds and a considerably treasury of funds we'd made off the trade marts [sic], and we built Constitutional Gardens,[45] which is a significant segment of the National Park up here.

DW: Okay.

---

[45] Constitution Gardens sits at Constitution Ave and 17th St. NW—site of the Old Main Navy Building.

JW: But anyway, you know, I drifted from one thing to another. I decided to run for the Senate, and so I'd launched a campaign shortly after that.

DW: Okay. Of course, Gerald Ford—did you know Gerald Ford before he was vice president up at the House?

JW: Yeah. I'll tell you one of the most interesting evenings. The year was 1960, the year of Nixon's first election for the presidency. He was sold a bill of goods on using a train to campaign.

DW: Right.

JW: He really didn't have his heart in it, but the president, the famous one that became president after Roosevelt, from Missouri—

DW: Truman.

JW: He had mastered the art of speaking from the rear of a train. Mind you, he campaigned there in the late forties, and this is the sixties, only ten or fifteen years, and trains and all those things were pretty much in the public domain.

So Nixon constructed a four-day train trip. We started somewhere, in my recollection, like Philadelphia Station or something, and it was just a small train, about five cars, six cars, sleeper cars, dining cars, observation car. I got picked to be the head advance man for the train trip, because, as you can see here in my library, my old model trains are up on the wall. I just loved trains and everything about it, and I was in seventh heaven.

Well, they'd worked out with modest success in that campaign, but we were on the road at least three days, I think four. But we were nearing the last stop, and I can remember as if it were last night, it was a furniture company—I had the name; just lost it—that manufactured metal furniture in Muskegon, Michigan, and the event was at nine o'clock at night. I had a series of assistants on every stop going up, and this one was carefully advanced. Then the Secret

Service had gone through. Everywhere we went with Nixon as vice president, Secret Service was with us, checked it out. So the old train—by this time, we're all pretty weary, been on that train for three days—pulls into the Muskegon railyards there right next to the plant, because heavy steel furniture, they wanted a railroad right there to cut down their handling of big heavy furniture.

DW: Makes sense.

JW: And I jumped off the train, met my assistants. "All set? Everything's good?"

He said, "Yeah. Come on, take a quick look at it."

And I ran into the big auditorium in the plant, right on the floor of the plant, all the machines and everything, and people all around in there having a good time, bands are playing, very patriotic. I said, "Okay. Give me a hand signal when you've got the crowd calmed down, and we'll bring him in. Then when he comes in, hit the bands and away we go."

Everything worked. I lined Nixon up, put him outside in the vestibule. We all got ready, and as soon as the guy came, [demonstrates], gave me the signal to come in, bands started, and we marched Nixon in.

We were unaware of the door that we came in, that above it was a balcony, which I'm not sure what the purpose was, but about two dozen young guys up there, mischief-laden, with raw eggs.

DW: Ugh!

JW: And they just pelted us with raw eggs. And here I am with the vice president of the United States, at the end of a *long* series of appearances. Now he's got raw egg all over him. But he was a tough guy in many respects. He said, "Come on. Let's wipe it off quickly." I had my handkerchief going, I grabbed this and that. I told them, "Get the bands louder." They were cheering. Pulled him up, we cleaned him up. He got up on the rostrum and gave his set of remarks flawlessly and got down and came out, went back straight to the train. I escorted him. The only time that he never turned to me and said, "Well done," or something, commending me for something. He didn't say a damn thing. Got on the train.

DW: Right.

JW: So I got on the train. Well, those trains, you've got to remember, each stop, you put on dignitaries so that they could be a part of the train ride. We had a load of dignitaries, and I didn't have time to check out all the people, who they were, because the distance between these stops was a half hour, forty-five minutes or something, and they all wanted to meet Nixon, all that stuff. I said, "Oh, shit. This is the end of my career."

So I went on back into the observation car, because the train now is steaming for wherever we were bunked for the hotels, and then the train was going along. We were being picked up by air and flown back to the next event. So I went back in this dim, dark observation car, and there were a handful of guys back there drinking beer, nothing rowdy. Because a lot of people just didn't see the whole thing happen. It was pretty well concealed. And I'm sitting there, and this guy engaged me in conversation, and he said, "You know, it's too bad this thing happened." He was one of the dignitaries.

I said, "Yeah. You know, you plan for it. We did everything by the books. Secret Service checked it out, local police. Nobody thought to go up in the balcony and make sure." Because people were doing silly things in those days, but no chance of any real pressure about getting shot or anything. It wasn't that. I said, "You know, I really put my heart and soul helping this man. It's been a long campaign, but it's all coming to an end now, and I guess this is the end of my career. I'll be fired in the morning."

The guy mumbled. I didn't even hardly look at him. He said, "Well, you know, you get fired, I'm gonna get fired."

I said, "What?"

Said, "Yeah, I'm responsible in some ways for this. I'm the local congressman."

I said, "Huh?" I looked at him, and there's Gerald Ford. I hadn't really focused on him. I said, "Oh, for God's sakes." So with that, we had another beer, and that started a longtime friendship.

DW: Okay.

JW: I'm actually getting this year the annual Gerald R. Ford Award.

DW: Okay.

JW: Quite an honor.

DW: Who presents the Gerald R. Ford Award? [laughs]

JW: Well, a *big* society.[46]

DW: That's a long-winded story about why you knew Gerald R. Ford.

JW: I'll give you a sequel to it. I can't give you the exact dates and everything. But the Secretary of the Navy in those days had tremendous leeway in naming ships.

DW: Right.

JW: And I've forgotten, but I had a heavy hand in getting that ship named for him.[47]

DW: Okay.

JW: And that's one of the reasons that his family wanted to honor me.

DW: So anyway, during this whole time period with the Bicentennial, Gerald Ford is running for reelection.

JW: Oh, yeah.

---

[46] Warner was the 2018 Gerald R. Ford Presidential Foundation Medal for Distinguished Public Service.
[47] The *Gerald R. Ford* is the lead class of a 21st century aircraft carrier.

DW: So he's trying to orchestrate this, and he's got this convention and he's being challenged by Ronald Reagan. So did you get to play in any of the politics around the '76 convention?

JW: I wasn't that involved. I mean, the Nixon defeat in '60, I did some things for him and then I got active in Virginia politics and helped Linwood Holton get elected governor, but I wasn't involved then. Nixon recalled me in the '68 campaign, and I ran his Washington office.

DW: Right.

JW: He's funny. He said, "You know, I want you to rent the biggest office building you can get."

I still called him vice president. "Mr. vice president, you can get a big office."

He said, "I got a purpose for it. I'm going to do my work in New York in the old hotel up there which is near my law office. I'm only going to have this many people. I own a lot of hanger-ons, wannabe politicians. Guess what? I'm calling *you* up to take 'em and give 'em a job. You get a big hotel and pack it."

We took the Willard Hotel, which was in bankruptcy, gut it out, cleaned it up. We put close to one thousand volunteers in that hotel.

He called me up, "Get this Spiro Agnew out. I don't want him in New York. Put him in the hotel, give him a big suite, keep him busy." He used to call me up and growl at me. "John, I got another one. Do it tenderly, but this John Eisenhower, he thinks he knows something about politics. He doesn't know anything about politics. Give him a big office and take care of him." That was the president's son.

DW: Right.

JW: And there was a couple others we packed in. It was a fascinating experience.

DW: Oh, we'll talk about—of course, Jimmy Carter becomes president of the United States, and you're going to be running for the Senate from Virginia for 1978. So we got two years of campaigning, and we can talk about that. Then we'll talk about the Senate and how the Senate works, how funding goes to, for example, Navy programs and projects. I think that's what's going to be very interesting to the eventual readers of this oral history.

JW: Well, the key to it is—and I'll stress this—that 30 years I was there—and I've checked this with the Senate historian; it's ironclad fact—70-plus percent of the membership of the United States Senate were World War II veterans—

DW: Right.

JW: —or a few Korean War veterans. I think just at the tail end of my time, Vietnam guys like McCain came in. That cohesion between men and—I always say "women." I don't think any women were involved in those days. We didn't have many for the early part of it, anyway. But that cohesion between persons who'd worn the uniform, you remember all of us, whether you're Army, Navy, Air Force, Marine Corps, goes through the same basic type of training, some more severe than others, but the fundamental principle that's drilled into your head, learn to know and respect the guy next to you, because there may be a time when your life is dependent on him taking the right steps.

DW: Okay.

JW: And that was the glue. When all the fighting on the floor and finally went down for a drink, that was the glue that brought us together to do the things. I think you'll be interested in that.

DW: I think that kind of leads to why we have a little dysfunctionality today, although it is encouraging that when you see some of these Iraq and Afghanistan War veterans are now—

JW: Oh, they really pull their weight. You notice how they gravitate together.

DW: Yeah.

JW: Because they've got that common training. But you see, the reason the numbers have gone down now, I think twenty-five, thirty veterans in the whole Senate, it's that we haven't been engaged, fortunately, in major wars.

DW: Right, right. No, I once sat down with the chief of legislative affairs, Gary Roughead, who went on to become—

JW: Oh, I knew Gary. Yeah.

DW: —Chief of Naval Operations, and I made the same observation, and he said, "You know, that was actually an abnormality that we had so many veterans because of World War II." What he said is that we're actually going back to a norm, that with the exception of the post–Civil War era and the post–World War II era, we really more have a legislative representative of what the population in the country is.

JW: Mm-hmm. It might be interesting, I've never done it, but you might go back and see what was post–World War I.

DW: Mm-hmm.

JW: I can find out from the Senate if they had any record of the number of veterans who came back. They were so abused, those veterans.

DW: Right. But World War I was so quick.

JW: Yeah, but we had five million men in uniform.

DW: That's right. That's right. Well, when you think about it, of course, Eisenhower became president. [laughs] Truman, World War I. But that would be interesting to see in the Senate and Congress in the late thirties.

JW: If there's a blip up.

DW: If there's a blip up. Let's close it there.

JW: We had a good session.

DW: That was.

[End of March 19, 2018, interview]

Interview Number 7 with Senator John W. Warner, USN (Ret.)
Date: April 23, 2018

David Winkler (DW): Today is April 23, 2018. This is David Winkler with the [U.S.] Naval Institute Oral History Program, with Senator John W. Warner at his abode.

I want to move decades forward, because in the news last week, the USS *John W. Warner* fired missiles against Syria, and I thought we'd be getting there eventually, but since it's in the news, I want you to talk a little bit about the whole process of the decision behind naming a submarine for you and taking that process to the christening, and then some of the things that you've done with the submarine in communications with the crew and what you've done as far as like setting up a fund to support the crew, I think are worth mentioning. So while that's in the news, I yield the floor to talk a little bit about the *John Warner*. First of all, when did you first find out? Whose idea was it to name a submarine after you?

JW: Well, I'm not certain how it was generated, except I plead not guilty. I never tried to seek recognition by way of naming anything for me, either in the Department of Navy or the Marine Corps, but others took it upon themselves.

For instance, I should back up. The Marines, a former commandant that I'd worked with very closely—mind you, I'd spent thirty years in the Senate, and it was well-known that I looked after the Navy and the Marine Corps. I don't know exactly what the word is, but I tried to address their needs, let's put it that way, and this was well-known from the four-stars down to the sailors and deckhands and grunts and Marines.

So the Marines elected to attach my name to a beautiful building, which is part of the University of the Marine Corps in Quantico, Virginia. It's basically a lecture hall and a study area for the student body going to the Marine Corps Institute, which is an offer of advanced learning given to a certain selection of Marines each year. It's a highly sought-after educational aspect to your career in the Marine Corps.

In the case of the Navy, I participated in the naming of many Navy vessels. Most of it were states, which were straightforward, simple, in the case that the *Virginia*-class were all states, and there was a little friendly politicking as to which states would get the names, but that's to be expected.

DW: When you were Secretary of the Navy, the *Virginia*-class at that time is a nuclear cruiser.

JW: That's correct. All your *Virginia*-class are attack boats.

DW: Now they're attack boats today, when you were Secretary of the Navy, they brought in—I guess the states were named for nuclear cruisers and they were naming submarines for cities.

JW: Yes.

DW: The *Los Angeles*-class.

JW: That's right. It's gone back and forth.

DW: Yep.

JW: It's a discretion with the Secretary of the Navy by and with the approval of the secretary of defense. The secretary of defense always sort of had a quiet hand in matters, but it was largely left, by tradition, to the Secretary of the Navy from the time of the first sailing ships. As to my own case, I truly did not try to get anything named for me. I felt that the opportunity to serve those five years and four months and three days were award enough to be with the men and women in the trouble spots of the world all those years, traveling and visiting with them, working with them when they got them back home.

But out of the blue, I got a call one night, five days left in my Senate term, fifth term in the Senate, and I was finishing up five terms, and it was the president of the United States, George Herbert Walker Bush, had moved on, of course, and his son, George W. Bush, had become president. It was George W. Bush who called me, and in a very friendly but cryptic manner said, "I've made a decision we're going to name a submarine for you in recognition of your very long service and the Navy secretariat," also in recognition of quite a few things I'd achieved internationally, like the Incidents at Sea negotiations, where I was the principal advocate for that and then made trips to the Soviet Union to work out the details with my counterparts in the Soviet senior staff of the Navy. That was quite an undertaking, took place two to three years. And there were other things that I was very much involved in, international. So, I mean, there was a flavor of my career, because challenges arose during my watch, and ostensibly and historically, I can say now, had met their goals as laid down in these various things. I wouldn't say "things." Really important historical steps taken by the Navy Department.

But George Bush was very cordial. He told me about it, and I thanked him very much, explained I wished he'd given it to someone more deserving, and I started down that, and he cut me off and said, "Guess what? I made the decision. I've got the right to do it. The decision's been made. This is my telephone call and my nickel we're spending, and the time of the call is up. So I'll say thank you again for your service. We're going to have the USS *John Warner*." The keel had just been laid shortly beforehand, and she was well under way in construction.

This beautiful submarine has come in to join our fleet, and my wife takes very humble pride in being the sponsor. She's very conscientious about it. She keeps in touch with the troops, the succession of commanding officers and executive officers and sailors and the like, and their families. We try making one trip a year down to the base to visit with them, picnic. And our family gathered together and set up a little permanent trust. I am always very quiet about this because not all the ships have it, but we felt that in this case, this ship deserved it because of my long association in the Navy Department. We took our own private funds and established a perpetual trust, perpetual in the sense of the life of the ship, and it pays a small stipend to the organizations that are annually holding, I should say, competitions for Sailor of the Year or, you know, different recognitions that both enlisted and officers are given for outstanding performance aboard the USS *John Warner*. And we broadened it; it can be used on other submarines too. So this whole experience has just been a joy in our life.

Then along comes the conflict in the Syrian war, and she is on her first combat patrol, having just finished about two years of graduate sort of exercises and training to quality [*sic*] them that they're combat-ready. You sort of think submarines are finished and crews go out on their initial shakedown cruise and so forth, but the actual qualification to be combat-ready, it's sort of the graduate school. That was completed, and lo and behold, they got posted to the Mediterranean. I jokingly said, "Well, you got what I call the 'candy-ass' mission." That was a Marine posting, and tours in that area, a wonderful opportunity to learn a lot of history about the very marvelous history of Europe and Mediterranean area.

And along develops this tension with Syria over their second gas attack, and I said to myself, well, this could be interesting, because the ship doesn't share with me, nor should it, all of their operational orders about what they're doing. They're a part of, I think, TAD [Temporary Active Duty] to Sixth Fleet, and I know full well, having so many years worked in that area myself, everybody loves port calls, the diversity of port calls, the history, and, by the large, the climate of that area is pretty good.

Then I was calculating if they did do this strike, that the president and chairman of Joint Chiefs of Staff would pick a diversity of targets and a diversity of launch platforms. It's all public now. All of that was done. Well, I did not do any interviews about it. I remained very quiet, deeply proud of the troops, and I simply said, "They are conducting themselves consistent with the naval tradition which originated two hundred-plus years ago: duty, honor, country."

[coughs] Excuse me. The old throat ain't what it used to be.

So that's about all I can add to that.

DW: Okay. Take a minute there.

JW: I just hope that—I mean, Syria's doing everything they can to block us from going in there to run some tests to verify the types of enemy or dangerous gas, other chemicals that were used against the poor civilians. I think they finally got in in the last seventy-two hours.

DW: I think so.

JW: But it's well-known that the Syrians did a lot of clean-up.

DW: The actual commissioning ceremony itself, how grand was that?

JW: Of the submarine?

DW: Yeah.

JW: Well, Ray Mabus was Secretary of the Navy. He planned it consistent with the others. I don't think it was any grander, except two reasons. I was a pretty colorful fellow and well-known in that part of the geography of the state, having been a senator for thirty years, so the attendance, understandably, was pretty substantial, and the weather was unusually good. Most of the ship and its inspections were done on time, so it was quite smooth. Then the current CNO was at that time the head of the segment of the Navy that handles all nuclear propulsion, and the ship fell under his jurisdiction, and he was just wonderful about it.[48] I had known him through the years as he advanced through the ranks. So I just can't imagine how anything could have been more exciting or done consistent with good law and order and traditions of the Navy and Marine Corps.

DW: Of course, the submarine was built at Newport News Shipbuilding. I guess now it's Huntington Ingalls Industries. I think it sets a relationship with—that's one of the major employers in the state of Virginia.

JW: At times, it's *the* major. If you discount the Department of Defense, which is the largest employer, yes, it is, and it's an integral part and has been for hundreds of years. I mean, it goes way back. Shipbuilding has been an important part of the economics of that region for a long time, and not only the building, but the manning of the ships. There's quite a bit of civilian shipbuilding down there, of course, nothing of the huge consequence of a warship, but some of the finer merchant vessels are particularly outfitted there. It's hard to compete with the Oriental market of shipbuilding today; that is, from hull up. That hull construction part and so forth can be done at such a comparably lesser price in the East, and it works. The systems work. But a lot of the outfitting and so forth is done down in Norfolk, and ship repair.

DW: Yeah. One of your portfolios as senator is defense contracting and, I think, looking out after the local industries, that their fair share of contracts go to Virginians?

---

[48] Admiral John Richardson had been the director of Naval Reactors before being selected to be the CNO.

JW: Well, I'd like to sort of revise it. My job was, in this Congress of the United States, to try to make sure not that Virginia got an *x* amount of it, but the allocations were done to companies that had a long history of performing well on these types of contracts, and, you see, there's no other shipyard in the United States—

In other words, my job was to just watch the contracting from the standpoint of making sure that it could stand the test of time and there was good reason for it. Members of Congress have to stand back, and the industry competitively bids these things. But Virginia is fortunate in the sense that it keeps and maintains—and believe me, it's a lot of overhead to carry in between major ship construction of naval ships, primarily. There's only two yards in America that are qualified to build submarines: it's a yard in the Newport News area and a yard up in Connecticut. Connecticut's had a long tradition, Connecticut, and then Maine's has a long tradition of building surface ships. We don't compete with the destroyer business.

DW: Right.

JW: So destroyers, but submarines, we finally worked out—and I was the one that started it, as a matter of fact, and came up with the idea—rather than Newport News and General Dynamics going through utter warfare over these naval contracts, just allocate one contract to one company this year, then to the other company the next year, but in the meantime, make them competitively bid these things. That's worked out very well, and it's maintained an industrial base of more than one yard, because it's hard to conceive, but someone could, some group or whatever, create such destruction in either location as to substantially degrade their ability to build for a while till the destruction is repaired. So you should have two yards.

DW: Because I guess with the *Arleigh Burke*, they build them down in Mississippi and up in Maine.

JW: That's correct.

DW: And I think that's going to be one of our challenges going forward, is that if we're going to build up to 3fifty ships, do we have the industrial capability.

JW: Do we have the industrial base.?

DW: Yeah. Because a lot of that's gone away over the past two decades.

JW: Yeah, but they're pretty good at reestablishing it. But, you know, the shipbuilding, it's more than a job, more than a trade; it's a skill. So much of it has been passed down from father to son, and grandfather to father and son. How many of these times I've been down there, and part of the ceremonies are to recognize Joe Smith, whose grandfather was in the yard in eighteen98, his father was in World War I, he was in World War II.

DW: Okay. So after going forward to the *John W. Warner*, lets pick up the narrative. I want to talk a little bit about running for Senate and the campaign. First of all, on the way home, I mentioned that another naval figure from your era, Admiral Zumwalt, who was the Chief of Naval Operations, attempted to run for Senate, I believe in 1976, right after he left office as CNO. He left, I think, in 1974. Admiral Holloway came in.[49] And that didn't go well. Do you have any observations about—

JW: Well, Bud Zumwalt, he had an interesting Navy career. We had our differences, but by and large—I won't go into the details, but the Navy, when I came and joined the Navy Department in '69, it was clearly and very well administered in the uniform side by World War II sailors.

DW: Right.

JW: They all knew each other. Most of the senior officers, if not all of them, had combat careers aboard the old-fashioned battleships, cruisers. Of course, there was a huge part of the Navy addressed to the landing craft, quite a good emphasis on landing craft. So it was a fine outfit and they all knew each other. It was a difficult transition for that group to quietly finish their work and step down, and then the new noncombatants coming along, the war having ended, World

---

[49] Admiral James L. Holloway III served as CNO from 1974 to 1978.

War II, rather abruptly and quickly, and while some of them had minor naval combat experience on the coastal assignments of Korea and Vietnam, by and large, nothing matched the old battleship-cruiser group and aircraft carriers. They were certainly coming into their own.

Zumwalt, he took a lot of rough treatment from me and others as he tried to shoulder the Navy. I felt he was trying to push it too far too fast. Anyway, he finished up, and suddenly he got it in his mind that everything he learned on the job in the Navy was applicable to the world of politics. He, of course, had done his testifying on Capitol Hill, but he'd never, ever been subjected to the city council, state legislature, members of Congress. He'd occasionally see members of Congress in his job with primarily the Armed Services Committee of the House and Senate. I doubt if he'd ever sat down—I'd moved on by the time he was preparing to leap into this thing. From day one, he was not cut out for the job.

There's one classic story I think that explains it. He was taking a group of reporters, as we always did, hired a bus and put the reporters on it and they'd go from stop to stop and watch you speak, shake hands, and write about the issues, this little crossroads of Virginia, what's their big problem. The bus is rumbling down in what we call the old traditional Southside Virginia, and this is where the last vestiges of the Civil War were fought at Appomattox, where Lee surrendered. You had Danville, where several prominent people came from Danville, Virginia. The bus was rolling down the road, on the subject of agriculture, and Zumwalt said, "And we're going to go down. You'll see the trees and the orchards where the peanuts are raised, because a lot of peanuts are raised in this part of Virginia." Well, peanuts are not raised on trees; they're raised underground. The first light of sunshine they ever see is when they're turned over—that's the phrase—the plow goes down and digs them up softly to let them begin to dry out in the sun. Well, I thought the press guys would rock and roll on the press bus. That story went far and wide. And he made so many little gaffes like that.

DW: The irony is that you had a fellow, another Navy man, from Georgia running for president at the same time.

JW: Jimmy Carter.

DW: Yes, who knew something about peanuts.

JW: He knew something about peanuts, that's for damn sure. Jimmy Carter's an interesting man. I met him first when I was chairman of the Bicentennial and I visited all fifty states and the governors, gave them a check for spending, and he couldn't have been more gracious to me. Little did I ever think he'd become president someday, but it happened by surprise.

DW: Well, you had met Elizabeth Taylor, and we talked a little bit about that. Just two follow-up questions on that. How do you go about proposing to Elizabeth Taylor?—

JW: Well, we were just down on the farm taking a walk quietly at sunset in the afternoon. She loved the farm because it reminded her of her birthplace in England. There's a small section of Middleburg [Virginia] where I lived, and it's the Upperville-Middleburg area, actually starts in Aldie through Upperville, three little villages in a row. They have a lot of stone walls. The agriculture in those days was mule or oxen, and you plowed your fields and you turned up these stones. And what do you do with them? So they took them one by one and made beautiful fences, and those fences, some of them were made two hundred years ago, are still standing today. And the same way in England. They have the Cotswold area, which is beautiful, old stone fences.

There was a lot about it she liked, so she was happy and she'd been visiting me quite a bit for a year down there, six months, I guess. So we were just walking along, and somehow it happened. She was overjoyed.

DW: Did you give her a ring?

JW: No. I said, "You've got so much jewelry now, I'll give you a wedding band." I think that's what I did, yeah. Gosh, I couldn't match all the stuff she had. I did give her a horse.

DW: Okay.

JW: And a horse had value of a pretty good ring.

DW: Okay. And then the actual wedding itself, that—

JW: Yeah. We decided we didn't want any big weddings, so we went out on the highest promontory of the land, on the back of the farm, and you could see down the valley of Virginia for probably twenty miles. Brought in the country minister and just my kids, her kids, and some of the farmhands. The press snuck in overnight and built tree boxes and slipped up there so they could get the cameras on it. But very quiet, nice wedding.

I made the mistake of—she's always late, so I figured she'd be late, and I strolled on up there. She was getting dolled-up and everything. So for lack of anything better to do, I'm sitting there. There was a field of fifty cows and heifers, which is the young offspring of a cow, and so I know how to call cattle. You call them [demonstrates], you know. You do it in the late fall and winter when you take some hay out. You start calling them and then they know when that hay's coming out, and you dribble the hay for an eighth of a mile so that they're not all banging into each other and fighting. If you're going out with a truck with hay on it and throwing a bale every fifteen, twenty yards, they come behind. So they're all out there.

Now Elizabeth arrives and the minister's escorting Elizabeth, and the cows won't stop chewing and hollering. I wasn't feeding them anything. So I called them all to come together and then didn't feed them. The minister, "I can't possibly conduct this ceremony with all this noise." So we had a dickens of a time getting them all quieted down so he could conduct the ceremony. Elizabeth got a big kick out of that. Hollywood did too.

DW: Yes. There was a show back then, I guess called *Green Acres*.

JW: She was a good wife, a wonderful woman, taught me a lot of things about how to handle oneself in crowds and press conferences and things. But particularly for a freshman senator in the vintage that I came in, boy, it suddenly consumes your life, and she was used to my saying, "Hey, let's fly to London for the weekend, see some of my friends." Stay a week, fly back, go to California. We were doing all kinds of things. It all dried up for me, so she ended up by herself. She very nicely, over a period of time, started talking to me, said, "I've just got to go back on stage. That's where I belong. And I'm not happy having something."

I said, "Go."

So she started that. Then we were commuting back and forth, and then we decided we'd just quietly split up. We stayed good friends, and I dated her fifty times afterwards in the years, talked to her ten days before she died.

DW: That was tragic. So you're running for office, and that's an asset, having Elizabeth Taylor, if she's on the campaign trail with you.

JW: Oh, she was good about campaigning. There's the old slogan, "They came to see Elizabeth, but they listened to me."

DW: Yeah. Talk about campaigning for the Senate in Virginia, because it is a huge state.

JW: Oh, yeah, a lot of territory.

DW: How do you go about doing that?

JW: I just had a little ol' broken-down bus and two beat-up old Lincoln cars. You don't want anything fancy. And I didn't go as far—well, I didn't have to because I had two pickups on the farm. I think I used them a little bit.

I'll never forget, a guy ran for the Senate in Virginia about twenty years ago, he went out and bought himself some designer blue jeans and a red pickup truck. He was a laughingstock. I mean, in the first place, it's a brand-new truck, he didn't know how to drive the thing, and he looked so silly in the designer blue jeans. Good guy, nice fellow, and, oddly enough, today he still owns the little farm that he bought and he's still got his old pickup truck, and I guess the blue jeans have been replaced. But he's a nice guy.

DW: So you kind of dressed the part.

JW: I had plenty of old clothes, because I'd been running my farms for years. Let's see. My first father-in-law gave me and my first wife a beautiful farm as a wedding present, and then I, as a boy, worked on farms right up until I went in the Navy. When I came out of the Navy and went to college, I didn't work on any farms anymore, but I'd hobnob around a lot of the horsey set and the farmers and this thing.

DW: So you're running for—okay, you mentioned before, before we started the interview—one reason I brought up Admiral Zumwalt is he tried to run for Senate without having prior elected office, and you're kind of in the same situation.

JW: Well, I did. It's interesting. But the Navy secretariat job, which I had over five years, gave me a lot of exposure in Virginia, as you said, as a consequence of the large shipbuilding industry, but on top of that, we have about ten major forts, Army, we have a big airfield, so the Air Force and the Army were very much a part of the state. We ranked, as a state, number five, six, seven, and up to one or two some years, in the number of defense contracts annually given by the Department of Defense, so we were a heavily oriented state to national security, and national security was a key issue. Particularly we were in the middle of the Cold War, and I'd been to Russia and I understood a good deal about how Russians operated, and that all pitched in. That's right, I'd never held public office—well, that is elected public office—till I ran for the Senate.

DW: Okay.

JW: They always laughed, "He parachuted in from up above."

DW: Because I guess you'd have residences in—well, you had the farm out in Middleburg, so you had residency.

JW: I have another farm at White Post, which is a little community down in Virginia, where we still have family has a lot of the farms down there.

DW: Okay. So, running. First you had the primary, and the convention—

JW: It actually was a convention, but it was conducted much like a primary. There were four of us, former governor Linwood Holton, former party chairman and a sitting state legislator, very able man. So my opponents in that duel had all been people who had had a lot of political experience, and they teased me about my absence of political experience.

DW: So in that convention, you didn't come out on top on that, did you?

JW: Well, I came out on top in the sense I came in second and only lost by about two hundred votes, and there were over ten thousand votes cast. That shows you how narrow it was.

DW: Mm-hmm.

JW: And I won—each of the others dropped out, and then I ran against the party chairman, wonderful man, and he eked me out by a couple hundred votes, I think three-hundred-and-some-odd votes out of ten thousand votes cast. In the Book of Guinness Records at that time, it was the largest political gathering in the history of America, the whole country.

DW: Okay. That was quite a convention you had. What was the draw of the convention?

JW: Just excitement. They had not had a political race like this, because it'd been all machine politics for years.

DW: Because you are seen here as this outsider with Elizabeth Taylor as a wife, you know.

JW: A lot of people who never thought about voting before decided they were going to vote.

DW: Okay. And then, of course, I guess the winner who won the primary, this convention—

JW: The guy beat me by about three hundred or four hundred votes.

DW: Yeah.

JW: I got up the next morning, went to his breakfast, and spoke on his behalf to the lingering delegates that always like to gather, a sleepless night, they were up way past midnight casting ballots. Wished him well and went back, gathered up Elizabeth. I was driving, drove her on back up to the farm. We unpacked all our stuff, said it was well worth it. We didn't regret it.

Actually, she had just been picked by the Irish government to become the Grand Marshal of the Dublin Horse Show, and she still had some ability to ride a horse, but she wasn't going to perform. But she was like a little girl with a new trunk of clothes. I mean, she was so excited about that thing, and, boy, she packed a suitcase, then the next day, there would be another suitcase. We had about fifteen suitcases stacked up in the hall of all her outfits to do this thing. I was going over. I was going to ride myself. I was pretty proficient in riding in those days.

I was up and giving a speech for Barry Goldwater up in the northeast part of the country, somewhere near Boston, and I got up and was watching the *Today Show* when they announced that he had been killed. His plane hit a tree coming in late at night to land.[50]

DW: Okay. So that means you're the runner-up. You have the nod.

JW: Well, but they still weren't comfortable with me because I wasn't a true dyed-in-the-wool conservative. Basically, I was conservative on national security issues, but, for example, right to life, I felt that that was a woman's decision and men should not try and superimpose their judgment. That was a big issue. I decided not to try and run around and shut up and dodge it. That's the way I feel. Matter of fact, I think I can remember this, the four of us were dueling, I probably took that position.

But anyway, I had this mystique of being Secretary of the Navy. That was a big deal, that plus Elizabeth. For a while, I sent her to one end of the state and I'd go to the other so we'd get two different press stories. She loved to campaign. She had the best—I talked to her on the phone three or four times a day. She was the wife that was very much involved in your life twenty-four hours a day. She was that type of woman. She couldn't get over the excitement she

---

[50] Richard Obenshain, having won his party's nomination to run for Senate to replace William L. Scott, died on August 2 when his small twin-engine airplane crashed in trees while attempting a nighttime landing approaching Chesterfield County Airport.

was in. She was made the—I guess it was—it wasn't Apple Blossom, but the annual big parade of a small town down in southwest Virginia, Tobacco festival.

DW: Okay.

JW: And each little town had its own product. Peanut festival. They had oyster festivals, peanut festivals, tobacco festivals, you name it. Apple festival, we had that. Anyway, it was one of these festivals and they made her grand marshal. It was a small town down in Southwest Virginia, but being small, they were very proud and they want Elizabeth Taylor. Well, all their cousins and half-cousins and wannabee-cousins all wanted to come to town to see her, so the little town that had maybe one thousand people turned out, they had three thousand or four thousand people. So the parade was set up, and I flew Elizabeth down. I wasn't with them. Got a little private plane, flew down. She had to change clothes in a funny little old motel, which was not much, and she said that was the hardest part. Even the bed hadn't been changed.

DW: Oh, my.

JW: But anyway, she turned out and bought a costume for the parade, and got in the back seat of a car with an open rumble seat. Bands were escorting here. The people were just loving it, going on, you know, block after block after block, and then the driver turns the car and speeds up and goes off. And she said, "What happened?"

He said, "We just finished the parade."

She said, "But it wasn't more than about eight, ten blocks."

Said, "Yeah, that was bigger than they intended it to be."

"Well, I bought this special dress for the whole thing."

"Well, ma'am, I think they all looked. They gave you a good ovation."

She said, "Yeah, but somehow—turn around. I want to go back through again."

So he turned it around, went back through again. They loved it. The town just loved it. She'd do funny little things like that, and it'd get all written up in the press.

DW: So she's campaigning. Also it's the fall, so you have—I know when I was in college up in Pennsylvania, I went to Penn State, so we had the politicians always came to the football games and worked the crowds there. Did you—

JW: Then we went to a few football games. Oh, no, we went to everything.

DW: Yeah.

JW: Horse shows and—we really campaigned hard. See, we only had ninety days from the death of this poor man to the election, and so we had to raise all this money, we had to campaign. It was every day.

DW: And you had, of course, that whole trip to Ireland went by the wayside.

JW: Oh, yeah. She never got over there.

DW: Yeah. Had to unpack all those suitcases.

JW: Yeah.

DW: So in the end, you wind up, I think, with a debate with your opponent, was Andy Miller? And was that here in Old Town Alexandria? Could you talk about how that debate went?

JW: Oh, yeah. It was a good, solid debate, but in the end, each of us had three minutes to summarize why Virginians should vote for me. Andy Miller got up and he said, "Well, I don't think I need three minutes. The one reason that you should vote for me is I was born in Virginia." And he didn't say anything more, and he went home and he sat down.

And my mother, who was eighty-some-odd years old, was there. And I got up and I said, "You know, Mother, stand up there. These folks would like to see you." All these gray-haired ladies stood up and they gave her a nice polite applause. I said, "Mother, could you tell me, did I have anything to do with where I was born?"

And she said, "Well, certainly you didn't have anything to do with it. Your father was a doctor and he worked in Washington at the hospital, and that's where you were going to be born. He was chief of gynecology. His wife couldn't go running around, so I wanted to be right there. I wouldn't let him deliver you, though, son." The audience is going like this [demonstrates]. That's true. She said his partner delivered.

I said, "Well, thank you, Mommy. I thought that'd be the case." So I said, "Folks, I didn't have anything to do with that, but I had everything to do about where I wanted to get my education. I went to my father's school, General Lee's school, Washington and Lee. I went to Mr. Jefferson's school for my law degree. My opponent, he left Virginia, turned his back on thirty-eight institutions of higher learning. He went north, north to Princeton."

This guy burst out in a sweat. The audience started stomping on the floor, "Go, go, go, go, Princeton!" I kept saying, "North!" I won it three days later, it was a Saturday, Tuesday vote. He's never gotten over it to this day.

DW: That was well played.

JW: Yeah. It fell into your hand. Made statewide story.

DW: You mentioned your father didn't deliver you. We're going to a dinner on Wednesday to honor J. W. Marriott. Is there a connection with your father and J. W. Marriot?

JW: He was a gynecologist. I don't have all the details, but it's factual. The original Bill Marriott, they started a small root beer/hot dog stand up on 14th Street, and they were patients of Father. Out of that simple beginning, the family and certainly your guest of honor this coming night, they built a magnificent United States corporation and hotel ownership all over the world.

DW: Okay. And your father had a little role in bringing that to fruition.

JW: I'm not sure whether he delivered this fellow. I never got down to that. See, Father died right after I got home from the Navy in World War II.

DW: Okay, okay. Are there some other notable individuals who your father brought into this world that you recall?

JW: Yeah, I still occasionally for a while met them everywhere. He had a huge gynecological practice, and he was one of the early pioneers in gynecology, because up until that point, the medical profession, everybody knew how to deliver babies, but then when they developed new science about how to save the life of babies in complicated cases, he became an expert and traveled all over this region of Virginia and Maryland, delivering. Local doctors would, "Call Dr. John. Get him out here, because I got one twisted in the breech and I'm in trouble."

DW: Okay. Any recollections off the top of your head of somebody that may have become—

JW: I can't pull it in right now, I mean people who achieved great notoriety, no, but I do hear that, "Oh, my grandma told me that it was your father who delivered me."

DW: You get those.

JW: Yeah. One popped the other day. It'd been two or three years since anybody said it to me. He practiced a lot in Alexandria because Alexandria didn't have any hospitals. They had a couple of clinics. The District of Columbia had all the big hospitals. My god, I can remember up here where as you cross Key Bridge, come into Virginia there, in that little community, they had a hot dog joint, a nice restaurant, steakhouse, a Dairy Queen, and a pawn shop. And now they've got these huge towers. See, they weren't faced with the building code in DC, no taller than the Washington Monument.

DW: That's right.

JW: And they built a small mini New York City over there.

DW: They do have a restriction, because you are flying into the airport.

JW: Yeah, but twenty-five, thirty stories.

DW: Shall we break it up?

JW: Yeah. It's such fun, though.

DW: Next time we'll talk about you coming into the Senate, and now that you're in government, how your outlook changes as far as—

JW: Sure.

DW: I think that'll be fun.

JW: We're up to the point I'm pulling the parachute and landing. Only won by one point. But I parlayed that into five terms. And nobody else has ever done that.

DW: A remarkable career.

JW: And then I'm the second-longest-serving senator. Harry Byrd. He's thirty-two and I'm thirty. It was a temptation to ride it out, because I was not going to have an opponent.

DW: You left in 2008?

JW: I was about eighty-two when I stepped down.

DW: Okay. I remember Strom Thurmond was in his late eighties.

JW: A hundred. Oh, no, I saw some of those fellows push it too far.

DW: Yeah. That's kind of a disservice to your state—you need to let a younger generation carry on.

JW: Oh, it's such a joy to work with you. Thank you for taking the time. You'll pull something together.

[End of April 23, 2018, interview]

Interview Number 8 with Senator John W. Warner, USN (Ret.)
Date: June 14, 2018

David Winkler (DW): Hello, this is David Winkler doing an oral history for the [U.S.] Naval Institute. Today is June 14, 2018. Why I have not put out my flag today—it's Flag Day—my bad. I'm here with Senator [John W.] Warner, former Secretary of the Navy Warner, continuing our interviews. A recent event that occurred is the anniversary of D-Day. Did you have some thoughts on that? Because Paulette French had brought that to my attention.

JW: Well, I remember going with Ronald Reagan. I was part of his official party, one of two or three senators asked to join, and it was a memorable occasion. Of course, it was on the 6th of June, and it would have been early in his tenure as President. Oh, I'll never forget we were with a famous congressman who had been there on D-Day, and he was a towering man of towering strength and highly respected in the House of Representatives. We were walking along, and all of a sudden, the Secret Service grabbed Reagan to protect his body, because suddenly, unbeknownst to anybody, some spectator down below had actually scaled the cliffs, and the Secret Service wasn't able to look over and see if it was going to be happening. Down below, I guess, we could have signaled, but anyway.

And this guy jumped up from coming over the cliff, "I made it!" and screaming happily. Everybody didn't know whether he—you know. And Reagan quickly was protected, and then we realized what had happened. He congratulated the guy. And he was on D-Day and scaled the cliffs. And he reenacted it.

DW: Wow.

JW: Then this other fellow, this congressman that was with us—I mean, picture going with Reagan, heavy press, heavy everything, and these incidents happen. Suddenly, this congressman shouted, "Stop, everybody! Stop! This is my hole!" And it was a rock formation and something else. This guy went over. He said, "This is where I scaled the cliffs, and only because I got in this hole was I able to protect myself until we were able to regain a greater security on top of the cliffs." And the fellow had completely joyously broke down. It was incident after incident.

And Reagan, you know, was a wonderful man. I got to know him quite well because he used to come down on the farm and ride horses with me and get out of Washington. He said, "John, I've got to get out of Washington. Give me a horse." And we'd go riding together on my farm. So he was a marvelous man, and he left a strong friendship, impact on my life.

DW: So that was D-Day. Then you mentioned, of course, recently was the 50th anniversary of the loss of Bobby Kennedy.

JW: Bobby Kennedy. Well, I was actually in University of Virginia Law School with Kennedy. I spent one year there with him. Then I got called back into active military duty in the Marine Corps. I joined the Marines two years earlier and got a commission on my graduation, and I was a second lieutenant, now first. I was called back to active duty.

But in that first year, I saw Kennedy quite a few times because I was fortunate enough to be invited to come over to his house and play football. And he and Ethel, they were just wonderful people. They shared their little house. There were very few married couples on the campus in those days, but postwar, students had wives. Rarely before World War II did students have wives on university.

DW: True.

JW: And she always had a full ice box of beer and Coke and sandwiches out. So through that, I got to know him.

Then in the campaign of 1960, he was advance man, of course, to his brother Jack, as I was advance to Nixon, and we were strongly competing each other. We'd have ways to kind of unsettle the other side, tactics we used.

But I remember two incidents. One, on about, I think, the second debate, Jackie Kennedy, whom I'd known slightly in my younger years because she was in the young group of sort of not teenagers, but young adults that we were growing up with in Georgetown in those days, she was pregnant, and the possibility of a delivery was in the scope of time of this debate scheduling. She wanted to come.

So I remember going over to the studio with Bobby to lay out different things to be agreed on, what was right and needed by both candidates as a prescheduler, and we talked about Jackie. I said, "I know her. Maybe we ought to build a little tent in the corner such that if she needs a rest or whatever, she's got some privacy, because this is going to be filled with press and everything else."

He said, "Bully good idea."

And then I remember the studio was located in a heavily congested part of the town, and we only had two or three parking spaces out front. By protocol, Nixon, as vice president, outranked the senator, so he had space for one, and it was in a side alley. Space two was given to Kennedy. I said, "You know, let's switch. You take space one, because if you have to get out in a hurry, I know the vice president would want to help." So we never forgot little incidents like that.

But the one time he did get me zapped is that there was a famous dinner given by tradition by the Archdiocese of New York, called the Al Smith Dinner.

DW: Right.

JW:—at the famous big hotel. I'll think of it.

DW: Waldorf Astoria.

JW: Waldorf Astoria. And the *Who's Who of America* [sic] attends, and it's bipartisan, everybody. I went over to see the monsignor to plan for it and assure him that everything was in order, but Nixon had particularly asked me to ask if we could not wear white-tie, because there are too many things attached to white-tie, and he didn't want any of that.

So I talked to the monsignor, and the monsignor said, "No. It's an inviolate rule. We've always had it, and that's the way." So, we acknowledged.

So the night of the thing, I had on my white-tie. I'm downstairs scoping out everybody coming in. I go up to get Nixon, and he's putting on his white-tie. I said, "I'll go down. I'll be right there and give you a call when they're ready to have you come," being the last of the guests to be accepted.

And I went down, and while I'm waiting, Kennedy came down and he and Bobby were in black-tie.

JW: And I said, "Oh, man, this is going to turn the tables."

So I rushed up and told Nixon, and he said, "John, I had a hunch they were going to stick it to us, and they did it."

I said, "Okay, I did the best I could, but you had to follow the monsignor's rules."

But the next day, the tabloids, "Black Versus White, Rich Versus Poor." And they identified clearly Kennedy as candidate of the people, Nixon the rich. He was very upset about it. So Bobby got me in the end. But then, you know, they won.

DW: So let's move forward to you're elected to the Senate and it's 1979.

JW: I was elected in the fall of '78 and took office in '79.

DW: So you take your oath on Capitol Hill with all the new senators.

JW: Class of about eighteen of us, eighteen or twenty.

DW: So as a new senator—

JW: First woman was in that Senate class in ten years since there was a woman in the Senate. There'd been a very wonderful, highly respected senator, Margaret Chase Smith of Maine, and she retired ten years, and there was a gap of ten years, no woman. Nancy Kassebaum, the daughter of the famous presidential candidate in the thirties, Alf Landon, who was a very good senator, stayed right continuously, reelected, and then married Howard Baker after, I think, both of them had left the Senate, yeah.

DW: So you're competing for different committees, the Senate Armed Services Committee.

JW: Luckily, I got it, but Howard Baker had something to do with that, I know. It's done fairly based on seniority, but he was the Republican leader. He had befriended me very strongly and was glad to have me aboard.

Because you realize there's an interesting footnote here. For one hundred years, the Democrats held both Virginia Senate seats. A hundred years. And there was a funny little congressman—nobody took him seriously—named Bill Scott. And I was beginning to be active in politics. I'd helped Linwood Holton. I was in his campaigns for governor. Other than that, I didn't have any real involvement. And Scott said, "I want to run for the Senate," and his seat was held by a man named Bill Spong, who was a very competent, able individual, but he felt he had such a stronghold that he just didn't campaign much, and it's one of those experiences where—and I was very much involved in helping him in his campaign. I think it was his idea; it wasn't my idea. I give credit to somebody else, but I was pivotal. He said, "I want to buy up every minute of radio time that's available for seventy-two hours prior to the election." Big money.

Well, I found an interesting guy. His name was Stets Coleman, lived down in a little village called Plains, Virginia, and very quietly I think he'd made quite a bit of money in the oil business, and he was a solid, true blue Republican. I remember going down and seeing him and saying, "You know, this is our one hope. We might be able to pull this thing off, because we're reading some of the stats, and radio is very impressive in this campaign. Spong hasn't done hardly any radio."

He says, "Okay, what do you need?"

I said, "I need a couple hundred thousand." And he gave me a check for a big one.

Bought up all the radio. We won by a fraction. So this unknown little congressman went in, and from day one, he just—and he'd been in the House for, I think, a term or two. It just didn't suit him and he was uncomfortable, and he made, sadly, some unintended errors, like he called a press conference one time to accuse the press. They claimed he was the dumbest man in the Senate. He called a press conference to prove he wasn't the dumbest man in the Senate. Well, they just recycled the story. But, sadly, he quit, and that's another reason the Democrats, "This time we're not going to lose the Senate seat again." So they really had mounted—they were going to threaten to put all guns on the seat. Then into the saga of my story, by pure luck.

DW: And we covered that.

JW: So I got to the Senate.

DW: So you got to the Senate and you got Howard Baker—

JW: But the Republicans admired me for accepting a challenge hugely.

DW: So, okay. You're on the Armed Services Committee.

JW: So I got a seat on that.

DW: And you're low man on the totem pole. We talked about seniority. It doesn't get much more senior than John Stennis.

JW: That's right. Oh, there were a couple of old-timers on there, wonderful group. Barry Goldwater.

DW: John Tower was the ranking member.

JW: John Tower had been on the longest, yes.

DW: Could you talk a little bit about John Stennis? Because he was a very popular man within the Navy.

JW: Well, I persuaded him—well, I don't want to say I alone, but I had a lot to do with him making a pivotal decision of being convinced that if we bought two super carriers at one time, we would save a considerable amount of money, knowing full well we had to go to a second one, and he gave us two super carriers. He had a lot of influence on the Appropriations Committee. At one time, he actually held the title of chairman of Armed Services and chairman of Appropriations. I don't know whether it was that or what it was. But he was one of the most gracious old-time southern senators you ever met, honest, hardworking. You know, he suffered the loss of his wife in 1983. I don't think he was married at that time. But anyway, I visited him in his home. He lived very modestly, all the way in Mississippi.

I'll tell you a funny story about him. He liked Willis Robertson, who was a Democratic senator from Virginia, and he'd always say to me [in pronounced southern accent], "You know that Dulles Airport. That was Willis' dream, and Willis had put in a bill to get the money to build that airport, and that bill worked its way up to the Appropriations, and we were in markup of Appropriations, and everything was going smoothly. I wasn't in Washington, but the staff was working on this thing, and the vote was the next day. Willis called me up and he said, 'John, I never will ask you for another thing, but you've got to get up here and you've got to make sure my airport gets in that bill tomorrow. *Please*, John!'" He says, "You know, I got on the all-night train from Mississippi to Washington, stayed on that train all night long and got here to Washington and cast that vote for my friend Willis Robertson, and he never forgot me. He always did what I asked him to do." That's the way they worked in the old days. So he's the founder of Dulles Airport. I mean, these stories have to amuse you.

DW: This is why we want to capture them. So the thing is, during this, you're in the last two years of the Carter administration. Now, you have—I guess Graham Claytor is Secretary of the Navy?

JW: Yeah, wonderful guy, interesting man.

DW: A railroad guy.

JW: Railroad guy, Virginia railroad man. The Claytor brothers were Norfolk and Western [Railway] men, and Norfolk and Western was a major line. It literally hooked Norfolk up as a port to the whole western infrastructure not only of Virginia, but on into West Virginia and out into the Midwest. Oh, he was one of the nicest guys I ever remember. You see in my room all these old electric trains up here? I'd get those trains and we'd go over to his house and put them on tracks at Christmastime, and we'd drink some Virginia Gentleman [bourbon whiskey] and play like teenagers with our electric trains. And he was a destroyer lieutenant on this destroyer that was the first on the scene to discover survivors of the *Indianapolis*. He used to tell me stories of that. "John," he said, "that was the saddest day of my life to pull these men up, just suffering terribly from excessive sunburn, dehydration, sharks, and few survivors."

DW: And, of course, you have CNO is Hayward, who you knew back from—

JW: Well, Tom Hayward was CNO, but he was my naval aide as under secretary and part-time as secretary.

DW: That's right.

JW: Wonderful man. He's still alive.

DW: Now, the one problem you had is you're pushing for these aircraft carriers, but President Carter was not on board with that.

JW: Well, I remember I got to know Carter slightly when I was chairman of the Bicentennial. I visited all fifty states to present the governors with contributions of federal dollars, and I got to know him slightly when he was governor of Georgia. I don't know. Carter was very big on submarines because he'd been a graduate of the Naval Academy, a submariner.

DW: That's right.

JW: So I can understand how he was looking after his chosen service. But we got it through.

DW: Now, you were in Manpower Personnel, Research and Development and Military Construction Subcommittees.

JW: And one of the most difficult assignments I ever had, I must mention this. It was the first bill introduced in the history of the Senate on military base closure, and I was junior man on the committee and on that subcommittee, and the power-to-be [sic], John Stennis and Tower on down, none of the other guys wanted to touch that bill in terms of writing it and being the principal sponsor, so I got literally tagged. You know, being a young freshman, eager to please, "Okay, so it's an important thing." I never thought through the ultimate politics of this thing. I mean, I hate to tell you, driving home tonight, you saw the result of it by remodeling this big fort down here.

DW: Right.

JW: Belvoir, where they quadrupled the size of it, and that traffic is snarled now, this little community, with snarled traffic out of that thing.

DW: Yes.

JW: But anyway, I'll never forget Howard Baker told me, "John, we're not going to let that bill on the floor unless it's bipartisan."

And Stennis came to me, "Bipartisan."

And Tower, "Bipartisan."

So it was moved by the Republicans, but what do I do? And I got—I can't think of his name now, but research, a freshman senator like me from Illinois, and you can check the books. But he was one of these youngsters like us, eager to please. [Alan Dixon]

JW: He only lasted one term, then got defeated, largely because of this damn bill. [laughs] I'm not kidding you. And he was, oh, excited to be cosponsor of a major piece of legislation. Well, both of us didn't realize what we were bringing down on our necks.

DW: Signing your own death warrant. [laughter]

JW: Yeah. So, oh, he's a nice fellow, very talkative. He was liked in the Senate. But he cosponsored it, and we got it out of committee. Then the result is, they made me be the principal sponsor of every one of the bills that had been written since then, and I wrote the last bill.

DW: Yeah, because it says here you had hearings in May. You're two months, three months in the job, and you're holding hearings on base closures.

JW: That's right.

DW: So how did that go? Do you just go to different communities and say—

JW: Well, you know, some profited, some lost. Of course, those that profited by closures, their bases usually got enlarged—

DW: Yes.

JW:—and profited in the sense it didn't get decapitated. It's a painful thing in America, painful but proud. People are so proud of their military installations. They may be mad at the president, but "That's our base. We took our children to that base. I mean, we were there. Our son served on that base." And people get really fixated on their bases, and they don't like it being closed.

DW: So were there any bases closed from this '79—

JW: Oh, yeah. Oh, yeah. It was a pretty sweeping and effective bill. In the long run, we do save money, and things change. For example, there's been a major shift over time between the number of ground troops versus the number of air support and airplanes and stuff like that. I mean, that grew from nothing in World War II to be a significant part of the military. It was the Army Air Corps until the Defense Reauthorization Act under Truman, and he created the Department of Air Force.

DW: The other, I guess, controversial bill that was being handled, or actually not bill, but was the treaty coming through on SALT II. I think initially you were not opposed to it, but I think you were trying to come up with a compromise, because what President Carter had presented was unacceptable. Eventually it does get voted down.

JW: Yeah.

DW: Could you elaborate a little bit about the discussions on SALT II?

JW: No, I can't remember those details, to be honest with you.

DW: Okay.

JW: I do recall being on many delegations. Tower made me take these delegations to the discussions we had with the Soviet Union in Geneva, and they were pretty colorful. I mean, they'd only shout at each other for an hour and then go off and party all over town, then come back and shout another day for a couple of hours, meantime keeping big staffs of arms controls measures, I think it was called.

DW: So during this time period, it's the period of the "hollow military," I guess they said, where—

JW: That was the famous Chief of Staff of the Army [Bruce Palmer, Jr]. I'll think of his name. Quite an interesting man. He really took a lot of heat, but he was right. The Army had all the bases and all the generals and everything, but down beneath, there wasn't that infrastructure anymore, they'd cut back so far. You ought to dig up his name. He came right after Westmoreland.

DW: Okay. Because with the election, of course, during your last year of Carter administration, he's running for reelection. Ted Kennedy, who's a colleague of yours in the Senate, is running for president, and I think, in retrospect, that hurt the president's reelection campaign. And then, of course, Ronald Reagan gets elected as president, and that's a whole different sea change. Then I think you don't take control of the Senate yet. No. John Tower takes control of the committee.

JW: Then we did take it.

DW: The "Reagan revolution" in—

JW: Eighty-four.

DW: Well, this is in 1981–'82, 97th Congress. John Tower was the chair. So Republicans must have took control of the Senate. Now you have a new—

JW: I think I became chairman of Sea Power Subcommittee, I'll bet.

DW: It says "Tactical Warfare Strategic and Theater Nuclear Forces chair."

JW: Is that it?

DW: Yeah. You get this guy [John Lehman] here [demonstrates] becomes the new Secretary of the Navy.

JW: Oh, yeah. That's his new book. When did it come out?

DW: It's been out for about a month.

JW: He always made a big fuss over everything he was going to say about me. I didn't know it was there.

DW: He calls you his "sea daddy."

JW: Is that what it is?

DW: In the front of the book, he lists a bunch of sea daddies, and you're on the list.

JW: Does that mean good or bad?

DW: That's good.

JW: I wonder who the sea daddies are.

DW: We're looking at John Lehman's latest book, *Oceans Ventured*.

JW: His father's first. Isn't that nice. Oh, Lieutenant Commander John Lehman Sr. Must have been his father. Burke, Warner, Zumwalt. God, I didn't know he put—Holloway and Tower. Isn't that something. Oh, John. He never sent me a copy, the rascal. Isn't that interesting. So I get two honorable mentions, both of them on page forty. Isn't this something—how does it read? Did you read it?

DW: I read it. I'm reviewing it for a Harvard publication.

JW: There's my picture.

DW: Yeah. It's a little choppy in the middle. Where this book makes a contribution is Lehman really makes a case that it was the military exercises that were conducted during the Reagan administration where they're really pushing forward towards the Russians that got the message across that we were very serious, and Ocean Venture was an exercise in 1981, where we simulated this striking capability against the Norwegians, and we were, you know, kind of faking it because we're pretending to deploy weapons we didn't have yet, but by the time '84–'85 comes along, we've developed these missile systems and kind of convinced the Russians that "if you come into Germany, you're going to be dealing with the Navy at your flanks."

JW: "It was one of the most successful agreements in the history of arms control." That's interesting. Isn't that interesting. Well, that's a tribute to you too.

DW: What's he talking about, Incidents at Sea?

JW: Yeah. You've got to use that quote for your own book.

DW: I don't know. Incidents at Sea really isn't an arms control treaty; it's more of a behavior control treaty. Because arms control is when you say, "You can only have so many missiles and you can only have so many widgets." Incidents at Sea says that "okay, you have those missiles, but you're not allowed to point them at each other." So it's a behavior. So I kind of wince when you say "arms control," because it doesn't limit anything. "You can have as many ships and planes as you want. Just don't point them at each other." People called it a confidence-building measure.

JW: Here's a little write-up about it. He starts off, "John Lehman, a former U.S. Navy aviator."

DW: That's right.

JW: I remember Moorer called me in and said, "This guy's no more an aviator than [unclear]." He was pissed. And [unclear] Logus [phonetic] and I had to get into it. I don't see how he got his wings.

DW: He talks about it in his first book.

JW: He may have been a crewman or something for a while.

DW: Right. Anyway, so he's the Secretary of the Navy. Well, he has to come before, I guess, you for confirmation hearings?

JW: I suppose so, yeah.

DW: And so how was the Reagan administration coming in with, I guess, Secretary Weinberger as Secretary of Defense?

JW: They all came in with a powerful commitment. I mean, they should have used Trump's "Make America Strong Again." Reagan, he outshined Trump on making America strong again.

DW: You mentioned you first met Reagan, I guess, on the campaign trail?

JW: No, I knew him as governor of California because I had some position, which I can't even remember, here in Washington, DC, area, greater metropolitan. We had a Republican Party of the Metropolitan Area, and we drew on Maryland, Virginia, DC, and I remember we gave a huge dinner for him as governor at the Mayflower Hotel. I'll never forget the night. I've got to tell you this story. And I think I had written him and asked him and he accepted, because I was dinner chairman. Well, he's coming, and we sold out. Boom! There wasn't a seat left. We turned people away.

He's in there now, he's come, and we're having a big cocktail party, people are shaking his hands and everything. This may have been the first time we met face-to-face, because I don't recall during the Nixon campaigns ever meeting him, at least I can't pull it out, as much as I traveled with Nixon, and Nixon never really had much to do with him. I don't know where he was in those days. I'm not doing this disparagingly; I just can't remember. But I remember this night.

He pulled me aside as the cocktail was beginning to wind down and the dinner was about to start. He says, "John, I always check the podium before I give any speech. Can we slip out the back door and let this thing grind on and let's go look at it?"

"Come on. Let's go." [demonstrates] We ran out across the hall. The dinner was across the hall in another big room. The waiters were all fixing the tables up.

He walked up to the podium and said, "Boy, I'm glad it's here. I've got to get it up an inch or two. I've got to have something so my cards don't slip off." So [demonstrates], I got the hotel turned upside down just getting any sort of things to get this, because he spoke with a pack of 3-by-5 cards. You knew that?

DW: No.

JW: He carried them. They were all dog-eared. I remember looking at this pack very well. I'll explain why. He had a magnificent way of taking one finger and flicking that card, and it had in big print so he looked as if he was extemporaneously talking and not reading any text. He was a master speaker that way. So many of these politicians get up and read, you know.

So we're fixing that, and he gets his cards out and checks them. Everything's got it going now. A waiter comes in with a whole tray of iced water on the thing, somebody bumps him, he bumps us. Bang! Down came the table. All these cards went on the floor. And at that moment, the doors opened for the crowd to come in, so the crowd came in seeing Reagan and Warner down on the floor picking up the cards. But he pulled himself back together, got the cards set up, and gave a flawless speech. But I'll never forget.

DW: So John Tower now takes over as the chair of the committee. Could you talk a little bit more about John Tower?

JW: John Tower was an interesting man. He was very proud of his naval career, and I say that respectfully. He was tough, and it was clearly the Navy benefited by having him in his position of leadership.

Let me do two things for a minute.

DW: Okay.

DW: Okay. We were talking about Senator Tower. He was a master chief petty officer in the Navy Reserve, I recall.

JW: Be careful. Here we go.

DW: Okay.

JW: He was chief petty officer boatswain's mate, which is, as you know, one of the rougher assignments. And somehow—I'm not entirely sure—he rigged it up so that he got appointed master chief when he was in the Senate.

DW: Okay.

JW: And he said, "Warner, guess what? You're coming over to the Pentagon with me and you're going to give me the oath of office as a former Secretary of the Navy." So he went over and the Navy put on a nice show. I gave him the oath of office. He said, "Don't you ever forget it. I'm a master chief."

I had to admire him. He had his faults, like all of us, but he was strong on national defense. Let's put it this way. He would have some trouble passing the "#MeToo" test today.

DW: Yes.

JW: Even at that point in life, he was somewhat haunted, but I don't think it was career-threatening. What finally dissuaded the president from—or was it the Senate from confirmation? I think a combination of both, was the allegations about his use of alcohol.

And out of the blue sky, Sam Nunn and I were given the very challenging task of leading a totally objective investigation, let the evidence speak for itself. One Saturday morning, in walked X, who had been a staff assistant to Tower, particularly within the state, and said that Tower was completely recovered and could handle the alcohol. The question was, "Well, was there a time when he had trouble?"

"Well, there was a time," this guy said, "that he used alcohol pretty heavily. As a matter of fact, I used to meet him at the airplane when he landed. His first request was, 'Where's my bottle of Jack Daniels?' And I would produce it. It would be by his side on that trip for that day." That guy really, I think, pulled the cord. "But he's recovered now." So the Senate just was uncomfortable.

DW: Unfortunately, there was a tragedy, because as I recall, he gets killed, Tower.

JW: He died in a plane crash.

DW: Yes.

JW: I was floor manager for his nomination, along with Bob Dole, and we did our best, but the votes weren't there. My recollection—the record will have to be the—is that some of the women did not vote for him.

DW: Okay. And by this time, there were more women in the Senate.

JW: There were several of them in the Senate, yeah. The votes are there. Somebody, all they've got to do is pull it up.

DW: Right. But as chairman of a committee—

JW: I thought he was a pretty good chairman, and the military had a lot of respect for him. Reagan appointed him, didn't he?

DW: Yeah. Well, it would have been—well, that's a question as far as appointments, but as chairman of different committees, that would be—

JW: That's Senate only.

DW: That's Senate only.

JW: This was a vote to be secretary of defense.

DW: And Reagan would have appointed him, and he didn't go through.

JW: Who took it? Weinberger took over?

DW: There was Weinberger and there was—I think it was—maybe this was Carlucci.

JW: Maybe Frank Carlucci took it when John was knocked out.

DW: That's right.

JW: Probably. Who turned out to be damned good.

DW: So during those first two years, you're now—the faucet is turned on as far as—

JW: Well, someone check my record. I was on the committee thirty years, and for fifteen of them, I was either ranking or chairman.

DW: Right. Right. Back in '81, you were still low on the totem pole, though.

JW: Yeah. Well, I'd only been there, what?—

DW: Three years. But right now the Navy's building up. Carter's last Secretary of the Navy was Edward Hidalgo.

JW: Yeah.

DW: Any recollections?

JW: Very little about him.

DW: Okay.

JW: We were all a little mystified, where he came from. Nice guy, but I don't remember anything particular about him.

DW: He kind of closed out the Carter administration as Secretary of the Navy.

JW: He just left with Carter?

DW: Then, of course, John Lehman came in, and he's the youngest Secretary of the Navy ever.

JW: Up to me. I think he replaced me.

DW: Actually, I did some research. I found there was a guy in the Franklin Pierce administration.

JW: Really?

DW: Yeah, a fellow by the name of Dobbin, I think was his name, who actually got the job when he was thirty-nine years old.

JW: I was forty-some. Well, that's interesting. Good for you.

DW: Lehman definitely, at thirty-eight years old, he was the youngest. Was there any concern about this young guy?

JW: Age had nothing to do with it. Generally, I thought he was a damn good secretary, but his forceful—I mean, he took off full speed when he got the mantle, and it was always breaking down, I mean with a hand brake, not take him down, but pull on the brakes to slow him down. He came up with, what, six-hundred-ship Navy?

DW: That was the push.

JW: The mantra. Would that be the phrase?

DW: The mantra and the Maritime Strategy.

JW: Well, the Maritime Strategy could have been anything that he wrote about. I don't know what that was. Did he have a special maritime that Zumwalt or somebody else hadn't thought of?

DW: Not really, although he takes a lot of credit for the Maritime Strategy.

JW: Is there such a thing as the Maritime Strategy? Didn't all of us operate under certain rules and stuff?

DW: That's true. The Maritime Strategy was a concept of aggressive warfare or posturing towards the Soviet Union rather than taking a more restricted defensive posture.

JW: Was there a line of demarcation where we're now under a new Maritime Strategy? Did he come in and frame it or something?

DW: He would argue that. I'd have to have him send you the book.

JW: Well, you can spare me the book. I've got too many things I've got to read. Although I would like to go through it. I'm interested in that "sea daddy" thing. He told me about that. But I'm surprised to see he put Zumwalt on there. Apparently, they may have had a détente or something. How do people look at Bud Zumwalt in history?

DW: Well, I think Zumwalt is a very—you either love him or you don't love him. The folks who don't care for him will argue he undermined discipline and morale. Those that favored or think positively of him argue that he enabled social change in the military as far as during an era when the nation was transforming due to cultural changes. For example, being more open, bringing on board minorities, opening ranks for women.

JW: Yeah. "Beer, broads, and bell-bottoms," or something.

DW: Well, that was the other thing, that he made these uniform changes that didn't go over too well.

JW: What were some of them? I've forgotten.

DW: Well, he replaced the bell-bottoms!

JW: I wouldn't let him do it on my watch, but as soon as I walked out the door—

DW: He went and got those bus driver outfits for the enlisted guys. They looked like bus driver suits. The idea was a twin-breasted overcoat, kind of like officers, and then the enlisted folks had the combination covers with the little crow on it. It just didn't look good.

JW: I don't remember.

DW: They looked like bus drivers. They did away with what we call the bell bottom, crackerjacks. Basically, in the 1980s we brought them back under John Lehman. I think under John Lehman we brought back that uniform. He did away with the beards in the Navy. I think Admiral Zumwalt was the one who allowed facial hair.

JW: Yeah. Did Lehman get rid of it?

DW: Lehman got rid of it, and it's because there were just too many scruffy beards.

JW: It was terrible.

DW: Part of the beard thing actually makes sense when you're dealing with gas masks and getting a good seal. So there are actually reasons not to have a beard. A beard had been a tradition, like in the submarine force. So those were some of the things that Lehman changed from the Zumwalt era, was the—

JW: Well, let me just—back up. When I stepped down, Middendorf took it.

DW: Right.

JW: So he succeeded Middendorf. Didn't Hidalgo come in?

DW: When you came in, you appointed Holloway.

JW: No, that's my last act.

DW: That's right. You appointed Holloway as your last act.

JW: Zumwalt was very much against it.

DW: To appoint Holloway?

JW: He did not want Holloway anywhere near.

DW: Really? Because Holloway was his VCNO.

JW: I guess Zumwalt was leaving, and I designate Holloway.

DW: Okay. I don't know who Zumwalt wanted to succeed him.

JW: He wanted Bagley.

DW: Okay, Bagley. Got it. But I think Zumwalt had put those uniform changes in—

JW: Oh, right away when he walked in.

DW: Right. So that was before—

JW: Before I got rid of him.

DW: Right.

JW: I was suffering through some of that.

DW: Yes. Okay. Yeah, I'll have to ask John Lehman why is Zumwalt one of his sea daddies.

JW: Isn't that ship a disaster?

DW: Oh?

JW: The destroyer.

DW: The destroyer. Well, I don't know if it's a disaster. It's just very expensive.

JW: Well, yeah. Cost is a significant thing, but if—

DW: You're not going to build a 3fifty-ship Navy if each ship costs—

JW: What is it, being a big destroyer and a small cruiser—

DW: That's because the size of it.

JW: And what else was built at the same time? A follow-on to the *Arleigh Burke*-class?

DW: That's what we're doing right now. Well, they were building these littoral combat ships.

JW: That's not working out.

DW: That's not working out too well. So they're going back, and I think they're looking to build corvettes or frigates.

JW: A corvette's a frigate?

DW: It's a small warship.

JW: Yeah, but, for instance, a *Burke* destroyer is a pretty well—Completely outfitted ship.

DW: Yes. We're continuing to build those. Flight three, I guess, is now in progress. Now, considering this is—think about it. We have a class of ship that has now been—we've been putting these out now for twenty years.

JW: Is the *Burke* that long?

DW: That's right. Mid-nineties. So it's a very successful design, and it's a technology that's improving with each ship.

JW: You haven't done any changes, really, in the superstructure or the hull. Maybe something.

DW: There's some changes as far as like the stack arrangements and some of the angles. The more current ships, you know, some of them have a flight deck for a helicopter, for example.

JW: Oh, do they?

DW: Yeah. So that's a change, give them an ASW capability.

JW: Got rid of your aft gun.

DW: Got rid of the aft gun, and you have the—the concern is that with all the frigates being decommissioned, you've lost your ASW capability, all those *Perry*-class.

JW: Well, hell, it was a good ASW weapons.

DW: Well, when you retired all the *Perry*-class frigates, which had the twin hangars on the stern, I think there were about fifty of those ships.

JW: Were there fifty?

DW: And, you know, that's a lot of ASW capability.

JW: Before ship life had ended for them?

DW: A little bit before. There's some talk about bringing back some of them to fill this 3fifty-ship gap time period, because if you just need a ship for presence, they're perfect.

JW: Yeah, that's a good phrase, "ship for presence."

DW: Yeah. But I think they did a study on that. I haven't heard anything from it.

JW: By the way, when you finish this thing, is it out there for the public? Can some guy come in and copy the damn thing, put his name on it, "I wrote a biography of Warner"?

DW: Well, I hope somebody would come in there and use this and then use everything else that's out there and write a biography.

JW: I hope they don't do that. No, I don't want a biography written.

DW: Well, somebody could if they wanted to. No, I think for people who are doing research on the history of the Navy in your time period, this is going to contribute to that.

JW: That's all right. That's what it's here for.

DW: That's what it's here for. So your insights are germane.

JW: I'm glad to see that Hayward was on as one of his sea daddies. He's a beautiful man. He was a wonderful aide to me. You know, he's a guy that—I was, unfortunately, divorced shortly after I became Secretary of the Navy. I was gone all the time. My wife just said, "Come on," and she shoved off. And he really took good care of me. I never will forget one time we used to have little confrontations, friendly ones. I said, "I want to go out to Tailhook."

He says, "You're not going."

"Who the hell do you think you are?"

He says, "I'm your naval aide, and I'm telling you you're not going." So he got a little rough.

Because some of the aviators said, "What's the matter with you? Why aren't you coming to our—?"

Thank God I didn't go. Because I was a bachelor, and what the hell. What happens in Vegas didn't stay in Vegas.

DW: So you're talking about as a bachelor Secretary of the Navy. That would have exposed you.

JW: Yeah.

DW: So, yeah, that later brings down—well, we can talk a little bit about that.

JW: What's the name of the guy that never got over it? He tried to stop—I've forgotten. One secretary.

DW: Right. Garrett. I did his oral history.[51]

JW: What did he say about that thing?

DW: Basically—and this is a recollection about fifteen years ago when I interviewed him—he was not served well by his, I guess, under secretary, J. Daniel Howard, who became Secretary of the Navy when he left.

---

[51] Henry Lawrence Garrett III served as the 68th Secretary of the Navy from May fifteen, 1989, to June 26, 1992. He resigned due to the Tailhook scandal. His oral history with the Naval Historical Foundation is yet to be published.

JW: Anyway, what did the Under Secretary fail to do? Report to him that it was all—

DW: I think that was the—the under secretary of the Navy, I think, released material and public information about it without clearing it through him, and it put him in bad light.

So this is a time period where now I'm part of naval history here and you're up there in the Senate, providing the funds to the fleet that I'm out there participating in. So, any observations about operations, the different weapons programs, Tomahawk? I think this is where Lehman writes in his first book we definitely got two carriers authorized, because he pushed that. It just made common sense. We're building *Spruance*-class destroyers.

JW: Did he give Stennis credit for giving him two carriers?

DW: I think he does in his first book, not in this book.

JW: Oh, another book.

DW: In this book, he talks all about strategy and big military maneuvers. Some of the characters he talks about in this book are some of the admirals, "Ace" Lyons, for example.

JW: He loved him.

DW: Yeah. I've met Ace Lyons. He's a colorful character. Who would be coming up to testify before the Senate Armed Services Committee during this time? Because Hayward would have been the CNO. Then he turns over to Watkins. Do you have any thoughts about—

JW: Watkins, a beautiful man, truly beautiful.

DW: He was a nuclear guy, right?

JW: Nuke stuff, under Rickover.

DW: I think we talked about in conversation that the relief of Rickover and the fact that you were trying to engineer a position—

JW: Well, I was working with Lehman. To Lehman's credit—is that in this book?

DW: Not this book. It's in the other book.

JW: Lehman worked hard, and I was supportive. I wanted to have Rickover put his talents to work in private industry, non-naval industrial base we had in this country, to encourage it, because the stronger the Navy is, the stronger this is or the stronger that is. They work together. Got a lot of money going into both, and it's the core reactor that counts. So I thought Rickover would be a splendid job in convincing America to expand its nuclear power. He just imploded, blew up.

DW: Yeah. [laughs] And Lehman talks about the meeting with President Reagan did not go well.

JW: Oh, no, my god. It's in this book, Reagan?

DW: Not this book. The other one.

JW: The other one.

DW: His first one, *Command of the Seas*.

JW: Yeah.

DW: That's his first book. Tower continues as the chairman. You also had—well, Stennis, I guess he must have left the Senate in '82 time frame, '83?

JW: I can't remember the year.

DW: Because "Scoop" Jackson becomes the ranking member from the Democrats in 1983.

JW: And is Tower the chairman?

DW: Yes. Jackson's a very—I remember him as a very imposing figure.

JW: Yes, he was. I thought, on the whole, he was a fine man, and Nixon should have picked him as his vice president.

DW: Mm-hmm. And the other person—and I'm right now doing some research. Just the other day, I was looking at the commissioning of the nuclear submarine *Atlanta*. You're actually at the ceremony because the ship is commissioned in Newport News, and Sam Nunn was the speaker.

JW: And his daughter was maybe the—yes.

DW: I think his wife may have been the sponsor, yeah.

JW: May be.

DW: So, your thoughts on Sam Nunn?

JW: Oh, a wonderful man, probably the most important senator to me of any senator. Chafee, I loved him like a brother. I literally loved that guy. Sam Nunn was a marvelous friend and a very trustworthy friend. We never had a cross word. We never tried to outscore the other guy. Absolutely seamless.

DW: Now, this area kind of contrasts to today, in a way, because I think the thought of the Senate is kind of—this organization where it's a brotherhood type of—although you now have some women coming in, where people are more reflective than the Congress, more courteous, respectful, versus I think today you have a little bit more—much more partisanship.

JW: Oh, gosh, it's terrible. Oh, no, we had a very good relationship, largely predicated on mostly we were all veterans, and, you know, the core rule of the veteran is the guy on your left or the guy on your right is going to save your life someday.

DW: Did Scoop Jackson serve?

JW: You know, I don't know.[52]

DW: Okay. Because he was out from Washington State.

JW: I don't remember it. He died so soon after he became ranking.

DW: I was in high school back then. [laughs] So, finally, in '85—well, let's see. Eighty-three, '84, '85, '86, this would have been Reagan's second term. He ran against a fellow colleague in the Senate, Walter Mondale. I don't know. Did you cross paths much with Mondale in the Senate?

JW: No, he was sort of quite senior and out of there shortly after I joined, on my recollection.

DW: Well, actually, he was Carter's vice president, right?

JW: I guess he was, yeah.

DW: Okay. So in '85, '86, Barry Goldwater becomes the chair, and Sam Nunn is the ranking member.

JW: Goldwater was a wonderful man, just all the way around, interesting, fine man.

---

[52] Henry M. Jackson was elected to Congress in 19forty and then joined the Army after the U.S. entered the war but was directed to return to Congress by President Roosevelt.

DW: He's getting up there in age right now, in the eighties, because he ran for president back in '64. He was Air Force reserve, one-star?

JW: Yeah, he had done his reserve work in the Air Force, and he'd become a general officer, yes. See this thing of Churchill behind me? The bust right behind me. He called me up to his office one day, and he said, "John, I want you to be among those to hear it first. I'm going to retire." I was very close to him, kind of his "When in trouble, call John," you know, when he was chairman. He really looked to me, and I did anything he wanted me to do. We became good friends, campaigned for me wonderfully when I ran for the Senate, everything.

So we're in the office and he was very down because he'd announced he's not going to run again. Said, "Look at all this stuff I've collected. I don't know what I'm going to do with it. Look around. If there anything you want, take it."

And I said, "Well, I've always been an admirer of Churchill." His bust was right over there.

He said, "It's yours. Churchill gave it to me himself." Churchill gave him that. And I put it under my arm, walked out of his office, put it down in my office, where it stayed until I left. That's the sort of guy he was. "Take it."

He was disappointed in his son Barry Jr. His son just never got traction. Seems to me his wife was ill and she wasn't able to come to Washington a lot. Towards the end, life crumbled around him a little bit.[53]

DW: One thing that he's noted for—

JW: Goldwater-Nichols.

DW: That's right. And I think you had some disagreements on that legislation. Your issues were?

JW: I can't remember. Too esoteric.

---

[53] Barry Goldwater Jr. served in Congress from 1969 to 1983 and lost his seat when his district was merged.

DW: I think John Lehman, in his previous book, talks about Goldwater, and he didn't care for it either, because I think it took some initiative away from the secretaries.

JW: Yes.

DW: As a former secretary, I think he probably—

JW: We were hanging on to our jobs and trying to protect them.

DW: Right. And I think it was putting much more power into the Joint Chiefs.

JW: You're right.

DW: So that's where you had some objections on Goldwater-Nichols. One thing that they brought back was the battleships.

JW: There used to be that guy—I think his name was Flood,[54] in the House. Every committee meeting—not every committee meeting. Every meeting of the conferees for the Senate bill, he would come in and demand to be five minutes' talk about the virtues of bringing back the battleship. He did it purely for being a horse's ass, having fun. I sat there through that five minutes. It was a ritual. Now, we didn't bring any of them back. We took some out of mothballs: *New Jersey*.

DW: *New Jersey*. All four of them.

JW: Dan Flood. Colorful old funny guy. See that picture of me up there? I'm in a flight suit. I'm in Korea, and my job was basic communications officer, but we had some old TBMs, and we gutted them out and put a photographer down in the belly turret under the belly of the plane, and

---

[54] Daniel Flood represented the Scranton area of Pennsylvania from 1955 to 1981.

then they had a seat behind the pilot, so there were eyes up and eyes down, and they let me do the eyes-up job. On that mission, I'm coming back. The reason that that picture's up there, the fellow to my right had just finished seventy missions and he was on his way home the next week, and they asked him to take one more mission. Killed him. I always put that picture up to remind me how close all of us were that were in that business.

But I remember on that mission, as on others, I often saw the battle wagons offshore, and it was a real sight to see that suddenly smoke. Had no sound up there.

DW: Right.

JW: And then you'd look in and you'd see the explosion.

DW: Had brought back the *New Jersey* from Vietnam, but that is a real short—

JW: Well, they made me get rid of it because it was shaking the peace table up in Paris. They were trying to solve the war and end it. Kissinger actually intervened and said, "Get that son-of-a-bitchin' ship out of there," because our peace table rattled every time you'd fire in. I mean figuratively, metaphorically speaking. They didn't like it because it was doing its job. We had the *New Jersey*. Then we didn't have any ammo. I told you that story. Or did I?

DW: I don't remember.

JW: Well, anyway, I'm sitting in my office, you know, and tracking how soon this thing can join the fleet, and I get a call from some obscure guy somewhere, said, "You know, my job is getting the ammo, and all the ammo we got stored is in no condition to put into a battleship today. It did not survive this long storage. I don't have a round to put in."

"Oh, god. Go out and get a contract. Don't care what it costs. Start building ammo."

We *barely* met the timetable to get fresh ammo on the ships. Then we sent them out and they were very effective. And they ordered me to turn them around, bring them back.

DW: Okay, okay. Now, getting back to the 1980s, we brought back the—and the Senate has to fund this. Now, you mentioned Congressman Dan Flood.

JW: He wanted new construction.

DW: Oh, he wanted *new* construction?

JW: Did you ever know your senator from Pennsylvania, wonderful man. We named a room after him in the Senate. He was minority leader for a while.

DW: Scott Hughes?

JW: Hugh Scott.

DW: That was before my time. He was there in the seventies, I think.

JW: He was a big, powerful man. He had the Mellon money. He really had it.

DW: Okay.

JW: He was their man. But he was a damn good senator.

DW: Yeah, he did well for Pennsylvania. Okay. So we talked a little bit—just tracking battleships as far as getting reauthorization approval. Was there any discussion about that?

JW: Nah. Nobody ever tried to—

DW: The case being made was that we needed these battleships because the Russians were building these—they were building some pretty impressive warships.

JW: I don't know that we ever made any case for them, because the Airedales just kept saying, "Hell, there's nothing they can do that we can't do better." And that's true, for far less money. I mean, that huge shell, you've got to be within twenty miles or forget it.

DW: But they also carry Tomahawk.

JW: Well, they probably put some Tomahawks on them, yeah, but you didn't need that platform. You could put Tomahawks on your oiler.

DW: True, true, true. No, but when they did bring back the *New Jersey*, it went down to—I think it operated off of Central America, and then it went over to Lebanon. I think for a shakedown cruise, it went around the world.

JW: Probably did.

DW: Now, speaking of Central America, Senate Armed Services Committee wouldn't have followed the—I guess it was the government with the Sandinistas in Nicaragua and what turns into—

JW: No, except I went down there. I remember going down with Chris Dodd. He was big on South America, and he conned me. They had to have a bipartisan delegation. I liked to horse around with ol' Chris. He, "Come on." Okay. So we went down. At that time, the Catholic priests that got murdered, they sent the two of us down to do an investigation. We couldn't find anything. All of them, closed-mouthed.[55]

DW: Okay. Why don't we call it a wrap for today—

JW: Sure. I had a good time. I enjoyed our conversation.

---

[55] Six Jesuit priests were murdered in El Salvador in 1989.

DW:—and regroup and pick it up. We'll get into the 1990s.

[End of June 14, 2018, interview]

Interview Number 9 with Senator John W. Warner, USN (Ret.)
Date: July 16, 2018

David Winkler (DW): Today is July 16 [2018], the day before the All-Star game here in Washington [DC]. So we've got David Winkler with the [U.S.] Naval Institute Oral History Program, with Senator John [W.] Warner, continuing our series of interviews.

We're now getting into the administration of George H. W. Bush. 1988, we have *glasnost*, openness with the Soviet Union, *perestroika*, and we're starting to look to cut down our expenditures, and one of the things they look at, we were looking at doing is shut down infrastructure. You did a round of closures when you first got into the Senate. You found out that wasn't very popular. So the Base Realignment and Closure Act of 1988 was kind of unique, that you set up, I guess, this board that would make a decision on the basis—it kind of took it out of the hands of the politicians, and then if there was a disagreement with the closures, there would be an appeal process. Is that my understanding of how that worked?

JW: Let me step back. Basically you got it right up to that last sentence.

DW: Okay.

JW: First, I'm a brand-new freshman senator, so to speak, and I had no knowledge of the procedures by which the several services could get rid of their property. Actually, I'll correct that. When I was Secretary of the Navy, I did have knowledge as to how we could get rid of excess naval property, and the individual secretaries were free to do it as they best saw fit for their services. That system seemed to work all right, although there wasn't a lot closed down because we were pretty well of a high tempo of operations during my five-plus years in the Pentagon, under secretary/secretary. But anyway, all you had to do was to make a recommendation to the SecDef. They were the veto in this thing. But it worked quite well. Of course, therein, individual members of Congress were very active in the debates that took place in the several secretariats from time to time.

Finally, now we're in a period where we are trying to get rid of a lot of infrastructure that was primarily put in place during World War II and was deemed excess property and a burden for them to heat, light, so forth, that goes with maintaining a piece of real estate. So the powers-to-be [*sic*] in Congress decided that they couldn't leave the matter to themselves arguing on behalf of their constituencies in the state, and the state arguing on behalf of the state interests. It was not feasible, it appeared to them at that time, to do the depth and length of closures that were necessary.

So Congress enacted the Base Closure Act. You should check for that date when it was put on the books. And along came the directions from the secretary of defense to the service secretaries to commence identifying those properties that they felt were suitable and should be closed. Then SecDef and the administration put together a commission, a Base Closure Commission, of individuals.

Now, here's an interesting point, you see, is you close military bases, you just don't want to turn it over to a lot of uninitiated civilians. I mean, not that they can't make decisions, but you need to draw on expertise. It was established that the commissioners were totally independent, but they would listen to the recommendations from the service secretaries and military of each service. Well, this system seemed to be working.

The law that was drawn up came before our committee, and the chairman directed me to review the law and consult with the members—as junior man, nobody else wanted to really be involved in it—and refine it before it actually became a final bill. I'm skipping back to pick that up, because there was a role of the Armed Services Committee in shaping this legislation at the direction of the secretary of defense. But we put it so that—and I think the president had the nominating power. We've got to check that point. It may have been SecDef. But to nominate persons to be on the Base Closure Commission. Then I think Congress had to give advice-and-consent to put them on. It's been a long time since I looked at this law. In any event, that's the way it worked.

The Base Closure Commission was absolutely independent, and they could accept or reject the recommendations of the service secretaries and the Department of Defense as a whole *and* initiate their own investigation, if they felt it necessary, to determine whether or not a piece of property should be closed. So it was quite a revolutionary piece of legislation, and I think it worked quite well the first time around.

The older senators knew that you were going to have a lot of trouble with your constituents, so they stuck me with it as junior guy, because none of the seniors wanted to fool with it, but I think other than to protect their own states' property. So I was the first. And a nice fellow, I think he was a classmate of mine from Chicago Alan Dixon, a senator from Illinois, he was a Democrat, and the two of us had to put this thing together and argue it on the floor and get it through. And it worked.

Lo and behold, I think in three years or some interval of that approximate length, the department decided they wanted to do it again, and they did it again. Well, they did, I think, five Base Closure Commissions during my thirty years, and by this time, everybody said, "Oh, John, only you can handle this." And then all of a sudden, I'm either the ranking or the chairman of the committee. And they kept saying, "Well, why would we want to get anybody else involved? You've done it so well." So I literally had a hand in writing all the five base closure laws. You had the original one, which remained fairly well intact. We polished up some of the rough edges each year and made it a separate bill. I'm not sure whether the bill, after the commission made its report, disbanded, I don't know, but I seem to think you had to pass—yes, I think the Congress required a new bill be passed for each of the five times it was done.

The last bill, whenever it was, my final years in the Senate, that was it. I remember fighting for my own state, kind of losing out on some of these things. But there was a mix of retired senior military on these commissions and civilians, because you wanted some military, ex, to give a military perspective, and you can believe that the [unclear] and their services kept pretty close contact with those guys.

But it did its job. A prime example is down here in my own state, Fort—what the hell's the name? Fort—down near the big thing, down at Mount Vernon.

DW: Fort Belvoir.

JW: Fort Belvoir. I mean, they just didn't do sufficient traffic studies, people studies. Where were they going to get the employees? They built the thing. They just tried to close down all the little small defense rental units wherever they were up here in northern Virginia and push them all into that one base, suddenly awakening to the transportation problems, which meant they had to build new highways and all kinds of new buildings. I don't think there was any cost saving reaped out of that. If there was, it's going to take many years before it'll show up.

So, now, that's the foundation I wanted to lay. What was the full question?

DW: I think you pretty much answered it, what your involvement was with the Base Closure and Realignment Act. I noticed in the 1990s, there was a massive one because at the end of the Cold War, and one of the big surprises that came out of that was—

JW: Fort Belvoir too.

DW: Yeah. Big surprise was everybody was expecting Great Lakes to be closed.

JW: I'm not sure how that got spared.

DW: Navy had three training stations: one in Florida, one in San Diego, and then you had Great Lakes, which I think they were surprised they were spared.

JW: You know, that's an interesting story, and I'm not sure how that happened, because I remember distinctly going to boot camp there in World War II, and I took sort of a special interest in it. Primarily they wanted to close it because it's slightly off the beaten path. There's quite a diversion from Chicago and main corridors of transportation up a little small railroad line. Well, it's not small. It's the main line of the Milwaukee road. But it has a lot of commuter trains on it, or did, because I remember it as a boy very well. But the Congress said, "We never want to hear another thing about base closure," and that was the end of it.

DW: Okay.

JW: We were never able to get another bill through Congress, although I don't recall of any real all-out efforts to get one passed.

DW: Yeah. I think the one thing you have to say about Great Lakes is, it's—

JW: It's so cold. The weather.

DW: It's cold. But also it does keep the Navy presence in the Midwest, and there's something to be said about that, because the interior of the country doesn't have an appreciation, I think, of sea power that the maritime states may. So I think an argument could be made for positioning—I think that's why Great Lakes was built there in the first place in 1911, to have a Navy presence in the Midwest.

JW: Is that when it was put up? 1911? Isn't that interesting. Well, there must have been a couple of powerful senators that decided that.

DW: Yeah, I think that was the case. I know somebody right now is writing their PhD dissertation on that topic, so we'll see—when the book comes out, we'll see what he says.

JW: That'll be quite interesting to read. I can testify—and you'd better bloody well put it in the book—I went there in the winter of 1945, before Germany capitulated. As a matter of fact, I'll digress a minute. And it was cold. I remember we used to fall out in the morning for formation, and many a time—we had these old wooden mock rifles, you know, we ran around with them—and you'd hear "Boom!" and you'd look around, and a rifle was on the ground, the guy slumping down, falling, just freezing, just from pure cold.

DW: Getting back to 1989, President Bush—well, you had the election. Ronald Reagan leaves office and his vice president, George Herbert Walker Bush, becomes president. Here's another fellow who has World War II experience.

JW: Very heroic experience.

DW: And, you know, you mentioned about this generation. At one time, I think 70 percent of the Senate had military service background from World War II.

JW: Or a few Korea and a few Vietnam.

DW: And he selects Dick Cheney to be his secretary of defense, and Colin Powell is the chairman of Joint Chiefs of Staff. One of the things that happens early during that administration is we have a tragedy on the USS *Iowa*, gun turret explosion, and I think the Armed Services Committee looked into that. Do you have any recollections about hearings about how the Navy handled the *Iowa* incident?

JW: Yeah, but what's your question?

DW: I guess the question is your recollection of the turret explosion on the *Iowa*.

JW: I remember it very well. It was such a sad, tragic thing. But my recollection, I was in the Senate then, and I remember the Armed Services Committee held extensive hearings. Frankly, there was no strong evidence clearly pointing to the cause of that accident, and the ship was withdrawn from active service in the fleet, put into a mothball status, but we kept open the investigation because we were running on just threads of evidence as to try and figure it out. I think to this day, no one has an understanding whether it was impurities in the powder bags that prematurely fired this thing or whether it was negligence in the gun crew. There was all sorts of spurious stories about maybe one or two of the guys were homosexuals and they were untrustworthy. Oh, god, it was terrible.

    I remember my naval aide, Carl Trost, who graduated number one in the Naval Academy class of whatever, he was my naval aide as under secretary and secretary. He bridged the gap. But he was CNO, and the whole thing just drove him crazy, he was so saddened by the whole thing. They just could not get their hands around solid evidence as to why this thing happened.

DW: Now, Trost being, of course, the CNO at one time, obviously I think you have a good relationship with the CNO because it's a personal relationship based on many years of knowing each other. So Trost was obviously—this happened on his watch. Any other recollections about Admiral Trost as CNO?

JW: Oh, he's just a marvelous man. I think he was well liked by the men. He handled these hearings beautifully. He's an exemplary chapter of history as CNO.

Then I had another aide, Tom Hayward, who was an aviator. Trost was a submariner and a Rickover man. And he made CNO. So I had the privilege of two CNOs, having served with them when they were Navy captains, as my aide. Wonderful men. There's a system in that building, and it's never been pencil put to paper as to how it operates, but they deep-select these young men and they spot them coming along and bring them up into the Department of Defense and make them aides to the secretariat, secretary, under secretary, for assistance, and same way they fleet-out aides for all the senior uniformed four-stars and others. But they just reach down and pick up these, and without a doubt, though maybe one was marginal, but I had so many of them, never any of my top aides were marginal, but they were just fine people. It's a system how the services believe in this civilian control. That's a constitutional function. But you get a lot of civilians that just don't have the experience of military training. They have to go through quite a learning curve. And these guys are excellent teachers.

DW: Okay. Later that year, the whole Eastern Europe collapses. November 1989 is the Berlin Wall, East and West Germany start looking at reunification. Senate Armed Services Committee, did this whole collapse of the Warsaw Pact kind of catch you by surprise?

JW: Well, we knew that it wasn't serving its purpose for Russia. Actually, a lot of it started in the internal Politburo itself. I guess there was some thinking, I expect from a standpoint of cash flow, that it was costing the Soviet Union some hard dollars to maintain these marginal countries. They were just struggling their way back after World War II. You had the population had to be fed and clothed and educated, the manufacturing industrial base had to be rebuilt, and then they were restive in terms of democracy on their own. So it all came to a head over there.

I remember I think Shirley Temple was ambassador to Hungary. And Poland was sort of the leader on it. The Poles were very—I have a high regard for their leadership. They have a very wonderful history of military. As you may know, the old—oh, gracious, come on, Warner. What is the term that we applied to the elite German officers? They were trained—they came from a little town up in Poland.

DW: Prussians? Prussia was a—

JW: Prussia. That was it. They were renowned to produce the finest officers for the European military.

DW: Right. I guess old Prussia now is territorially part of Poland. I guess that's what you're referring to. Yeah, there's a legacy there. Well, the other factor you're dealing with Poland is, of course, the pope is Polish at the time, so Pope John Paul II has a lot of sway in fermenting [*sic*] resistance to, I guess, the communist government. So anyway, I imagine it must have been fascinating looking at this whole collapse of the Soviet empire—

JW: Oh, yeah.

DW:—and what to make of it.

JW: Yeah, no question about it. I remember going over on a CODEL. Strom Thurmond led the CODEL, and we were the first parliamentarians in the world to be invited to come in and meet Gorbachev. Bob Byrd headed the delegation, and it was a very senior—I was the most senior man on it, together with Sam Nunn. We were the two most junior men, picked only because we were at that time, he was chairman, me ranking Armed Services, but we were fortunate to get on it. I mean, it was an education.

But we went there, and I remember Gorbachev coming in and very politely announcing that he would stay for one hour, and Strom Thurmond and Bob Byrd had to cut up that time. He gave the Senate one hour, and then he was a loner; no one else spoke but him. Then he would reply, but that wouldn't subtract from our hour. There was a timekeeper in there. It was one of the funniest experiences that occurred. We all marched in in a line of strict seniority, and I was the actual tail gunner in the whole thing, but I was so happy to be on it. I mean, the eyes of the world were on it. And televisions had pooled, and one and only one Soviet camera would do the filming and then give it to the others, unedited, just gave them raw footage. Claiborne Pell was the top Democrat under Byrd, and he inadvertently, in coming in, rather than take his seat right away, he stood and he didn't realize it—he was engaged in conversation, just one of these things that happened—he put his back against the television camera, and this live film going back to the United States and the rest of the world suddenly went blurred. They went crazy trying to figure out what had gone wrong mechanically with the equipment, and turned out it was Claiborne. He was just standing with his back against the camera. And the camera guy was petrified. He didn't know. Being under the thumb of the Soviets, you didn't have a lot of initiative. But, finally, anyway, just a little side effect.

DW: So you had a chance to meet Gorbachev. Obviously, I guess he made—

JW: Very impressive man, very impressive.

DW: And this, I assume, was in Moscow?

JW: Oh, yes, right in the Kremlin.

DW: Okay, okay. Now, during your time in the Senate, you had an opportunity to make several of these, I guess, overseas trips. Was this perhaps one of your more memorable ones?

JW: Yes, by all means.

DW: Okay. So you recall, I guess, he wanted to be more open in trade, and I think that was break down the barriers?

JW: Well, yeah. I've forgotten. I think we were basically—I mean, we had some discussions on issues like Incidents at Sea, things like that, and it was a very friendly—Bob Byrd and Strom Thurmond, I remember Strom started to run over his time. Byrd had to stop him. Each of them took five minutes. But I think we had a nine-man delegation. Now, ended up I was given four minutes.

DW: Okay. So you had the fall of the Berlin Wall. The other event during the Bush administration, of course, was the Iraqi invasion of Kuwait. That happened August 2nd, 1990. I think that's the first time we did the general recall for the reserves.

JW: Well, I can't remember that. I can't give you an answer to that. You mean—

DW: We had 50,000 reserves recalled to active duty.

JW: What year was that?

DW: Nineteen-ninety, in reaction to the Iraqi invasion of Kuwait.

JW: I guess we did call up some, yeah. All right. I remember, of course, working on the piece of legislation for George Herbert Walker Bush. He wanted the authority of the Congress as the Constitution provides, and there had not been a single instance where Congress had declared war since the original resolution—not original, but *the* resolution used by Congress declaring war in 1941—

DW: Right.

JW: —after Pearl Harbor. But that was the last time that constitutional provision was ever invoked. This time, Byrd and—well, let's see. George Mitchell was his leader. Well, yes, he was majority leader, because he was the one that directed us to find out how the Senate could support President Bush by having them write up a UN resolution, thereby bringing in all the UN countries, and if the UN ordered it, then it could draw troops from the ranks of any of the member nations. That's where we came in. That was pretty clever. But they only passed by five votes, you know. *Huge* pushback on getting involved in that war. Sam Nunn went against the bill. It was my bill. I drew it up. And George Mitchell. Both went against it.

DW: Interesting. Why do you think the pushback?

JW: They did not feel that this justified the United States committing its forces. Since then, I think Sam Nunn has gone on record saying it was the one vote in his entire career that he wished he hadn't made.

DW: Okay, okay. Well, everybody was in favor of putting troops in to defend Saudi Arabia. That was [Operation] Desert Shield. What this legislation enabled basically was the follow-on, [Operation] Desert Storm, which occurred in January 1991, which is the liberation of Kuwait. So I guess that was the pushback—there wasn't total support for liberation of Kuwait, from what you're—

JW: Well, there wasn't total support for committing U.S. forces in harm's way. I mean, everybody wanted Kuwait liberated. We're not the ones to do it.

DW: Got it. Okay. Fair enough.

JW: But the "no" votes, once the decision was made to give the authority to President Bush, during the implementation of that call-up and utilization of forces, those who had protested and voted against the resolution pitched right in. The past is prologue.

DW: Yes. No, and I guess after the success of the campaign, I guess Norman Schwarzkopf came before the committee and testified about the—he was a colorful character.

JW: He was as fine an officer as I ever knew in my life. Did I tell you the time that we—the operation was what, twenty-something days?

DW: That's right.

JW: And it was planned and tactically executed with absolute precision, and although we never anticipated that the Iraqi forces would capitulate so quickly, I think we felt they were going to put up a fight, but, oh, my god, I remember I took five successive CODELs over there in a period of thirty days because everybody back home wanted to hear their senator went over and looked at this victory, a total victory.

On the fifth time I was over there, Schwarzkopf met every CODEL. The SS started going before the House finally got itself organized. I'm packing up the fifty CODEL and bringing them back. We managed to stay in country only about twenty-four, at most forty-eight, hours. The community were actively mopping the place up. It was dangerous. There were IEDs all over the place, and you didn't need a lot of members of Congress wandering around willy-nilly. So anyway, the fifth one is finished, and I'm packing them up and I'm planeside, and Schwarzkopf always faithfully met every CODEL, personally lectured to them, answered their questions, and then he was always present when they were leaving. So this last CODEL was all packed up and we're leaving. Schwarzkopf invited me into a little office he used to have at the airport, and he said, "Warner." He literally grabbed my shirt. He said, "Don't you bring any more CODELs. We don't need it. I got a job to do here, and I don't want any more. We've given you five CODELs. That's it. Is that understood?"

I said, "I think you've got your point across."

DW: During these CODELs, did you get out to units out in the Persian Gulf, the Navy units?

JW: Yes, I went aboard—I felt obligated to—each member of the CODEL picked one of five or six options to go up with the troops, and it modified as time went on over thirty days. We were really joining troops and everything and structured a reserve force to stay in place in case some more trouble broke out somewhere.

But I went out aboard the USS *Wisconsin*, and I remember to this day they were so pleased that some guys went out, and I took two Virginia congressmen. Their CODEL was in town, so I looped it up to them, and they were always very grateful to me. We went aboard in a helicopter, and the ship had actually fired several occasions in anger; in other words, fired in on anger. One of those battleship shells, when it goes off—we weren't doing the firing now.

DW: No, I remember somebody brought video back from the *Wisconsin*, and basically the Iraqis had all their gun emplacements very well camouflaged and hidden, and the way they targeted these bunkers was that there was some guy with a meal truck who would just drive along and knock on this door in the sand, and a door would open and somebody would come out and grab the meals, then close the door. The plotters on the *Wisconsin* would put an *x* on their chart, then they would follow that guy to the next bunker, and systematically the *Wisconsin* took out the Iraqi defenses because of this guy with his little meal truck was doing the spotting for them. So they did a remarkable—that's the last time, I guess, the battleship was used. *Wisconsin* was based here in Norfolk, I recall.

So, okay.

JW: Is that a wrap?

DW: Yeah, I think that'll be a wrap for today.

[End of July 16, 2018, interview]

Interview Number ten with Senator John W. Warner, USN (Ret.)
Date: September 12, 2018

David Winkler (DW): Today is September 12th, 2018, and yesterday was the 17th anniversary of 9/11 [2001]. 9/11, to most people in this country, is kind of like December 7th [1941] for the generation that was around then. You kind of remember where you were, what you were doing. And I think that's how I want to open up, given that this was the 17th anniversary yesterday. How do you recall that day?

Senator John Warner (JW): I recall that day as if it occurred yesterday. I was giving a speech to a group of corporate executives in the modern office building that is directly facing the White House on H Street, with the Farragut Squarae being the only intervening plot of land undeveloped between this building and the White House. It commands a magnificent view of everything, the whole of Washington, up in this penthouse, glassed-in penthouse.

In the course of speaking to about thirty or forty senior executives, eight, eight-fifteen or something in the morning. I noticed—as any speaker that's done as much as I and others have, is able to almost have a second knowledge of how the audience is reacting to your remarks by the way they're squirming, looking or not looking and not squirming, or whatever the case may be, and I noticed this audience was distracted through the glass doors by women who ordinarily were doing their duties before printouts and machines and so forth, all running around furiously. I just knew that there was something unsettling going on, to the point it was just about to disrupt what I was endeavoring to do.

A woman opened the door and said very politely to me, "Senator, I urge you to call your office right away, because I think you'd better advise your guests that you'll have to depart."

And I was somewhat taken aback, but I did call the office and they told what little they knew, that the Capitol was getting ready to close its doors and send everybody home, and perhaps I'd better return fast to wrap up my office, which I did. I went down and got in my car, and a young man who was driving my car with me sped down there, and we could tell by the streets—everybody was driving through lights and all kinds of things—that something was going wrong.

We couldn't learn it from the radios, but when I got there, I saw the members of the Senate were in an orderly way departing the Capitol Building very quickly, and I soon learned that there'd been an attack somewhere, and it wasn't clear in mind just how or who perpetrated the attack, but that there was some thought that the [sic] Washington—namely, the Capitol or the White House—would be the next target.

Well, then the facts came together pretty quickly, and we were told by the majority leader that the chambers would be closed, the building would be secured, and he suggested that we send our staffs home, and that there had been this attack. By now, I'd gotten to a television set, where I was able to visualize and share with others what was portrayed on the screen very dramatically and very professionally, the buildings burning.

I met with Carl Levin. Carl was then chairman of the committee. I was ranking. We decided that we would try, for the benefit of those senators who were not leaving their offices and closing them up, who might want to come and learn about this, and given it was a national defense issue, that the two of us should be the conveners.

So we got a hold of the attorney general and one other cabinet officer and asked them if they'd come to Capitol Hill and brief the Senate. Then we put out the word to the Senate offices that this briefing would take place here in short order. We gathered together probably—oh, head of the CIA was there, and I remember Bill Webster was CIA director. He'd only been director five days, I think. And the attorney general was a former senator from the Senate. And both of them sat there as best they could and told us quite frankly that within the informational loop of the administration, there were no facts over and above what was being visualized on the television.

So we adjourned the meeting and thanked them very much, and I turned to Carl and I said, "You know, Carl, I feel like I want to call Rumsfeld up. I spent five years of my life in that building." By this time, the second hit had hit the Pentagon, and you could see the smoke. "I think I'll call him and just have a chat with him, say that Capitol Hill sends its prayers, and that we ought to as soon as possible get a message out that we're up and running here in this country."

And damn if I didn't get him right on the phone. He said, "John, I'll tell you what. You'd be a great help to me because I'm periodically going out here and comingling with the rescue workers who are still bringing out wounded and bodies and so forth. Your presence would be helpful."

And I said, "Okay, Rummy. I'll be there."

I spoke to Carl Levin, and he said, "Well, if you're going, I guess I'll go too." So the two of us jumped in Carl's car, an old beat-up car that he had, and drove over the 14th Street Bridge. There wasn't another car on the bridge. But we could see the building and the fires still leaping up in the skyline from the building.

So we got there and assimilated ourselves with Rumsfeld, and we spent the balance of the afternoon doing what anybody could do to comfort some of the victims and be present as they were bringing out the rest of them.

Then Rumsfeld said, "Well, I think we've done all we can do here. Let's go down and get into the subterranean command post in the building and just begin to monitor things. It'd be helpful to have you two guys, because I never know when I'll need a little reinforcement on the absence of a lot of knowledge which the public could understand, it happened so quickly, to gather facts."

So we went down, and there was myself, Levin. And the chairman of the Joint Chiefs was in an airplane circling Washington. He could not get clearance to land. The president of the United States was in a plane circling Washington at quite a distance out, hundreds of miles away, but the president was quite anxious to get down and into the White House as fast he could, and he, every fifteen minutes, would call Rumsfeld on his hotline to say, "Have you fixed it so I can get in?"

And Rumsfeld was repeatedly telling him, "I have no control whatsoever over air space in Washington. That's FAA's exclusive."

And the president was not irate, but really hot-tempered.

Finally, Rumsfeld gave the phone to me, said, "Here. This is your friend John Warner. He can reinforce me."

And I explained that we'd checked it out. And the vice chief of staff, who later became chief, the Air Force general, chief of staff, was in the room with us.

And then at about ten OC at night, the president did get down and did say a few words, and he called Rummy and said, "Get up, you and Warner and Levin, and get on the tube and reinforce that we're up and running and you're in the building where the actual hit was taken."

So we did it, and it was a fascinating thing, experience, on fifteen minutes' notice, get ready to put together about ten or fifteen minutes of remarks divided between four of us. The vice chief spoke, and that was projected all over the world. So that was a day I'll never forget.

There was a reproduction of those film clips on television the other night, very good show. Did you see it?

DW: No, I missed that one. I saw it, though, on the TV. Yeah, I missed that program.

JW: I remember it very well. Then we delved back into how it could have happened, and to this day, it's just unbelievable how that thing—how simplistic the plan was to do it.

DW: No, that leads to the differences today, of course, there was the—I guess they stood up a commission to look into that. We're talking John Lehman was involved in that commission, and a couple others. Some of the recommendations, Department of Homeland Security and—

JW: Oh, the fallout was quite productive.

DW: And the whole revision of national intelligence establishment is all fallout out of that. And obviously you had a role in that.

JW: A minor role.

DW: No, of course, other fallout from that is we immediately go into Afghanistan. We're still there seventeen years later.

JW: Yes.

DW: And in 2003, we wound up going into Iraq. So that's two of the fallouts. Events leading up to that, one of them was the attack on the *Cole* back in 2000, and I think that was one you held hearings on?

JW: We went into extensively that situation, yeah.

DW: What are your recollections? I think one of the controversies or how do you view the command responsibility, I think there was—

JW: Yeah, it was not unlike, you know, the *Indianapolis* case, where the old naval tradition, the commanding officer is responsible, irrespective of whether he was rightfully trying to take a little rest or whatever it was. It's his fault. So you had to sort through that.

You know, the other one was when the Iraq plane, using a French Exocet missile, blew up a destroyer over in the Far East.

DW: That was the *Stark* incident, right? That was back in the '83, '84 time.

JW: Oh, gracious. The president [Reagan] called me up and said, "What the hell is this all about?"

I said, "Mr. President, I'm following it, as everybody else."

He said, "Well, you and John Glenn—now, John Glenn knows aviation. You, Secretary of the Navy, you know surface warfare. You two guys saddle up and get over there *tonight*."

And I said, "Yes, sir. We'll do that."

To make a long story short, we got a plane and we were out of there that night, and we visited six countries, Israel being the seventh, to reassure them that we weren't going to quit. In the meantime, we were trying to get certain nations—like the UAE was very helpful—to help us tow this disabled ship to a port and begin to get such instantaneous maintenance on it to stop the flow of water into the hull till we could get around to sealing it and pumping it out. And we managed to do all that, just flying all around in a Gulfstream airplane, visiting heads of state and then checking on how the ship was coming along. It killed, I think, some thirty-five guys and wounded another thirty.

DW: I think so.

JW: A lot of death on there. And to this day, it's never been clear, other than Iraq did it, they confessed it was not an act of belligerency, but how in the heck they could induce some young aviator to go down there and fire that missile. And then also everybody was very impressed with their missile, because it entered the ship's hull and set off secondary fires to the explosion, and that's where we suffered the most damage. Smoke got into the breathing system in the ship, and a lot of people were subjected to that acrid acidified smoke

DW: It was kind of interesting because that's the same missile, when you think about the time frame, as the Brits had just been down to the Falklands and those same missiles were used by the Argentines.

JW: That's interesting.

DW: And they had taken out some of the British frigates. There was an argument made that some of our Bath-built frigates—

JW: Could use some redesign.

DW: Yeah. But were able to stay afloat. That was the contrast to the British ships that [demonstrates] went down. So that's a good insight into the *Stark* incident.

There's also the "*Sammy*" [Samuel] *B. Roberts* incident, where the *Sammy B. Roberts* in April 1988 hit an Iranian mine and holed the ship. So that was a case which we immediately struck back with Operation Praying Mantis and took out these Iranian platforms. The Iranian navy came out, and we basically sunk a couple of their frigates.

JW: I remember well Glenn—they asked us to go down to that area and look at the Straits of Hormuz and get some understanding of the restricted sea lanes that vessels needed to get through, and the Iranians had shore mounts of a missile system. I've forgotten the name.

DW: Silkworm?

JW: Silkworm, yeah, all along there, and the ships were just sitting ducks, I mean, because they were rigidly contained in a line. There was no maneuvering to make targeting more difficult.

I'll never forget, Glenn said, "We've got to do this covertly."

I said, "Well, of course, everybody here would know it."

He said, "Yeah, but let's rent one of these dhow fishing boats, rent the whole boat, and go out in that and put on old clothes."

"Sounds like a plan."

We found some old fisherman and persuaded him to forget catching fish that day. We'd give him a pocketful of cash if he took us out in his dhow right into the sea lanes. Those little fishing vessels dart amongst the ships quite nicely, just doing their catch at the same time. And here Glenn and I were, two senators out in the channel, and you could see the Silkworm system in the whole thing.

DW: So this is in the aftermath of that *Stark*.

JW: Mm-hmm.

DW: There's a couple of interesting trips I noticed. I think you went to Somalia one time?

JW: Yeah, Carl Levin and I went down there because there was a lot of questions as to whether or not we wanted to put any U.S. troops in it. Jim Jones was SacEur.[56]

DW: Right.

JW: And Jim called me up—yeah, I think this is it—and asked if I would divert from a trip that I was on, a CODEL, and would I go down, join Carl Levin and then go in. And we did do that, had a very interesting experience on it. The capital of that area was just all blown up. The embassy was a fortress, nothing but machine guns up in the second-floor windows of the embassy. The ambassador and the Marines were the only American people left in the embassy. We were damn

---

[56] General James Jones was Marine Corps commandant and remained on active duty to take on the Supreme Allied Commander assignment.

proud of that, Glenn and I both being ex-Marines. So we did send back a kudo for that man, and that ambassador was very impressive.

The question was should we send forces, and we made the decision and relayed it to Jones to send some ships down to do a little—what's that term we use? It's a naval term that we use when ships are used as standoff to warn people.

DW: Show the flag?

JW: Yeah. Carl, he's a good trooper, wonderful man. I adore him to this day. And Carl says, "You really think we ought to go in?"

"Yeah."

And there was a four-star naval officer or a four-star Marine, he was sort of an odd fellow. How he got his fourth star, I wasn't sure, not that I'm denigrating him, but what his commands were. He's still around. I met him at McCain's funeral, as a matter of fact. Hadn't seen him in twenty, fifteen years.

He said, "You two senators want to go in on my watch and get blown up? I don't think that's a good idea."

DW: Was this General Crist?[57]

JW: Yeah. Well, this guy and I went back and forth. We finally rigged up a scheme that if we went down and went in through Ethiopia, which was neutral, and then came in the back way, we'd avoid some of the more dangerous areas. So we did it. Here Carl and I and the admiral, who finally went along with it, he went over not exactly with us, but he wasn't more than one hundred yards away from us the whole time, because if it was going to happen, he wanted to be sure that all were present and accounted for.

I'll never forget, the ambassador, the U.S. ambassador to Ethiopia was our escort officer, and the president of Ethiopia, the ambassador said, "We can't just bring two senators wandering in his country and not start at the top and make our manners." So we agreed that we would go up

---

[57] Marine General George Crist commanded Central Command between 1985 and 1989.

and meet him. So we did. And in the course of the meeting, fully composed and very presidential, he said, "Gentlemen, it's a coincidence that you're here today, because at this end of my building I have one man stationed, and at the opposite end I've got another stationed. The man at this end is Alamati [phonetic], and he is the head of the rebel forces." And the other end was Colonel so-and-so, who was the head of the opposing forces. He was a British-trained—wouldn't be Indian, but he'd be local whatever.

DW: Right.

JW: But he was trained at Sandhurst and everything. "And they're here trying to negotiate a treaty between the two of them."

I said to Carl, I said, "Carl, you know, this is interesting."

Carl says, "Yeah, but we've got to watch out. We can't do diplomacy."

"No, but we can do courtesy."

So we turned a courtesy call into a diplomatic call, and we met with these two guys together in the same room. They were very composed and collected, and it wasn't a long meeting, but nothing particularly emerged from it.

Then we went on in. And while we were there, it got a little shaky. There was mortar fire. We were put in a cement bunker, and mortars were dropping all around us. The general was a little uneasy. I don't know what that trip ended as fire zone [unclear], but anyway, we did it.

DW: I think eventually we did put some Special Forces in there.

JW: Then I talked to Jones, and he sent down a contingent of ships, small ships, that were housing the Marine battalion that was in country in the Med, and they were on their way from the Med back to CONUS on a normal six-month rotation, and he turned them around and brought them back and did standoff of the embassy, and that scared those people back into the hills like you wouldn't believe it. And the thing finally got under control. But the presence of those ships was something I remember.

DW: I think this was, what, the final year or so of the George H. W. Bush administration? Like '91 or something, '92?

JW: Herbert Walker.

DW: Yeah.

JW: Yeah. And it was rather funny. I said to Jim, "I'm on a CODEL, something else that I'm doing."
> He said, "Well, I'll lend you my Gulfstream so you and Carl can get around."
> "Okay." So we did that.
> And I'll never forget our CODEL plane stopped at an island about three hundred miles off the African coast, a well-known refueling station for ships and aircraft, that's all it is, and the Gulfstream flew me and then waited there until my CODEL plane came in and scooped me up and took me back out. Then that plane took off, and in the takeoff pattern—can happen just accidental—they flew through some seagulls and ingested two seagulls in engines and had to do an emergency landing. [laughs] And Jim Jones' plane was on the beaches for weeks until they could figure out how to get the plane off and bring in engines to replace down there. Oh, my god. Funny stories.

DW: So that was one CODEL. I think the other in the nineties, a major one you were involved with is in the whole Adriatic, Bosnia, Serbia—

JW: Oh, yeah. I went with Bob Dole on that one. Oh, my gosh, we had quite a trip through that area, yeah. There were interesting times, yeah.

DW: So the one into, I guess, Serbia, you were looking at that whole situation. Yugoslavia broke up. You had the situation with—

JW: Tito pulled out, just folded his tent, and this thing fractured, and you went back to the classic old religious dispute between several religions, and that whole thing was predicated on religions.

But you had the ruthless head of one faction. His name was Milosevic. And the other gang was represented by in-and-out people. Nobody seemed to keep the job very long. But they were inferior in size and training. It was a pitiful thing.

You know, one of the interesting things I carried away with from that chapter of my career, nobody in America knew anything about the Balkans. I didn't know a great deal about it. I had not been in that country. It was just a piece of the world map that nobody paid any attention to.

DW: What's interesting about—because especially this is the 100th anniversary of World War I, is the affinity that Russia's had with Serbia, Russia has always had this tight bond with Serbia, and listening to the Russians talk today about this fractured relationship between Russia and the United States, one of the things they point to is that in the 1990s, the NATO operation against Serbia was something that soured them on relations with the West. They've always been protective of Serbia.

JW: They really were.

DW: Yeah. No, we accidentally, I guess, launched—

JW: I think I conducted three CODELs into that country to do a crash learning course for as many senators as I could get, because it was getting antsy and NATO was getting involved. So one time I was over there, Clark was Commander-in-Chief, American Forces Europe,[58] I think, and it was the crusty old Sandhurst British admiral named Jackson, known for his crustiness, but a very able soldier who had proven himself under fire in more battles than one. And Clark didn't want to bring in some heavy tanks, because he felt that would be a symbolism of escalating it more danger than that, and he and Jackson got in an argument. Jackson wanted to bring in heavy tanks as a show of force. And these guys, they were arguing so bitterly, I beckoned to the military aide to these guys and said, "Let's step away and let them have it." I walked off about twenty paces out of earshot. But they damn near got in a fistfight.

---

[58] Army General Wesley Clark.

DW: Geez.

JW: And then Clark was right, because—this is one of those little fascinating vignettes—he and I had, the day before, been on a trip together in a helicopter, where he took engineers out and landed in the vicinity of where bridges which linked these ravines, had to have the engineers determine what weight they could bear before they would collapse by a heavy armada of tanks. It was quite interesting. It came back there was hardly any of them over which we dared take a tank, and they'd been up for centuries.

DW: I was about to say, some of these bridges have been up since the 13th century.

JW: Thirteenth century, yeah. So Clark said, "What the hell would I do with a whole battalion of tanks and making a perfect target stored away somewhere till they could fix the bridge?"

DW: Did you ever do any CODELs with Senator McCain?

JW: Mm-hmm. I took him on his first CODEL right after the first Gulf War. He was very respectful to me in every way. You've got in there how I'd gotten him into the schools.

DW: Right.

JW: He told me, frankly, he operated better with just another senator, and I said, "Go ahead. Kick off on your own." And he and Lindsey [Graham] started doing a lot together.

DW: Okay.

JW: They started their trips. A lot of the things that John did, I didn't get a direct relevance to what the Senate was trying to do, some of those conferences on economics and stuff like that, but he loved it. And he did some good for this country to run our flag up.

DW: With his recent passing, do you have any special recollections about his service in the Senate?

JW: Well, it was quite an interesting service. I mean, John was the champion of the "Let's get something done. Just exactly how you get from A to B to get it done, that's irrelevant. Just get from A to B. Show some concrete results."

He had some interesting pieces of legislation that were very valuable for this country, did a good job, but he was irascible and his own man, and finally, leadership went along with some of the things he thought were never possible. He was quite a guy.

Just complete off the record, off the side here, what did we do for Ted Kennedy? I was part of his funeral. I flew to Boston with quite a few senators. We had a beautiful service in one of the cathedrals up in Boston, and that was it.

Then along comes Bob Dole. What do you do with him? I mean, he's certainly courageous as any of them were. Everybody pulling his hair out right now. How do you do that? Bob never allowed any memorial of his to be shown, you know.

DW: Well, I have to talk to Senator Dole soon. I'm going to be doing that project with the World War II Memorial. So I want to interview him about the role he played afterwards. But I guess he's not in the best of health.

JW: Well, I'd like to retract that. I talked to him last night.

DW: Oh!

JW: We're working on an Op-Ed together. The thesis is let's put aside whether they're Democrats or Republicans or Independents. Give the veterans a fair chance to join the Congress, because—and this is the language he likes, but I wrote it—tattooed on each of their hearts, from the moment they step into a military uniform, are those three words: duty, honor, country. And it never comes off. It's with them. And in later life, they'll put the "duty, honor, country" forward rather than getting lockjaw on some of these party caucuses that won't let anything happen.

DW: I did see something on BBC News the other night that there are quite a few veterans who served in Iraq and Afghanistan, women, who are in both parties who are candidates for office.

JW: I'm all for it. I'm a part of the movement. I went through that.

DW: So we covered—we talked about 9/11, we talked a little bit about Senator McCain, and we talked about some of these CODELs to Somalia and Adriatic. Going into Iraq, obviously you supported that. Any reflections now?

JW: It seemed to me to be the right thing to do, particularly the first time when Saddam Hussein drove into Kuwait. That was such a clear manifestation of invading another territory of another land. And that thing was pulled together right. First we operated on the thesis you are part of a team of the United Nations. Each member of the team abided by the mandate that the UN chamber wrote regarding this is what's happened, this is the mission of the UN forces, and once that's achieved, out of there.

But in this country, in order to utilize any forces like that of ours in harm's way, you've got to get the Congress involved, at that time anyway. Now they do it surreptitiously. So, oh, no, that was a moment in time.

DW: Okay. You were mentioning earlier, and I was just thinking about this, that President Reagan used to come back to your farm to do horseback riding. During the early years of his administration, he's a movie star and you're still married to Elizabeth Taylor. That must have been interesting, having—

JW: Oh, yeah, they were great friends. I mean, I would be with them, and the two of them would just disappear and have a chat themselves about old times.

DW: I guess that was one of your regrets when that marriage broke up, is you didn't have that—

JW: Well, the marriage, it broke up for good reasons. She was a grand campaigner for me in the Senate, wonderful, and really worked hard. I'll put in a little story to color this in a minute. But when I got elected, the full reality of the commitment that you make by doing in as a junior senator just came upon us so swiftly. I had a pretty good idea about it, but she had no idea about it, because in Hollywood, when they did a Senate film, they used whatever clothing was necessary to look like a senator, then hang it up in a room and forget it. But she was not facing the fact that I had to wear that uniform night and day, and I didn't get home every night for dinner, and I wasn't able to go on all the trips she had, wonderful invitations all over the country we got. I couldn't do that. What a shock for her. So we went through a quiet divorce, but we don't call it a divorce anymore.

DW: I guess I could ask, your current, Jeanne, I guess you've been married for, I guess, at least a decade. Now, was there a time that Barbara Walters and you had—

JW: Yeah, we did a little tap dancing. We had two dances, one before Elizabeth and then after Elizabeth and I split.

But Elizabeth wanted to go back on films. She wanted to go to her native land. She was born in England, lived much in England and Ireland, Scotland, and she liked films over there and she enjoyed doing films on the continent. I was commuting to Europe. I'd leave Thursday night, miss a vote, maybe, and get on that plane and go over there, and get back Monday afternoon, and she would do the same thing to come visit me. Finally, she said, "We're good friends. We get along. We got it all solved. Why don't we just split the sheets and stay friends?" And that's what we did.

DW: Okay, okay. And then you knew Barbara Walters from before and afterwards as friends.

JW: She was a lovely lady, absolutely. My first dancing with her was, so to speak, I was just trying to learn to campaign. I was head of the Bicentennial. She was interested in the Bicentennial, as were all the media in those days, because it was a successful program, not just because of yours truly, but the concept.

DW: Right.

JW: So a *lot* of television that I did. And she'd watch me on television and then call and critique me. "Why did you do that with your hands? Take your hands and get them out of the film. Keep your head up. Don't let the chin drop. Watch that voice. You don't have to roar up and down. Keep it modulated." The famous one—she listened to radio. She says, "The way you do radio is to picture that you're sitting on a settee for two people, one at one end, one at the other, and you're having a conversation with that person next to you, and just speak as if you were on a settee and stop trying to project your voice through the microphone." And it worked like magic. My radio rates went up.

DW: [laughs] So, basically, she was a coach.

JW: Oh, yeah.

DW: So I guess you had interviewed with her or done an interview with you, and she kind of took a liking?

JW: Yeah, it developed into a very beautiful and genuine romance for two or three years in the beginning, a year and a half or so afterwards, but we realized—she said, "You know, that old adage, you can take the boy out of the country, but you can't take the country out of the boy. You do love farms." She used to come down on my farm, spend weekends with me, and we didn't do all the country partying and everything. She'd bring two suitcases of books and speeches, lock up in the library, and stay in the library the whole time, maybe take a walk in the evening with me. That was her idea of going to the country. We had a good pool. She enjoyed that. But as far as going to the races or going down watching the horses work out or get on a horse, much less get on a horse, she didn't want anything to do with it.

DW: Sounds like that old show *Green Acres*, you know.

JW: Yeah. But I still talk to her every so often. I think—I'm not sure, but I think she's had a stroke. You don't see her anywhere anymore. Lovely woman.

DW: I remember the gossip, the social commentary where your names came up from time to time.

JW: Oh, yeah. But it was a genuine relationship between two people.

DW: Good.

JW: And she said, "I admit I love everything you showed me and everything. I've just got to be back on Fifth Avenue."

DW: Just like [singing the theme song from *Green Acres*], "Farm living is the life for me."

JW: Yeah. A great lady. She had a beautiful apartment. We had good times together. We took lovely Christmas vacations. And then she had a number of friends abroad who would entertain us beautifully overseas, in France and England, things like that.

DW: Her background, she grew up where?

JW: Who?

DW: Barbara Walters was from New York originally?

JW: She was a New Yorker all the way through. Her father owned a series—not a series, I think one or two nightclubs, and she never fully acknowledged it, but my little bit of research showed that they were speakeasies in Prohibition. It all works out.

DW: It does. It does. And I guess Jeanne, her first husband was a Navy captain who—your current wife.

JW: Yes. Very fine man. He was a good personal friend of mine. He did very well. He was an assistant secretary of commerce. He worked in the White House. He was very much a part of the

Eisenhower-Nixon period. He just lost his life suddenly, unexpectedly. She wouldn't date me. I kept trying to get—Thad Cochran knew her husband like I did, and Thad lived a few blocks from where they lived. I deputized Thad to get me a date, and he said, "Okay, but you behave yourself. I'll get you the date."

And I'd keep calling. "How about now?"

"She's not ready now."

DW: Okay, okay. When did you wind up giving up the farm?

JW: The children really were not that much interested in it, and a farm is a huge drain economically and decision making, and I used it until I got to the point where the commute had deteriorated so much because of the development of new housing along all the arterial roads leading out to Middleburg. In the old days, I could go back and forth between Georgetown and Middleburg in less than an hour without batting an eye. Now it had gotten up to an hour and a half.

Then when I was Secretary of the Navy, Mel Laird passed an edict that you had to be within one hour of the Pentagon, unless you had written permission. And my first farm, which I raised the kids on, which we still own, my son owns it now. My son and daughter divided it up. That was an hour and a half. So then that's when I had to move from Middleburg and get off the river, which I loved, Shenandoah. We kept the land. Of course, the kids now have it. And we moved to Middleburg, and that worked out. I could get there within less than an hour.

DW: You had a house, I guess, in Georgetown when you were Secretary of the Navy.

JW: When I was Secretary of the Navy, I did. I had a big house in Georgetown that I actually built, in the sense that I studied architecture in engineering school, got a good architect, he did the work, but I'd sketch it and built it. And the wife at that time, whom I still see and we have good relations—we all go to family dinners about every ninety days—she wanted five children. And when the third child came, my son, she very casually said, "I don't want any more. Too much work." [laughs]

And I said, "Well, we're building a house for five bedrooms. I guess we're going to have plenty of guests, aren't we."

DW: I think there was an episode where when Zumwalt was coming in, you snuck him in.

JW: Oh, yeah, we hid him in the house.

DW: We talked about that.

JW: For forty-eight hours. He was under tight lip, and nobody talked to him till the president talked to him.

DW: So then you had a place in Old Town, didn't you, Alexandria?

JW: Yeah. Then we moved into Georgetown. Then when I ran for the Senate, I sold the main big farm, and Mark Warner, who, oddly enough, had come in late in the scene as an opponent, picked up on it and said, "He sold his Virginia property." Well, it was true, but I still owned property on this side of the mountain, but that didn't count. I wasn't living on it. And he was trumpeting that no end. So I quickly moved everything I had to Alexandria.

DW: Okay. This is a political move, literally.

JW: Yeah, political move. I don't regret it. I enjoyed Alexandria.

DW: Were you over on—what was it?

JW: I was on 35th Street in Georgetown.

DW: Okay. But in Alexandria, were you like Prince Street?

JW: No, I was over in an apartment house which was on the outer fringe of Old Town. But then when I married Jeanne, we bought a little house together, which is right on the border of Old Town, but our address is still Alexandria, Virginia.

DW: Fairfax County.

JW: Yeah.

DW: So that apartment building is why you have your relationship with that—you'd occasionally drop off clothes at that one dryer.

JW: That place, I do. Still use it.

DW: Okay. Well, we can wrap it up for today.

JW: All right. I don't want to get there too early to this event, because it's tiring. Oh, god, they drained me last night. I was so tired.

[End of September 12, 2018, interview]

Launched in 1969, the U.S. Naval Institute's award-winning oral history program is among the oldest in the country. Used in combination with documentary sources, oral histories offer a richer understanding of naval history through candid recollections and explanations rarely entered into contemporary records. In addition, they help depict the atmosphere of a particular event or era in a manner not available in official documents.

The nonprofit Naval Institute accomplishes its history projects through contributed funds and gratefully accepts tax-deductible gifts of all sizes for this purpose. This support allows the Institute to preserve the life experiences of today's service men and women so they may enlighten and inspire future generations.

For information about opportunities to underwrite Naval Institute oral history projects, please contact the Naval Institute Foundation at 291 Wood Road, Annapolis, Maryland 21402; by phone at (410) 295-1054; or by e-mail at foundation@usni.org.

AD-1 Skyraider, 21, 21n4
Adams-class destroyers, 64
Adriatic region, 190, 194
Afghanistan War and Afghanistan War veterans, 108–9, 184, 193–94
Agnew, Spiro, 35, 38, 107
agriculture in Southside Virginia, 118
Air Corps, U.S., ix
Air Force, U.S.: Defense Reauthorization Act and Department of Air Force creation, 140; successor to Army Air Corps, 43, 49; Virginia airfield of, 122
Air Force, U.S. Department of the, 40
aircraft: anti-aircraft fire during Korean War, 21–22; logs of flight time, 24; multi-engine planes, 49; return from Korea on, 24; types used in Korea and Vietnam, 21–22, 21n4
aircraft carriers: activities on during Vietnam War, 53–54; authorization for, 136, 138, 158; *Forrestal* role in Bicentennial celebration, xii, 90–91, 95; *Gerald R. Ford*, 106, 106n48
Al Smith Dinner, 133–34
Alaska, 15, 15n1
alcohol, 147
Alexandria, Virginia: debate with Miller in, 126–27; home in, vi, 199–200
Alvaraz, Everett, Jr. "Eve," 56
American Airlines, 31
American Freedom Train, 95–96, 96n43
American Revolution Bicentennial Administration. *See* Bicentennial celebration
Amherst, Virginia, ix
Anacostia Naval Air Station, 19, 19n2
Andrews Air Force Base, 19n2
anti-aircraft fire, 21–22
Archdiocese of New York, Al Smith Dinner, 133–34
Argentina, 186
Arleigh Burke and *Arleigh Burke*-class destroyers, 116, 154–55
armed forces: adventure of being in, 24; age for enlistment in, 5; base closure bills and closing military bases, 138–40, 168–72; enlistment and draft for World War II, 4–5; feelings of citizens toward military facilities, 140; first in, first out policy in, 9, 14; "hollow military," 141; incentive

for joining, 5; interdependency of military and working with fellow serviceperson, 8–9, 12; recruitment for, 5; reserves recalled to active duty for Iraq operations, 176–77; stickers on front doors for family member in, 4; train travel to port of embarkation, 6; veterans elected to and service in Congress, 108–10, 172, 193–94

Army, U.S.: Army Medical Corps, 2; "hollow military" comment by Chief of Staff of, 141; interservice tension with Marines, 52–53; service of father in, ix, 2, 9; Virginia bases of, 122, 139

Army, U.S. Department of the: career staff of, 40; Secretary of the Army, 40, 43

Army Air Corps, U.S., 5, 43, 49, 140

Army suit, not dressing children in, 9

Arnold, Benedict, 74

ASW capabilities of ships, 155–56

Atlanta, 160

Atlantic Fleet, 14

Atomic Energy Commission, 72

Australia, 64

Bagley, David H., 58, 58n21, 153

Bagley, Worth H., 58, 58n21

Baikov, Ivan Ivanovich, 67, 67n25

Baker, Howard, 134–35, 136, 139

Balducci's, v

Balkans, 190–92

Banshees, 21, 21n4

Base Closure Commission, 169–70

Base Realignment and Closure Act (1988), 168–72

Bath, Maine, 186

battleships: ammo for, 164; capabilities of, 165–66; decommissioning of, 9, 14–15; new construction of, 165–66; pocket battleships/battlecruisers, 15, 15n1; return to service of, 163–66

Bayonne, New Jersey, 14–15

BBC News, 194

beards, 152

behavior control agreement, 144

bell bottoms (crackerjacks), 152

Belleau Wood, Battle of, 53

Bicentennial celebration: administrator of American Revolution Bicentennial Administration role, xii, 34, 55, 86–87, 89, 96, 119, 138, 195–96; cocktail party dinner thrown by and plates made by France for, 89; commemorative events in states and foreign countries, xii; congressional and executive branch support for, 86–87, 88; dismantling agency at end of, 102; enthusiasm across the country for, 88; events and travel on July 4th, 89–93, 95–97; feelings about being involved in, 87–88, 89, 96; heads of state attendance by, 96–97; intellectuals, Nixon concern about Bicentennial celebration planning by, 94; invitation to Queen to attend, 88, 96–97; items made to commemorate Bicentennial, 89; offices of, 34; organizational structure and staffing to support, 88, 90, 93–94, 95; ringing bicentennial bells coast to coast by ringing bell on the *Forrestal*, xii, 90–91, 95; Senate confirmation of appointment as administrator, 88; swearing in as administrator by Ford, 89; trademark/logo for, 88–89; travel related to, 87–88, 119, 138

biographical tribute by Cox, ix–xiii

Black Sea: Bosporus Strait and mines in embankment, 60; *Yorktown-Caron* incident in, 60

black-tie, white-tie, and the Al Smith Dinner, 133–34

Bolling Air Force Base, 19n2

Bolshoi, 82–83

Bosnia, 190

Bosporus Strait, 60, 60n23

Bowsher, Charles, 46, 46n17

Boy Scouts, 3, 6, 8

Brezhnev, Leonid, 82–83

Bryant, Jim, iii

Buckingham Palace, 97

Budd, Martha. *See* Warner, Martha Budd (mother)

Buick, 16

Bulge, Battle of the, 1, 5–6

Burke, Arleigh, 143

Burton, Richard, 101

Bush administration and George Herbert Walker Bush, 112, 172–73, 176–80, 190

Bush administration and George W. Bush, 112–13, 182–84

Byrd, Harry, 129

Byrd, Robert "Bob," 85, 175–76, 177

cabinet and sub-cabinet, forming of, 38–43

California: Nixon campaign for governor of, 34; Nixon trip to vote in, 30–31; Reagan as governor

of, 145
California, 72n29
Calvert, James "Jim," 74, 74n30
Cambodia, 52
Campaign Annex, 35. *See also* Willard Hotel, Washington, D.C.
canned food, 6
Cannon's steam house, 17–18
Capitol: 9/11 attacks and closing of, 181–82; swearing in as Bicentennial celebration administrator on steps of, 89. *See also* Congress, U.S.
career: admission to the Bar, x; decision to be a lawyer, 18; Hogan & Hartson (Hogan Lovells) law firm, xi, xiii, 27, 27n9, 28, 33, 35, 80; international lawyer organization membership, 80–81; law clerkship, x, 17–18, 26–27; leave of absence from law firm, 35; private law practice, x; pro bono cases, 27, 35; regulatory interests of law firms, 35; U.S. Attorney Office appointments, x–xi, 26–28. *See also* politics
Carlucci, Frank, 148–49
Carter administration and Jimmy Carter, 107, 118–19, 137–38, 140–41, 149, 161
caviar, 65, 84
Central America, 166, 166n56
Central Command, U.S., 188n58
Chafee, John: aboard *Constitution* in irons on Charles River, 79–80; death of, 29n11; effectiveness and success of, 44; military service of, 29; relationship with Warner, 160; resignation of, 29, 50; responsibilities of, 43–45; as Rhode Island governor, 29, 44; Rickover opinion about, 58; Secretary of the Navy appointment, 29; war protest assessment by, 47
Charles River, *Constitution* in irons on, 79–80
Charlottesville infantry unit, 19
Cheney, Dick, 173
Chesterfield County Airport, 124n51
Chevy Chase Country Club, 32
Chicago: changing trains in, 7–8; Democratic Convention in, 36; lost votes in 1960 presidential election, 31–32; VE-Day and service as shore patrol in, x, 12–13
Chief of Naval Operations (CNO): appointment decisions for, 50; Armed Services Committee

meetings with candidates for, 52; Clarey nomination as, 50; Hayward as, 81n38, 138, 158, 174; Holloway as, iv, 58, 117, 117n50, 153; Moorer as, 49–50, 58, 68; Richardson as, 115, 115n49; Roughead as, 109; Trost as, 173–74; Watkins as, 74, 74n31, 158; Zumwalt as, 50, 50n19, 58, 68, 117–18, 150–53

China, template for agreements between U.S. and, iv

Christ Church, Farragut Square, 89–90

Churchill, Winston, 162

Circuit Court of Appeals, U.S., District of Columbia Circuit, x, 26n8

Civil Service, 39

Clarey, Bernard Ambrose "Chick," 50, 50n18, 53, 68

Clark, Wesley, 191–92, 191n59

Claytor, Graham, 137–38

Cleopatra, 101

Clifford, Clark, 39, 39n16, 46

Cobra, Typhoon, 91, 91n42

Cochran, Thad, 198

Cold War: secret negotiations with Soviet Union over, 36; travel related to, 87

Cold War at Sea (Winkler), iii

Cold War Gallery, National Museum of the United States Navy, v

Cole, 184–85

Coleman, Stets, 135

Command of the Seas (Lehman), 144, 158, 159, 163

Commencement–class escort carriers, 23, 23n6

communication equipment, 10

Communications Officer service, x, 20–22, 20n3, 163–64

Congress, U.S.: Armed Services Committee of, 118; aspirations to serve in, 89; Bicentennial celebration support from, 86–87, 88; CODEL visits to Iraq, 178–79; Ford service in, 103, 105; hearings for appointees, 41; Laird service in, 28, 40; legislative representation of the population in the country, 109; 9/11 attacks and closing of the Capitol, 181–82; ship designs for post-war shipbuilding, 15; swearing in as Bicentennial celebration administrator on steps of Capitol, 89; veterans elected to and service in, 108–10, 172, 193–94; war declaration legislation and authority

of, 177–78, 194. *See also* Senate, U.S.
Connecticut, 116
Conover, Mary, 32n13
conservative politics and right-to-life views, 124
Constitution Gardens, 102, 102n46
Constitution in irons on Charles River, 79–80
Corsairs, 21, 21n4
corvettes, 154–55
Coskey, Ken, 56
Cosmoline, 23
Cotswolds, 101, 119
cows, 120
Cox, Samuel J., ix–xiii
crackerjacks (bell bottoms), 152
Crist, George, 188, 188n58
cruisers, 58
C-SPAN, v
Cunard International Hotel (Novotel, London West), 61–62, 61n24

Danville, Virginia, 118
D-Day anniversary, 131–32
De Gaulle, Charles, 63
debate in Alexandria, 126–27
Declaration of Independence, 90
Defense, U.S. Department of: base closure bills and closing military bases, 138–40, 168–72; career staff of, 41–43; Carlucci as secretary, 148–49; competition in, 68; Director of Ocean Affairs appointment, xi; Distinguished Public Service Medal and citation from, xi–xii; EOB offices of War Department, 39, 39n15; Laird as secretary, xi, 28–29, 36, 40; as largest employer in Virginia, 115; Schlesinger as secretary, 58; screening and selection of people to work in, 29, 38, 40–43; Secretary of Defense meetings about Vietnam, 48; ship-naming role of Secretary of Defense, 112; Tower nomination as secretary, 148; Weinberger as secretary, 144, 148; women working in, 41
Defense Reauthorization Act, 140
Desert Shield, Operation, 178
Desert Storm, Operation, 178
d'Estaing, Giscard, 89
destroyer escorts (DEs), 23, 23n6
destroyers, 154–55
discipline and skills of discipline, 18

Distinguished Public Service Medal and citation, xi–xii
Dixon, Alan, 139
Dobbin, 150
Dodd, Chris, 166
dog mascot, 23
Dole, Bob, 148, 190–91, 193
draft boards, 35
drug culture, 54
Dublin Horse show, 124, 126
Dulles Airport, 137
Dunn, Bob, v

East Germany, U.S. Ambassador to, 78n37
Easter Offensive, 54
Eddie, Captain, 11
Eddie test, 11
education: abilities as student and not finishing high school, 8, 11; academic life, enjoyment of, 18; electronics school training, x, 1, 10, 11–14, 17, 92; G.I. Bill, 9, 16, 18; naval justice refresher course, 25; University of Virginia Law School, x, 17–18, 19, 26, 28, 30, 127, 132; walking to school, 4, 6; Washington & Lee University, x, 9, 16–17, 127; Wilson High School, 4, 6
eggs, getting pelted with during campaign stop, 104–5
Ehrlichman, John, 31
Eighth and I Streets, 29, 29n12
Eisenhower, Dwight D. "Ike," 33, 61, 96, 96n44, 109
Eisenhower, John, 35, 38, 107
Eisenhower Executive Office Building (EOB), 39n15
El Salvador, 166, 166n56
El Toro base, 22
electronics school training and electronics technician duty, x, 1, 10, 11–14, 17, 92
engineers and engineering, 18, 35, 46, 72
Ethiopia, 188–89
Europe: collapse of Eastern Europe, 174; VE-Day and service as shore patrol in Chicago, x, 12–13
Executive Office Building (EOB), 39, 39n15
Exocet missile, 185–86

F2H Banshees, 21, 21n4

F4U Corsairs, 21, 21n4
F9F Panthers, 21, 21n4
Falklands war, 186
Fallon, Admiral, 77
farm at White Post, 122
farm in Middleburg, 30, 34, 100–102, 119–20, 121, 122, 132, 196, 198, 199
farms, summer work on, 7
Farragut Square, 34, 89–90, 181
federal government and presidency: cabinet and sub-cabinet, forming of, 38–43; industry interest in hiring people with government experience, 46; Joint Chiefs reporting to President, 43–44
FFG-7 frigates, 64
Finch, 72n28
fireworks, 93
Flag Day, 131
Fletcher School of Law and Diplomacy, Tufts University, 76–77, 77n36
flight jacket, 5, 24
Flood, Daniel "Dan," 163, 163n55, 165
Folger Nolan Investment and Securities, 31
football games, 126
Ford, Gerald: Bicentennial celebration administrator appointment and swearing in by, xii, 89; congressional career of, 103, 105; enthusiasm for Bicentennial celebration, 89, 92; events and travel on July 4th with, 89–92; foundation of and medal awarded to Warner, 106, 106n47; Michigan stop on Nixon's campaign trip, role in, 105; reelection campaign of, 106–7; relationship with Warner, 103–7; ringing bicentennial bells coast to coast by ringing bell on the *Forrestal*, xii, 90–91, 95; ship named for, 106, 106n48; swearing in as Bicentennial celebration administrator by, 89; Vice President role of, 89; World War II service as deck officer about small carrier, 91, 91n42
Ford car, 22–23
Formosa, 61
Forrestal, xii, 90–91, 95
Fort Belvoir, 139, 170
France: Bicentennial celebration plates made by, 89; Bicentennial celebration–related travel to and role of, 87, 89; Gallipoli campaign, 60; military facilities in, 63; NATO withdrawal by, 63; relationship with French Navy, 62–63

Freedom Train, 95–96, 96n43
French, Paulette, vi, 131
Friends of the World War II Memorial, iv
frigates, 64, 154–56, 186
furniture company in Muskegon, Michigan, 103–5

Gallipoli campaign, 60
Garrett, Henry Lawrence, III, 157–58, 157n52
General Dynamics, 116
Geneva, 141
Georgetown home, 198–99
Gerald R. Ford, 106, 106n48
Gerald R. Ford Foundation Medal for Distinguished Public Service, 106, 106n47
Germany: Autobahn system in, 96n44; East Germany, U.S. Ambassador to, 78n37; pocket battleships of, 15, 15n1; reunification of East and West and fall of the Berlin Wall, 174, 176; surrender of, 13, 172; training of German officers, 174–75; World War II battles, 1, 5–6
G.I. Bill, 9, 16, 18
Glenn, John, 185, 186–87, 188
gold star stickers, 4
Goldwater, Barry, 33–34, 124, 136, 161–63
Goldwater, Barry, Jr., 162, 162n54
Goldwater-Nichols act, 162–63
Gorbachev, Mikhail, 85, 175–76
Gorshkov, Sergei, 81–82, 82n39
government. *See* federal government and presidency
Graham, Lindsey, 192
Great Britain: Bicentennial celebration–related travel to and role of, 87, 88, 89; Cotswold area, 101, 119; Falklands war, 186; force multiplier deterrent role of British ballistic submarines, 62; Gallipoli campaign, 60; invitation to Queen to Bicentennial celebration, 88, 96–97; knighting by the Queen and visit to Buckingham Palace, 97; London visit and dinner at Cunard hotel, 61–62, 61n24; nuclear submarine development by and information sharing with, 62; Taylor's birth and life in England, 101, 119, 195; visits to and relationship with Royal Navy, 61–62
Great Lakes Training Center: arrival at, 8; battlefront footage showings at, 12; benefit of Navy presence in Midwest, 172; closure of, discussions about, 171–72; formation at, 12;

history of, 172; lesson on looking out for fellow serviceperson, 8–9, 12; reading and writing ability of boys at, 8, 12; train trip to and box from mother, x, 7–8, 11–12; training at, 10, 171, 172; weather conditions at, 12, 171–72

Green Acres, 120, 196, 197

Griffith Stadium, ix

grocery delivery by wagon, 6–7

Grosvenor Square, 61

Guadalcanal, Naval Battle of, 11, 29

Guam, 24

Guam, 15, 15n1

Guiness Records book, 123

Gulfstream aircraft, 190

Haig, Al, 86–87

Haldeman, Bob, 31

Hartson, Nelson T., 27, 27n9

Hawaii, 15n1

Hayward, Tom, 81, 81n38, 82, 138, 156–57, 158, 174

helicopters: evacuation from embassy rooftop in Saigon, 55; Huey helicopters for evacuations of injured men, 51; visiting ships from, 53–54

Hetu, Herb, 93

Hidalgo, Edward, 149, 152

Hogan & Hartson (Hogan Lovells) law firm, xi, xiii, 27, 27n9, 28, 33, 35, 80

"hollow military," 141

Holloway, James L., III, iii; CNO appointment and service, iv, 58, 117, 117n50, 153; Naval Historical Foundation role of, v; relationship with Warner, iv; sea daddies status of, 143; Veterans History Project interview with, iv

Holton, Linwood, 107, 122–23, 135

Holy Loch, 61

Homeland Security, U.S. Department of, 184

Hormuz, Strait of, 186–87

horse-drawn ambulances, 2

horses and horse shows, 100–102, 119, 124, 126, 132, 194

Howard, J. Daniel, 157–58

Huey helicopters, 51

Hughes, Scott, 165

Hull, 91, 91n41

Hungary, 174

Huntington Ingalls Industries (Newport News Shipbuilding), 115–16
Hussein, Saddam, 194

Illinois, 139
Incidents at Sea (INCSEA) Agreement: as behavior control agreement, 144; ceremony for, 79; discussions on during CODEL, 176; fortieth anniversary meeting for, iii–iv; interviews about, iii; Kasatonov dinner at Warner home during negotiations, 99–100; Laird selection of Warner for meetings for, 68–69; meetings and negotiations for, iii–iv, xi, xii, xiii, 36, 53, 54, 65–68, 77–84, 112–13; signing agreement for, 81–82; signing of as member of Presidential Party at Moscow Summit Meeting, xi; success of agreement, 143–44
Incidents at Sea (Winkler), iii, 36n14
Independence Hall, Philadelphia, 90
Indianapolis, 137–38, 185
Ingersoll, Stuart H., 91n42
intellectuals, Nixon concern about Bicentennial celebration planning by, 94
interdependency of military and working with fellow serviceperson, 8–9, 12
international lawyer organization membership, 80–81
interstate road system, 96
Iowa, 173
Iran, 186–87
Iraq: CODEL visits to, 178–79; invasion of Kuwait by, 176–78, 194; Navy units in Persian Gulf targeting bunkers in, 179–80; 9/11 attacks and operations in, 184; reserves recalled to active duty for operations in, 176–77; *Stark* attack by, 185–86; war declaration legislation and vote in Congress, 177–78, 194
Iraq War veterans, 108–9, 193–94
Iron Curtain, highest-ranking American associated with military to go behind, 84
irons story on *Constitution*, 79–80
Israel, 185
Italy, 63, 64

Jackson, Henry M. "Scoop," 28, 28n10, 39, 160, 161, 161n53

Japan: bombing of and end of war, 13–14; order for invasion of, 1; Pearl Harbor attack by, ix, 3, 4, 72, 177, 181; relationship with and exchange and information sharing programs with, 64; trips to, 61
Jeep carrier, 23
Jesuit Priests, murder of, 166, 166n56
John Paul II (pope), 175
John Warner, xiii, 111–17
Johnson, Lyndon B., 34, 35, 38
Joint Chiefs and Chairman of the Joint Chiefs, 43–44, 163, 173, 183
Jones, James "Jim," 187–90
Judge Advocate General program, 25

K Street, 27
Kasatonov, Admiral, 82, 82n39, 99–100
Kassebaum, Nancy, 134
Kennedy, Ethel, 132
Kennedy, Jacqueline L. "Jackie," 30, 34, 132–33
Kennedy, John F. "Jack," 28, 30, 34, 132–34
Kennedy, Robert F. "Bobby," 28, 30, 132–33
Kennedy, Ted, 141, 193
Kissinger, Henry, 36, 53, 79
knighting by the Queen and visit to Buckingham Palace, 97
Korean War: anti-aircraft fire during, 21–22; bomb damage assessment observer duty during, xiii, 20–21; Chosin Valley battle, 20; Communications Officer service in, x, 20–22, 20n3, 163–64; deferred reporting dates and student deferments, 19, 26; five days to prepare for going overseas for, 22–23; G.I. Bill eligibility for service during, 18; interview about service during, iv–v; Jeep carrier for travel to, 23; living conditions during, 20; pilot losses during, 21–22; return from on plane, 24; service during, x, xiii, 1, 18, 20–24, 20n3; start of and orders to report, 19; veterans elected to and service in Congress, 108, 172
Krulak, Charles Chandler, 52, 52n20
Kurth, Ronald "Ron," 81, 81n38
Kuwait: Iraqi invasion of, 176–78, 194; libration of, 178; troops to support operations in, 176–78

Laird, Melvin R. "Mel": on CNO appointment decisions, 50; congressional career of, 28, 40; distance between home and Pentagon, rule about,

198; Distinguished Public Service Medal and citation for service from, xi–xii; military service of, 28–29; Secretary of Defense appointment, xi, 28–29, 36, 40; transition office role, 29, 30, 46; war protest, sending Chafee and Warner to, 47; Warner selection for INCSEA talks by, 68–69; Warner swearing in by, xi

Landon, Alf, 134

law librarian, assistant, 18

Lebanon, 166

Lehman, John: books written by, 75; *Command of the Seas* (first book), 144, 158, 159, 163; Goldwater-Nichols act, opinion about, 163; Maritime Strategy role of, 75n33, 150–51; Navy aviator status of, 144; 9/11 commission role of, 184; *Oceans Ventured*, 75n33, 142–44, 151; oral history of, 75; portrait of in Rickover's office, 74; relationship with Rickover, 73, 74, 75; relationship with Warner, 75; sea daddies of, 142–43, 151, 154; Secretary of the Navy appointment and tenure, 73, 142, 144, 150–51, 163; unform changes under, 152

Lehman, John, Sr., 143

Levin, Carl, 182–84, 187–90

Lexington, Virginia, x, 16–17

Library of Congress Veterans History Project, iv

Lincoln Highway, 96n44

Linebacker, Operation, 53–54

Los Angeles General Airport, 30

Los Angeles–class submarines, 58, 112

Lovell, John Spencer, 27n9

Lyons, "Ace," 158

Mabus, Ray, 115

Mack, William P., 70–71, 71n27

Magna Carta, 96–97, 97n45

Maine, 116, 134, 186

Marine Air Wing, 1st, 1, 20n3; Marine Air Group 33, x, 20n3

Marine Attack Squadron VMA-121, x

Marine Corps Barracks, Eighth and I, 29n12

Marine Corps Commandant, 29n12, 52, 52n20, 187n57

Marine Corps Institute, 111

Marine Corps Reserve, U.S., x, 19, 24–25, 32, 40, 132

Marine Corps, U.S.: building named for Warner at

University of the Marine Corps, 111; Chosin Valley battle losses and need for officers, 20; decision to stay in reserves and decision to leave, 24–25; devotion of Warner to Sailors and Marines, 111, 114; discharge from, 26, 32; enlistment in, 1; friction between Sailors and Marines, 23; G.I. Bill eligibility for service in, 18; interest in joining, ix, 9, 11; interservice tension with Army, 52–53; interviews about service in, iv–v; OCS at Quantico, 18, 20; officer commission in, 18–20, 132; paperwork, orders, and informal processes, 22; Radio Tech School at Quantico, 20; service in, xi, 32, 40, 132; service in Korea in, x, xiii, 1, 18, 20–24; Somalia embassy operations role of, 187–88; visits to bases in Vietnam while serving as Under Secretary, 50–54; World War I service in AEF, 52–53; years of active duty and missing retirement from, 25, 32

Marine Fighter Squadron VMF-321, 19

Maritime Strategy, 75n33, 150–51

Marriott, Bill, 127

Marriott, J. W., 127

Mayflower Hotel dinner for and speech by Reagan, 145

McCain, John, 56, 57, 98–99, 108, 188, 192–93

McCain, John "Jumpin' Jack," 56, 98–99

McKee, Kinnaird "Kin," 75, 75n32

McNamara, Robert, 39, 46

Medal of Honor, 98

Mediterranean operations, 87, 113–14, 189

Mellon, Catherine "Cathy": children of, 25, 28, 32, 87, 97, 99, 198; divorce filing of, 24–25, 97–98, 99–100, 156–57; farm as wedding gift from father of, 121; feelings about Marine reserve duty, 24–25, 32; Georgetown home with, 198–99; meeting and marriage to John, 32–33; Vietnam War opposition by, 97; watching parade leave White House after Kennedy death, 34

Mellon, Mary Conover, 32n13, 34

Mellon, Paul, 32, 32n13, 34, 121

Metropolitan Club, 1

Miami, 35

Middendorf, 152

Middleburg, Virginia, 30, 34, 100–102, 119–20, 121, 122, 132, 196, 198, 199

Midway, Battle of, 49

military bases, closing of, 138–40, 168–72
Military Occupation Specialty Code (MOS) 2502, 25, 25n7
military system of politics, 43
Miller, Andy, 126–27
Milosevic, Slobodan, 191
Mississippi, 116, 137
Missouri, 14
Mitchell, George, 177
Monaghan, 91, 91n41
Mondale, Walter, 161
Monterey, 91, 91n42
Moorer, Admiral, 49–50, 58, 68, 144
Mormon Tabernacle Choir, 92
mothers, toast to, 67
movies, 6
Movietone News, 6
Muskegon, Michigan, 103–5

national intelligence establishment, revision of, 184
National Mall, iv
National Maritime Historical Society Washington Awards dinners, vi
National Museum of the United States Navy: Cold War Gallery of, v; Dunn and Warner interview at, v; Naval Historical Foundation receptions at, vi; Warner support for, xiii
National World War II Memorial, iv, 193
NATO: Brussels headquarters of, 63; conferences for, 44; French withdrawal from, 63; Jones as Supreme Allied Commander in Europe, 187–90, 187n57; Naples location of NATO South, 64; Serbia operations of, 191–92; Stavridis as Supreme Allied Commander in Europe, 76n34
Naval Academy, U.S.: Carter attendance and graduation from, 138; engineering building named after Rickover at, 70–71; Rickover experience at, 71–72; superintendents of, 70–71, 71n27, 74n30
Naval Air Station Anacostia, 19, 19n2
Naval Air Station Patuxent River, 19n2
naval courts and boards, 69
Naval Forces Europe, Commander in Chief (CinCUSNavEur), 61–62
Naval Historical Foundation, iii, v, vi, 75, 77
Naval Institute Press, iv
Naval Institute, U.S.: oral histories project of, 75–

76; Stavridis role with, 76n34, 77
naval justice refresher course, 25
Naval Observatory, iii
Naval Research Laboratory, 10
naval review, international, 95
Naval War College, 81n38
Navy, U.S.: birthday of, 1; decision to join over other branches of service, 9; devotion of Warner to Sailors and Marines, xii–xiii, 111, 114; discharge from, x; electronics school training and electronics technician duty, x, 1, 10, 11–14, 17, 92; enlistment in, ix–x, 1, 6, 7, 9, 11; friction between Sailors and Marines, 23; interviews about service in, iv–v; Judge Advocate General program, 25; Laird service in, 28–29; Persian Gulf, units in, 179–80; reenlistment in, 1, 11; service in, xi, xiii, 40; 600-ship Navy, 150; social change in, 151–52; 350-ship Navy, 154–56; train to Great Lakes Naval Station and box from mother, x, 7–8, 11–12; training in and success in life, 1; unform changes under Zumwalt, 151–52, 153; VE-Day and service as shore patrol in Chicago, x, 12–13; wearing uniform on leave and after discharge, 15–16
Navy, U.S. Department of: administration of uniformed side, 117–18; assistants in, 45–46; competition in, 68; Crystal City offices of Main Navy, 70; EOB offices of, 39, 39n15; flag board and woman as admiral, 41–42; public exposure of, 44; rats and Main Navy buildings on Constitution Ave., 70; responsibilities over Sailors and Marines, 41–42; screening and selection of people to work in, 40–43; Secretary of Personnel Management, 46. *See also* Secretary of the Navy (SECNAV); Under Secretary of the Navy
Navy Cross, 49, 68
Nevada, 72n28
New Jersey, 163, 164, 166
New York: Al Smith Dinner by Archdiocese of New York, 133–34; Bicentennial celebration and Tall Ships regatta in, 90–92, 93, 95
New York University Medical School, 2
Newport News Shipbuilding (Huntington Ingalls Industries), 115–16
newspaper delivery, 6–7
Nicaragua and the Sandinistas, 166
9/11 attacks (2001), 181–84

Nixon, Pat, 31

Nixon, Richard M.: Al Smith Dinner attendance by, 133–34; Bicentennial celebration administrator appointment by, 55, 86–87, 89, 96; California trip to vote, 30–31; CNO appointment by, 50n19; continuity of succession in 1960 presidential election, 31–32; election of, 38; enthusiasm for Bicentennial celebration, 89; governor campaign of, 34; Haiphong harbor mining, speech about, 99–100; inauguration and oath of office of, 39; intellectuals, concern about Bicentennial celebration planning by, 94; Moscow visit with, 67–68, 82–84; presidential campaign in 1960, v–vi, xi, 28, 29–32, 33, 35, 86, 103–5, 107, 132–34; presidential campaign in 1968, 28, 30, 35–36, 38, 86, 107; presidential debate of, 29–30, 132–33; rats on Main Navy buildings on Constitution Ave., 70; resignation of, 89; return to Washington after 1960 election, 31–32; Under Secretary and Secretary of the Navy appointments by, xi, 29; train trip for 1960 campaign, 103–5; transition office of, 28, 29, 30, 38–43, 46; vice president selection by, 160; Watergate consequences and concern about Bicentennial celebration, 86

nomenklatura, 83

Norfolk and Western Railway, 137

Norway, 143

Novotel (London West, Cunard International Hotel), 61–62, 61n24

Novotel, London West (Cunard International Hotel), 61n24

nuclear power: British nuclear submarine development, 62; civilian nuclear power industry and demand for training in nuclear science and safety, 45; confidence in civilian industry and Three Mile Island incident, 74; force multiplier deterrent role of British ballistic submarines, 62; nuclear-powered ships, 45; Rickover role in, 58, 58n22, 72–75; Rickover role in civilian nuclear power under Reagan, 73–74, 75, 159

Nunn, Sam, 85, 147, 160, 161, 177

Nutter, G. Warren, 68, 68n26

Obenshain, Richard, 124n51

Ocean Venture exercise, 143

Oceans Ventured (Lehman), 75n33, 142–44, 151

Okean-70 exercise, 65
Okinawa, Battle of, 29
Okun, Herbert "Herb," 77–78, 78n37
Old Executive Office Building (EOB), 39, 39n15
Op-Ed on veterans serving in Congress, 193–94

Pacific Fleet, Commander in Chief (CinCPac), 50, 50n18, 53
Palmer, Bruce, Jr., 141
Panthers, 21, 21n4
Patuxent River Naval Air Station, 19n2
PBY Catalina, 49
peanuts, 118–19
Pell, Claiborne, 175–76
Pennsylvania: Penn State, 126; senator from, 165; Three Mile Island incident, 74
Pentagon: distance between home and Pentagon, rule about, 198; hospital, original intent for building, 41; 9/11 attack on, 182–84. *See also* Defense, U.S. Department of
Perot, Ross, 98
Perry-class frigates, 155–56
Pershing, John, 52–53
Persian Gulf, 179–80
Philadelphia, 90
Pierce, Franklin, 150
Pierre Hotel, New York, 28
Plains, Virginia, 135
pocket battleships/battlecruisers, 15, 15n1
Poland, 174–75
politics: conservative politics and right-to-life views, 124; intense interest in federal government, 35; Nixon aide, service as, 28, 33, 86; Nixon campaign, caliber of people involved in, 38; Nixon presidential campaign roles, v–vi, xi, 28, 29–32, 33, 35–36, 38, 86, 103–5, 107, 132–34; party affiliation, 33; regulatory interests of law firms, 35; transition office of Nixon, 28, 29, 30, 38–43, 46; Virginia politics, activities in, 107. *See also* Senate, U.S.
Powell, Colin, 173
Praying Mantis, Operation, 186–87
presence, ship design for, 156
President's Chapel (Christ Church, Farragut Square), 89–90
Prettyman, E. Barrett, x, 26–27, 26n8

Priests, murder of, 166, 166n56
Princeton, 127
prisoners of war (POWs): decision about conviction and court-martial of, 55–56; meeting with wives of, 45, 48, 55, 98; organization to help families of, 98; return to U.S. from Vietnam, 55–57
pro bono cases, 27, 35
professional careers and social structure in America, 18, 35
Prussia, 174–75

Quantico, Virginia: building named for Warner at University of the Marine Corps in, 111; memorabilia in museum in, 24; OCS at, 18, 20; Radio Tech School at Quantico, 20

radio technician duty and communication equipment, x, 1, 10
rationing and ration stamps, 3–4
Reagan administration and Ronald Reagan: cabinet during, 144; committment and success of, 144; D-Day commemoration event with, 131–32; governor of California role of Reagan, 145; Mayflower Hotel dinner for and speech by Reagan, 145–46; nuclear-power program under, 58; presidential campaign and election of, 107, 141–42; "Reagan revolution," 141–42; relationship with Warner, 132, 145; Rickover role in civilian nuclear power under, 73–74, 75, 159; *Stark* incident during, 185–86, 187; Taylor relationship with Reagan, 194; Webb as Secretary of the Navy under, xii
Reagan National (Washington National) Airport, 19, 19n2
Red Cross, ix, 2
Rein, Charlie, 80
Republican Party of the Metropolitan Areas, 145
Revolutionary War, 64
Rhode Island, 29, 44
Richardson, John, 115, 115n49
Rickover, Hyman G. "Rick," 58, 58n22, 62, 68–75, 72nn28–29, 75n32, 158–59
right-to-life views and conservative politics, 124
Robertson, Willis, 137
Rockefeller, Nelson, 92–93
Rogers, Bill, 77–78

Roosevelt, Franklin D., 161n53
Rossiya Hotel, 81
Rota, Spain, 63
Roughead, Gary, 109
Rowland, Ross, Jr., 96, 96n43
Rumsfeld, Don "Rummy," 182–84
Russia. *See* Soviet Union/Russia

Safety at Sea talks, 77. *See also* Incidents at Sea (INCSEA) Agreement
Sailor suits, dressing children in, 9
St. Albans, 3
SALT/SALT II Treaty, 78n37, 140–41
"Sammy" [Samuel] B. Roberts incident, 186–87
Sandinistas and Nicaragua, 166
Saudi Arabia, 178
Scharnhorst (Germany), 15n1
Schlesinger, James R., 58
Schwarzkopf, Norman, 178–79
Scott, Hugh, 165
Scott, William L. "Bill," 124n51, 135
sea daddies, 142–43, 151, 154
seasickness, 23
Secret Service, 103–4, 105, 131
Secretary of Personnel Management, 46
Secretary of the Navy (SECNAV): aides to, 138, 173–74; appointment and tenure as, iv, v, xi, 29, 38, 61, 86, 87, 88, 112–13, 122, 168; career staff of, 42; ceremony at Marine Corps base for, 29; Chafee as, 29, 50; Claytor as, 137–38; Distinguished Public Service Medal and citation for service as, xi–xii; divorce while serving as, 97–98, 99–100, 156–57; feelings about service as, 88, 96; Garrett as, 157n52; Hidalgo as, 149; Howard as, 157; Lehman as, 73, 142, 144, 150–51, 163; Mabus as, 115; press conferences and public exposure of, 44–45; relationship with Under Secretary, 43–45; responsibilities of, 41–42, 43–45; ship naming role of, 106, 111–15; transition from Under Secretary, 54; travel and overseas visits while serving as, 60–61, 87, 97, 98–99; Warner service as, ix, xiii; Webb service as, xii; Winter service as, xiii; woman as admiral, decision about, 41–42; youngest men to serve as, 150
Senate, U.S.: age of people serving in, 129; Appropriations Committee on, 136–37; Armed

Services Committee of, 118, 136, 166, 169, 173; Armed Services Committee service, v, 51–52, 134–35, 136, 149, 158; base closure bills and closing military bases, 138–40, 168–72; Bicentennial celebration administrator appointment as path to, 87, 96; Bicentennial celebration administrator, confirmation as, 88; campaign for and election to, vi, xii, 103, 107–8, 117, 121–27, 129, 134–36, 194–95; Chafee service in, 29; CODEL diversion to Somalia, 187–90, 194; CODEL visits to Iraq, 178–79; CODEL visits to Russia, 85, 175–76; CODEL visits to Serbia, 190–92; confirmation hearings of, 144; contracts for Virginia businesses while serving in, 115–16; demands of commitment to and marriage to Taylor, 120–21, 194–95; Democrats in Virginia Senate seats, 135, 137; dumbest man in, 135; friendships and relationships in, 29, 160–61; length of service in, 129; lesson on interdependency of military in, 8–9; Manpower Personnel, Research and Development and Military Construction subcommittee, 138–40; oath of office as new senator, 134; retirement from and tribute to service in, xii–xiii; Sea Power Subcommittee, 142; service in, ix, xii, 107–8, 112, 129; Tactical Warfare Strategic and Theater Nuclear Forces chair, 142; time requirements for service in and marriage to Taylor, 120–21; veterans elected to and service in, 108–10, 161, 172, 193–94; war declaration legislation and vote in, 177–78, 194; women serving in, 134, 148; Zumwalt campaign for, 117–18, 122

September 11 attacks (2001), 181–84

Serbia, 190–92

Seventh Fleet, 61

Shenandoah region, 198

shipbuilding industry, 115–17, 122

ships: ASW capabilities of, 155–56; designs and capabilities of, 154–56; destroyer escorts (DEs), 23, 23n6; guns on and sizes of guns, 15; Jeep carrier, 23; loss of ships from a typhoon during World War II, 91, 91nn41–42; morale on during Vietnam War, 53–54; naming after living people, xiii; naming of, xiii, 106, 111–15; nuclear-powered ships, 45; ship designs for post-war shipbuilding, 15; ship-building program after

Vietnam, 58; 600-ship Navy, 150; 350-ship Navy, 154–56. *See also* battleships; submarines
Shoemaker, Bob, 57
sidearms, love for, 19
Silkworm missiles, 186–87
Silver Star, 49
Sixth Fleet, 64
Smith, Margaret Chase, 134
Somalia, 187–90, 194
South America, 166
Southeast Asia, trips to, 61
Southern Command, U.S., 76n35
Soviet Union/Russia: alliance with Japan against, 64; CODEL visits to, 85, 175–76; drinking at banquet given to honor Warner in, 66–67; female guide in, 83; food in, 65, 84; Geneva discussions with, 141; growth and capabilities of Soviet Navy, 64–65; international lawyer organization trip to, 80–81; Leningrad banquet and visit to Navy installations, 66–67; Moscow visit with Nixon, 67–68, 82–84; Navy riverine force during World War II, 65–66; Rossiya Hotel stay, 81, 84; St. Petersburg naval facilities, 65; secret negotiations with, 36; Serbia, Russians bond with, 191; Stalingrad, supplies for, 65–66; Stalingrad, visit to, 82; U.S. Embassy in Moscow, 84; Warsaw Pact collapse and, 174–75. *See also* Incidents at Sea (INCSEA) Agreement
Spain: relationship with Franco and military facilities in, 63; Rota base for submarines, 63
Spence, 91, 91n41
Spong, Bill, 135
Spruance-class destroyers, 158
Stark incident, 185–86, 187
State, U.S. Department of: EOB offices of, 39, 39n15; INCSEA meeting role of, 77–78; Rogers as secretary of, 77–78; screening people to work in, 38
Statue of Liberty, 90
Stavridis, James G., 76–77, 76–77nn34–36
Stennis, John, 136–37, 138–39, 158, 159
stickers on front doors for family member in armed forces, 4, 6
Stockdale, Jim, 57, 98
Stockdale, Sybil, 55, 98
stone fences, 101, 119

streetcars, 4
submarines: British nuclear submarine development, 62; Captain Eddie service on, 11; Carter service on, 138; conditions aboard, 49; force multiplier deterrent role of British ballistic submarines, 62; INCSEA agreement and operations of, 68; *Los Angeles*-class submarines, 58, 112; Navy Crosses to submariners, 49; nuclear submarines and losing men in submarine force, 45; Rota base for, 63; ship-building program after Vietnam, 58; sponsorship of and perpetual trust for *Warner*, 113; torpedo accuracy and malfunctions, 49; *Virginia*-class fast attack submarine, xiii, 111–17
Swan Lake, 82–83
Syria, 111, 113–14

Tailhook, 157–58, 157n52
Tall Ships regatta, 90, 93, 95
Taylor, Elizabeth "Liz": back injury from fall while riding a horse, 102; birth in England and love of the farm in Virginia, 101, 119, 195; campaigning for Senate with, 121, 123, 124–26, 194–95; death of, 121; Dublin Horse show invitation to, 124, 126; horseriding experience and love for horses of, 101–2, 124, 194; lessons learned from, 120; marriage to, vi, 97, 102, 120, 124–25; meeting and escorting to reception, 97, 100; proposal to and wedding ceremony, 119–20; relationship with Reagan, 194; split with and relationship with after split, 120–21, 194–95; time spent on farm with, 100–102
TBM aircraft, 163–64
technological and communication equipment advances, 10
Temple, Shirley, 174
Tenleytown, 4
Tet Offensive, 99
Texas, lost votes in 1960 presidential election in, 31–32
Three Mile Island incident, 74
Thurmond, Strom, 85, 129, 175–76
Tito, 81, 190
Today Show, The, 124
Tomahawk program, 158, 166
torpedo accuracy and malfunctions, 49

Tower, John, 136, 138–39, 141, 142, 143, 146–48, 159–60
trains/railroad system: American Freedom Train, 95–96, 96n43; Nixon campaign trip on a train, 103–5; Norfolk and Western Railway, 137; trip to Great Lakes Naval Station and box from mother, x, 7–8, 11–12; troop train priority over passenger trains, 6; Truman campaign trip on a train, 103; during war, 4
Treasury, U.S. Department of, 39
Tribute to a Generation (Winkler), iv
Trost, Carl, 173–74
Truman, Harry S., 39n16, 103, 109, 140
Trump, Donald, 144
Tufts University, Fletcher School of Law and Diplomacy, 76–77, 77n36
Turkey, 60, 61

Under Secretary of the Navy: aides to, 138, 173–74; appointment and tenure as, v, xi, 29, 38, 40–41, 61, 86, 168; Distinguished Public Service Medal and citation for service as, xi–xii; first day in office and seeing casualty report, 41, 42; Howard as, 157–58; Moscow visit with Nixon, 67–68; relationship with SECNAV, 43–45; responsibilities of, 41–42, 43–46, 48; ship-building program, concerns about as, 58; transition to Secretary, 54; travel and overseas visits while serving as, 50–54, 60–61, 87
Uniform Code of Military Justice, 69
Union Station, 25
United Arab Emirates (UAE), 185
United Nations (U.N.) resolution, 177, 194
United States Attorney: Assistant U.S. Attorney appointment, x, 28; Special Assistant to the U.S. Attorney appointment, x; trial lawyer service in Washington, D.C., office, x–xi, 26–27
United States Court of Appeals, 26n8
United States (U.S.): clothes manufacturing during war, 15–16; exciting period in after end of war, 16; national intelligence establishment revision, 184; Nixon and continuity of succession in presidential election, 31–32; social structure in and professional careers, 18, 35; 250th birthday of, xii
University of the Marine Corps, 111
University of Virginia Law School, x, 17–18, 19,

26, 28, 30, 127, 132

Valley Forge, 90
Vice Chief of Naval Operations, 50n18
Vietnam and Vietnam War: aircraft used in, 21, 21n4; battleship use during, 164; casualty report from, 41, 42; ceasefire, peace negotiations, and treaty to end, 53, 54–55, 164; Easter Offensive, 54; evacuation of injured men from fire base, 51–52; Haiphong harbor mining, 99–100; Linebacker operation, 53–54; morale on on ships during, 53–54; opinion about involvement in, 34–35; outlook for war, 39, 47–48; phasing out involvement in, 47–48; political structure in South Vietnam, 47–48; protests, civil unrest, and home front turning against, 36, 47, 54, 97; riverine forces in, 50; Secretary of Defense meetings about, 48; Tet Offensive, 99; veterans elected to and service in Congress, 108, 172; visits while serving as Under Secretary and Secretary, 50–54, 87, 97, 98–99; war protest assessment by Chafee and Warner, 47; Webb service during, xii; Zumwalt service during, 50
Vietnam Memorial, iv
Virginia: agriculture in Southside Virginia, 118; building code and height of buildings in, 128–29; contracts awarded to businesses in, 115–16, 122; convention for Senate run in, 122–24; debate with Miller in Alexandria, 126–27; Defense Department as largest employer in, 115; farm at White Post, 122; farm in Middleburg, 30, 34, 100–102, 119–20, 121, 122, 132, 196, 198, 199; festivals in small towns in, 125; home in Alexandria, vi, 199–200; military facilities in, 122, 139; shipbuilding industry in, 115–17, 122; stone fences in, 101, 119
Virginia-class cruiser, 58
Virginia-class fast attack submarine, xiii, 111–17

wagons for grocery delivery, 6–7
Waldorf Astoria, 133–34
Walters, Barbara, 195–97
War College, 56, 57
Warner, Jeanne (wife): Alexandria home of, vi, 199–200; dating of, 198; first husband of, 197–98; marriage to, 195, 200; sponsorship of *Warner* and perpetual trust for submarines under, 113

Warner, John W.: allowance while growing up, 6; birth and early life of, ix, 3–7, 126–27; children of, 25, 28, 32, 87, 97, 99; death of, ix; divorce from Cathy, 24–25, 97–98, 99–100, 156–57; farm work experience of, 121–22; knighting by the Queen, 97; languages, struggle with, 17; legacy of, vi, xiii; loss of father and feeling cheated, 16; meeting and marriage to Cathy, 32–33; success of and strong parents, 1; tribute by Cox, ix–xiii; *Virginia*-class submarine naming for, xiii, 111–17

Warner, John W. (father), 154–56; abilities as student, 16, 17; biography of, 156; cancer diagnosis and death of, 15–16, 127; car ordered by, 16; connections and friends of, 127; delivery of notable people by, 128; education of, 2, 9, 16, 17, 127; family of, ix; feelings about doing oral history with Winkler, 130, 156; medical training and career of, 2–4, 30, 127–28; meeting and marriage to Martha, 2–3; money left after death of, 17; move to Washington, D.C., 3; permission to enlist in military, ix, 5, 6, 9, 11; seeing off at the train, 7; World War I service of, ix, 2, 11, 51

Warner, John William (grandfather), ix

Warner, Mark, 199

Warner, Martha Budd (mother), ix; debate attendance in Alexandria, 126–27; dressing son in Sailor suit, 9; meeting and marriage to John, 2–3; money for after death of John, 17; move to Washington, D.C., 3; permission to enlist in military, ix, 5, 6, 9, 11; Red Cross work of, ix, 2; seeing off at the train and giving a box to open later, 7–8, 11

Warner, Mary Tinsley (grandmother), ix

Warren, Earl, 80

Warsaw Pact, collapse of, 174

Washington, D.C.: All-Star game in, 168; Bicentennial celebration events in, 89–90, 92–93; birth and early life in, 3–7; British embassy in, 96; building code and height of buildings in, 128–29; Constitution Gardens in, 102, 102n46; electronic circuit problem during Bicentennial celebration event in, 92; grocery delivery by wagon for mothers in, 6–7; layout of, 4; lifestyle in Cleveland Park, 7; 9/11 attacks (2001), 181–84; rationing during war and staying in own part of city, 4; Republican Party of the Metropolitan Areas, 145;

stickers on front doors for family member in armed forces, 4, 6; Willard Hotel use for Nixon campaign, 28, 35, 38, 107

Washington & Lee University: academic achievement at and graduation from, 17; admission to with help of father, 16, 17; credit for work in Navy, 17; education at, x, 9, 16–17, 127; education of father at, 2, 9, 16, 17, 127; graduation from and Marine Corps commission, 18–19

Washington Cathedral, 3, 6

Washington National (Reagan National) Airport, 19, 19n2

Washington Navy Yard, 11

Watkins, James D. "Jim," 74, 74n31, 158

Webb, James, xii

Webster, Bill, 182

Weinberger, Caspar, 144, 148

Westmoreland, William, 141

White House, parade from after Kennedy's death, 34

White Post, Virginia, 122

Whitehouse, Sheldon, xii–xiii

white-tie, black-tie, and the Al Smith Dinner, 133–34

Willard Hotel, Washington, D.C., 28, 35, 38, 107

Wilson, Woodrow, 52, 95

Wilson High School, 4, 6

Winter, Donald, xiii

Wisconsin, 179–80

Woodrow Wilson High School, 4, 6

World War I: Gallipoli campaign, 60; number of men in uniform for, 109; 100th anniversary of, 191; Pershing and Marines in the AEF, 52–53; service of father during, ix, 2, 11, 51; veterans elected to and service in Congress, 109–10

World War I Commission, 2

World War I memorial, 94–95

World War II: battlefront footage from, 12; battles in Europe, 1, 3, 4, 5–6; bombing of Japan and end of, 13–14; clothes manufacturing during, 15–16; D-Day and event to commemorate, 131–32; demobilization after end of, 9, 14–15; Dunn and Warner interview about Pearl Harbor attack, v; end of, 1, 9, 10, 14–15, 172; enlistment and draft for armed services for, 4–5; enlistment in Navy during, ix–x, 1; Ford's service as deck officer about small carrier during, 91, 91n42; 40th anniversary of end of, 85; gold star stickers on front doors during, 4; interview about service during, iv–v; Laird service during, 28–29; loss of ships from a typhoon during, 91, 91nn41–42; Normandy invasion, 5; odd jobs during, 6–7; Pearl Harbor attack by Japanese, ix, 3, 4, 72, 177, 181; rationing and ration stamps during, 3–4; service during, x, xiii, 1, 10, 13, 40; Soviet Navy riverine force during, 65–66; stickers on front doors for family member in armed forces during, 4, 6; technological advances and communication equipment for, 10; total involvement of country in, 3–4, 6–7; VE-Day and service as shore patrol in Chicago, x, 12–13; veterans elected to and service in Congress, 108–9, 172; war declaration after Pearl Harbor attack, 177

World War II Memorial, iv, 193

Yemassee, South Carolina, 25
Yorktown-Caron incident, 60
Yugoslavia, 190

Zumwalt, Elmo "Bud": CNO appointment and service, 50, 50n19, 58, 68, 117–18, 150–53; hiding in Georgetown home, 199; legacy of and opinions about, 151–52; maritime strategy under, 150; Navy career and Vietnam service of, 50, 117; relationship with Holloway, 153; relationship with Warner, 57–58; sea daddies status of, 143, 151, 154; Senate campaign of, 117–18, 122; unform changes under, 151–52, 153

www.ingramcontent.com/pod-product-compliance
Lightning Source LLC
Chambersburg PA
CBHW080614170426
43209CB00007B/1432